NANCY BERNKOPF TUCKER
and WARREN I. COHEN
Books on American-East Asian Relations

A NANCY BERNKOPF TUCKER AND WARREN I. COHEN BOOK ON AMERICAN–EAST ASIAN RELATIONS

Edited by Thomas J. Christensen
Mark Philip Bradley
Rosemary Foot

Michael J. Green, *By More Than Providence: Grand Strategy and American Power in the Asia Pacific Since 1783*

Jeanne Guillemin, *Hidden Atrocities: Japanese Germ Warfare and American Obstruction of Justice at the Tokyo Trial*

Andrew B. Kennedy, *The Conflicted Superpower: America's Collaboration with China and India in Global Innovation*

Anne F. Thurston, ed., *Engaging China: Fifty Years of Sino-American Relations*

Nancy Bernkopf Tucker was a historian of American diplomacy whose work focused on American–East Asian relations. She published seven books, including the prize-winning *Uncertain Friendships: Taiwan, Hong Kong, and the United States, 1945–1992*. Her articles and essays appeared in countless journals and anthologies, including the *American Historical Review*, *Diplomatic History*, *Foreign Affairs*, and the *Journal of American History*. In addition to teaching at Colgate and Georgetown (where she was the first woman to be awarded tenure in the School of Foreign Service), she served on the China desk of the Department of State and in the American embassy in Beijing. When the Office of the Director of National Intelligence was created, she was chosen to serve as the first Assistant Deputy Director of National Intelligence for Analytic Integrity and Standards and Ombudsman, and she was awarded the National Intelligence Medal of Achievement in 2007. To honor her, in 2012 the Woodrow Wilson International Center for Scholars established an annual Nancy Bernkopf Tucker Memorial Lecture on U.S.–East Asian Relations.

Warren I. Cohen is University Distinguished Professor Emeritus at Michigan State University and the University of Maryland, Baltimore County, and a senior scholar in the Asia Program of the Woodrow Wilson Center. He has written thirteen books and edited eight others. He served as a line officer in the U.S. Pacific Fleet, editor of *Diplomatic History*, president of the Society for Historians of American Foreign Relations, and chairman of the Department of State Advisory Committee on Historical Diplomatic Documentation. In addition to scholarly publications, he has written for *The Atlantic*, the *Baltimore Sun*, the *Christian Science Monitor*, *Dissent*, *Foreign Affairs*, the *International Herald Tribune*, the *Los Angeles Times*, *The Nation*, the *New York Times*, the *Times Literary Supplement*, and the *Washington Post*. He has also been a consultant on Chinese affairs to various government organizations.

JOHN T. DOWNEY,
THOMAS J. CHRISTENSEN,
AND JACK LEE DOWNEY

LOST IN THE COLD WAR

The Story of Jack Downey,
America's Longest-Held POW

COLUMBIA UNIVERSITY PRESS

NEW YORK

Columbia University Press
Publishers Since 1893
New York   Chichester, West Sussex
cup.columbia.edu

Library of Congress Cataloging-in-Publication Data
Names: Downey, John T., 1930–2014, author. | Christensen, Thomas J.,
1962– author. | Downey, Jack Lee, author.
Title: Lost in the Cold War : the story of Jack Downey, America's
longest-held POW / John T. Downey, Thomas J. Christensen,
and Jack Lee Downey.
Description: New York : Columbia University Press, 2022. |
Includes bibliographical references and index.
Identifiers: LCCN 2021060329 | ISBN 9780231199124 (hardback) |
ISBN 9780231552950 (ebook)
Subjects: LCSH: Downey, John T., 1930–2014. | Korean War, 1950–1953—
Secret service—United States. | United States. Central Intelligence
Agency—Officials and employees—Biography. | Korean War,
1950–1953—Prisoners and prisons, Chinese. | Prisoners of war—
United States—Biography. | Prisoners of war—China--Biography. |
Korean War, 1950–1956—Military intelligence—United States. |
New Haven County (Conn.)—Biography. | Cold War.
Classification: LCC DS921.5.S8 D69 2022 | DDC 951.904/28—
dc23/eng/20220405
LC record available at https://lccn.loc.gov/2021060329

After being ahead of the game age-wise all my life, I'm appalled by the realization I may find myself behind.

—Jack Downey, letter to Rufus Philips, October 10, 1952

CONTENTS

NOTE TO THE READER

THIS BOOK contains the memoirs of John Thomas "Jack" Downey, an American CIA officer who was captured during the Korean War and held prisoner in China from November 1952 until his release in March 1973. He wrote these memoirs in secret in the spring of 1982, and his family discovered the manuscript after his death in 2014. They are published here as they were found, without amendment or correction. Some discrepancies or inconsistencies have been acknowledged through notes to the text.

Interspersed among the chapters of the memoir are analytical chapters written by Thomas J. Christensen, a professor at Columbia University, an expert in Sino-American relations, and a former senior state department official responsible for policy toward China. These chapters trace global politics and diplomacy during the Cold War, and they explore just how Jack Downey came to be the longest-held prisoner of war in American history.

The book closes with an afterword from Jack Downey's son, Jack Lee Downey.

LOST IN THE COLD WAR

1

A PERFECT AMBUSH

WE HAD a bomber's moon, and the landscape below was bathed in a flood of light that made it featureless. The great, conical bulk of the Forever White Mountain (Changbai Shan) loomed out of this ether as our plane, an unmarked, fixed-wing propeller-driven Douglas C-47, reached the northern finger of North Korea that points toward the Soviet seaport of Vladivostok. The snow-covered volcano seemed to be larger than the sky. We turned ninety degrees to the left heading west. Our crossing of the border into the territory of the People's Republic of China (PRC) went undetected and we headed for the predesignated drop zone. A few minutes after midnight we spotted our Chinese agents' signal, three fires in single file. For the first time since we had taken off from Seoul, South Korea, I began to feel tense. Our pilots, Bob Snoddy and Norman Schwartz, turned the plane straight at the fires. Dick Fecteau and I grabbed the supply bundle and manhandled it past the winch, which was bolted to the cargo door. We watched the supply parachute open and drift toward the fires. We swung north to make a wide circle while the agents retrieved the bundle and assembled the pickup poles and ropes. Our loop carried us near the Manchurian city of Forever Spring (Chang Chun). We saw its lights in the distance and, as we drew closer, whole swathes of its brightness abruptly blinked out. Apparently, we had been detected now. Within a minute or two, the entire city had hidden itself in darkness, afraid of our tiny presence.

At one o'clock we reapproached the drop zone. As planned, I took a length of rope attached to my parachute harness and tied the loose end to a metal brace inside the cargo area. The rope was to be my lifeline in case I should slip from the door opening while thrusting the hook pole into its sleeve outside the fuselage. Because of the rope, I wore only a reserve parachute on my chest. I reminded myself the reserve chute ripcord did not pull automatically. I felt for the ripcord ring to memorize its position, just in case I would have to bail out. We made one pass over the drop zone, straining to see any activity on the ground. We saw nothing but the signal fires telling us all was in order.

We circled one last time and descended for the pickup. Snoddy and Schwartz straightened their course and the C-47 swayed from side to side as they flattened its path for the retrieval, Fecteau crouched at the winch. We had worried that the engine might not start after four hours exposed to the frigid air, but it coughed then caught. I stood over Fecteau, pole in hand. The cold wind raced past the cargo door. We were thirty feet above the ground, and we could see that it was covered with light snow. An electric bell, the pilot's ready signal, rang insistently. I leaned out into the wind and slammed the pole into position and locked it into the sleeve with a twist. I looked for the colonel and thought I saw him, hunched between the tether poles. We hit the rope and lurched upward.

At the same instant, the darkness was broken by flashes of gunfire. There was no mistaking it, even though the roar of wind and engine drowned out the reports of rifles and machine guns.[1] I knew we were being fired on because tracer bullets punctured the fuselage and flew by my face like tiny comets. I stood mesmerized as they came through the floor, through the door, and through the sides of the plane. I didn't think to move. It flashed through my mind that I hadn't been to confession and I was conscious that my groin felt terribly exposed. Suddenly, I sensed the C-47 had ceased climbing. It hung in midair and shuddered, a clumsy bird stricken at its moment of greatest striving. I felt the nose dipping then leveling. I fell toward into the sleeping bags and blankets behind the pilot's cabin. Stumbling, I called out for Bob and Norm, there was no response, only the sounds of the plane crashing through the woods. I couldn't tell when the plane hit the ground or why it didn't cartwheel. I only knew the battering and noise stopped and that we were no longer moving.

A sheet of flame quivered like an orange, red and blue waterfall in front of me. I must have stood and moved, for the next moment I was outside the plane. I tried to move away and was brought up short. Fecteau appeared at my side and helped me slip out of my harness. Together we stumbled toward a stand of young trees, where we tried to get our bearings.

The nose of the plane rested against the base of a small hill. Snoddy and Schwartz were nowhere to be found. I knew the gunfire had been concentrated on the cockpit, and there seemed little chance they could still be alive. I wondered whether our crash landing was luck, or if one of them had died a hero, bringing the plane in level and switching off the engine to prevent an explosion.

Through the trees, I saw a stream.

"What do we do?"

"I dunno—follow the stream down to the Yalu?"

At that moment we saw a single Chinese soldier emerge from the woods near the burning C-47. He carried a rifle and aimed at us as he approached and shouted a single, harsh syllable. I reached for my revolver as Fecteau and I edged out of the trees and into the clearing. As the soldier moved toward us, others began to appear from all directions at once. I knew immediately that resistance was useless. I dropped the revolver and raised my hands over my head. We were led into the flickering light cast by the burning C-47. Without warning, an officer stepped forward and struck Fecteau across the face. It seemed to have no impact. It was only a sound swallowed by the night. We were searched, and our hands were tied behind our backs. I wondered whether they would shoot us then and there but assured myself it was more likely that they would take us somewhere for interrogation. Soon the order was given to move out. We left the plane burning and walked away in single file.

I had come to the Far East for adventure, but now I had more than I bargained for. Later, when I remembered the crash, one frightening thought stood out among the rest. It wasn't the tracer bullets or the ride through the treetops or the fire. It was the lifeline. What if the plane had gained more altitude after being hit and I had tried to bail out? I would have jumped and fallen only the length of my lifeline. Then I would have dangled, watching the ground rush toward me and waiting for the plane to crash on top of me.

Two years of merciless interrogations, leg irons, solitary confinement in a 5′ by 8′ empty cell, and three thousand pages of written confession later, I find myself standing in line with the other defendants in a military courtroom.

"Be still," I commanded myself. "Don't let them see the trembling. They will take it as a sign of fear." Perhaps it was fear. But I told myself I was shaking from pain. For weeks I had an infected toe and the Peking[2] prison treatment of antiseptic applied with soiled cotton had done nothing to cure the inflammation, which now was raging so badly it hurt to stand. I tried to hide my shaking inside my baggy prison uniform, and when the court called me forward to identify myself, the confident tone I intended emerged as a near shout.

"John Downey, New Britain, Connecticut, United States of America," I declared. The tribunal of judges in military uniforms stared sternly down from their high rostrum. Along the opposite wall, a hundred Communist Party officials were grinning, evidently pleased to be the privileged witnesses to the sentencing of a pair of American CIA agents and their Chinese collaborators.

We stood in a long row before the judges. The nine Chinese defendants, all former army officers whom we had recruited after they fled the Communist revolution, had parachuted into the Manchurian mountains in the summer of 1952. The Korean War was stalemated and we hoped our guerrillas would find support for a counter-revolution, though we had been able to find little evidence such support existed. Dick Fecteau and I had been ambushed on a nighttime rendezvous with the guerrillas. The C-47 we were flying in was brought down by two anti-aircraft 50's and small arms fire. The two pilots had been killed in the crash landing and Fecteau and I were captured. That was at midnight of November 29, 1952. Now it was two years later, the war had ended, but we did not know it, and neither our families nor our government knew we were still alive. For two years the Communists had held us in isolation, each in solitary confinement so strict that for months we were allowed to stand only to be fed or to go to the toilet or to be questioned. The interrogation lasted eighteen months, and its conclusion with coerced confessions of "crimes against the people of China," had led to a trial and now this sentencing.

As I stood before the judges, I tried to prepare myself for the worst. I knew the Chinese regarded us as spies, not prisoners of war, yet I was convinced they had to consider the diplomatic consequences of our imprisonment. On the basis of nothing but my own conjecture, I assumed that our release could be negotiated. But even another year in prison was unpleasant to contemplate. Five years would be an ordeal I hoped I could find the strength to endure. I was only twenty-four years old, a middle-class college kid who had been willing to risk death in a war against Communist aggressors, but not to watch his life slip away day by day in a prison cell whose sole furnishings were a nine-inch high plank bed and a chamber pot, where boiled vegetables were the main diet, where the only visitors were lice and maggots, where there was nothing to read except propaganda tracts, and where there was no one to talk to except interpreters who used their broken English relentlessly to reform my errant imperialist mind. Ten years under such conditions would be impossible. It would be the same as death. Beyond ten years, I could not think.

While I played this dire numbers game and tried to cope with my throbbing toe, I listened to the solemn drone of the court proceedings. Only statements deemed pertinent to Fecteau and me were translated into English. Occasionally our names bobbed up in the stream of Chinese. My name was pronounced *Tahn-nye* and Fecteau's was *Fe-ke-toe*. Suddenly, I realized the preliminary speeches were over. The center judge of the tribunal fixed his eyes on the Chinese agent at the farthest end of our row. He pronounced the sentence and it was repeated in English. "Life." I had no time to conjure the implication of the sentence before the judge turned to the next agent in line. He also got life. I felt as though I had been clubbed from behind. I retained enough of my wits to hear the third agent, who was a radio operator, receive twenty years. The severity began to sink in. A few minutes before, a ten-year sentence seemed inconceivable. Now ten years seemed a slap on the wrist. The judge addressed another agent. He got life. And the next? Death. Inwardly, I staggered again. I heard another death sentence, perhaps two more deaths, when I realized the judge had arrived at Fecteau.

During our trial, defense attorneys for the Chinese agents had argued that they were the dupes of the "American Imperialists," that I was the real criminal and that Dick was my chief accomplice. The judge pronounced the sentence, Fecteau got twenty years. Immediately, I knew my sentence would be more severe. I would either be condemned to life in prison or death. The judge was now looking in my direction. I concentrated on holding myself steady; I was too flooded with sensation to feel normal fright. Every nerve in my body blazed with electric fire. I looked at life and death, and I braced myself. The interpreter listened to the Judge speak. I held my breath. "Life." Life imprisonment was the punishment ordered by the court.

I exhaled, and my body drained with relief. I became aware again of my throbbing toe. The command was given to leave the courtroom. We pivoted to the right and marched out. I did not have the chance to see the reaction on any of the Chinese agents' faces. Once we were outside the courtroom, Fecteau and I were led into a small antechamber where we were told to sit on the floor.

Fecteau was black with bitterness. "Well, it looks like my wife will die childless," he said.

"I don't believe it," I answered, my voice surprisingly high. "New Year's amnesty." I was grasping for straws of hope, trying to retrieve a future.

"There's no way I'm spending twenty years here," said Fecteau, as if anger could alter his sentence.

We knew talking was forbidden, but when a guard gestured for silence, Dick swore at him viciously. He had nothing left to lose. The guard jabbed his hand at a wall clock. My overheated imagination leaped to a conclusion. "It's bugged!" I hissed at Fecteau. He looked at me oddly. Moments later, we were separated for the return trip.

Back in my cell that evening, the jagged emotions I had felt at the sentencing flattened to the lowest despair ever. I felt as if a granite slab had been laid across my heart. I was not thankful for having been spared a death sentence. All I could think was that my life would never be my own. I imagined a stooped, white-haired American, shuffling about the prison corridors, doing menial chores and speaking a pidgin tongue to guards one-third his age, all the way into the next century. They would regard him as a curious relic from a time they learned about in history class. He would be too infirm in body or in spirit to pose any escape threat. The image was so vivid. The old man seemed to be standing there in my cell. I prayed I would not become that old man, but even if I didn't and my sentence were commuted, it seemed likely I would be locked up for years. My youth would be taken from me and I could not imagine what good the rest of my life would be.

I must have looked as bad as I felt, because a guard was posted at the window to my cell and he stayed there all night. My jailers may have worried that I would try to kill myself. The thought did cross my mind. But I had been raised to believe suicide was the ultimate sin. Even in that deepest despair I could not consider suicide seriously. The guard's passive face was the last thing I saw before I fell asleep.

The clanging prison bell woke me the next morning and before long the sun was shining and some of my optimism returned. I began to think less of the hopelessness of a "life sentence," and more of what hope remained to me. My release still might be negotiated, if not soon, then in a year or two. A few years seemed nothing now. Perhaps there would be an amnesty or a change in the Chinese government.

I was occupied with such musings when the interpreter came to my cell. I noticed he was thin and pale, obviously a member of the upper class, who, before the revolution, had been sent abroad to be cured of tuberculosis. Despite his lost privilege, he embraced Communism zealously and his inbred arrogance was now overlaid with political piety, an unattractive combination. He was gloating as he spoke to me.

"What did you think of your sentence?" he asked.

I told him I thought it was severe, much tougher than I expected. I didn't expect any sympathy from him and I didn't get any.

"You could have been sentenced to death," he said, suggesting he personally thought the court had been merciful. Then he went on, "Of course, you understand there is no hope for any reduction in your sentence, or any chance of appeal. But there are ways you can help yourself. Your conditions can change."

He was still gloating, but he had told me more than he had intended, and I was elated. After two years of interrogation, I had become experienced at fencing with interpreters, and I knew most of their psychological feints and thrusts. If this fellow threatened that there was no hope for an early release, it could only mean that there was. As for what he said about better conditions, I took that to mean that if I behaved myself and answered whatever questions the Chinese might have left to ask me, I could get better food or other minor prison amenities. But at that moment I was immune to such pompous wheedling.

"Look, if you've got questions, I'll answer them," I told the interpreter. "But not because I want any favors from you. The only thing I want is to be left alone."

If I was going to spend one more year, or fifty, in their prison, I'd be damned if I would give the Chinese the opportunity to pretend they were humanitarian captors. I'd shut myself away from them. My own prison would be far tighter than any they could ever provide.

2

AN AMERICAN HERO ON A FOOL'S MISSION

Thomas J. Christensen

OHN T. DOWNEY was an American hero. He was brave and daring, steadfast and loyal. In November 1952, as a CIA officer during the Korean War, he willingly, almost eagerly, put himself in extreme danger. Along with three American colleagues, he entered enemy airspace in Northeast China. Their mission was to recover a Chinese agent who had been inserted there earlier to gain intelligence, sow political discord, and weaken the Chinese war effort.

Downey had volunteered the year before while still an undergraduate at Yale, committing himself to become a paramilitary officer for the CIA, a new branch that was just four years old at the time. Although he was technically not a soldier, he trained like one with elite forces in Fort Benning, Georgia. And though he was not a soldier, most soldiers do not face the sort of danger that Downey and his three colleagues rather cheerfully accepted on that fateful November day.

Downey's faith in his nation endured across his twenty-one years of incarceration in the People's Republic of China (PRC). The CIA-authorized history of his ordeal appropriately called his dedication "extraordinary fidelity."[1] It was only the historic trips to China by National Security Adviser Henry Kissinger and President Richard Nixon in 1971 and 1972 that would change the geostrategic calculus of

U.S.-China relations sufficiently to secure the release of Downey and his colleague Richard Fecteau, the only survivors of that 1952 mission. From the Nixon breakthrough until the end of the Cold War, the United States and the PRC entered into a loose partnership to counter their common Soviet enemy. In that new environment, Fecteau was released in 1971 and Downey in 1973. Not only was Downey's spirit unbroken, but upon his release he rather quickly put his harrowing experience behind him, enrolled in Harvard Law School, started a family, and eventually became a judge in his home state of Connecticut.

His dedication after his release is all the more remarkable because he had every reason to be bitter at his own government. The mission that stranded him in Manchuria was quixotic in the extreme. The four of them—Downey, Fecteau, and two American pilots—had been sent to scoop up an anticommunist Chinese agent using a recovery system by which a passing plane would catch a line tied to the agent and yank him skyward. To label Downey and Fecteau's involvement in the mission a mistake would be an insult to mistakes. Neither had any useful language training nor any relevant education on the politics, history, or geography of mainland China. Neither was Chinese, so they would stick out like a sore thumb if their plane were to crash, which it did. And if they were captured, they both knew far too much as CIA case officers to maintain the plausible deniability of ignorance under coercion. They were indeed shot down. The pilots were killed in the crash, and Downey and Fecteau were ambushed at the pickup point by Chinese forces.

Two technicians were initially assigned the mission of exfiltrating the Chinese operative, which made sense. They would have been better trained with the equipment than Downey and Fecteau, and they would not have known the details of CIA training missions in China; therefore, their capture would have carried fewer national security risks. They might also have had a better chance of being released along with U.S. prisoners of war from the conflict in Korea. Downey writes that he had flown into China once before in October for a less dangerous resupply mission. He had maneuvered himself as a volunteer on that mission out of a simple desire for adventure. He also suggested that this action was a violation of the rules for CIA case officers

A Douglas-C-47 Skytrain with a hook for snatch pickups.

flying over China. He and his commanding officer were concerned that his participation might be discovered.

In Downey's recollection, two Chinese nationals were considered for the task but ultimately rejected. But the former CIA historian Nicholas Dujmovic writes that it was actually the two American technicians who were initially assigned to the flight but their security clearances were deemed insufficient. Downey and Fecteau, with the highest level of clearance—which carried with it much more valuable operational knowledge for the Chinese government to extract and a very clear designation as spies—were ordered on the flight in their stead. In a sense, then, the technicians knew too little to be sent into harm's way, but Downey and Fecteau, in retrospect, knew far too much.[2] Supporting this account of a last-minute change, one history of the airlifts into China said that they were trained "hurriedly" in how to operate the recovery system, which had recently been used to rescue downed pilots in North Korea.[3]

Is it too harsh to judge the decisions that led to their capture as foolish? Even the CIA seems to think they were. Since that 1952 operation, no American officers were again sent into the airspace over communist China on paramilitary intelligence operations,[4] even though the CIA continued to involve itself in paramilitary operations in China for years through foreign proxies, mostly ethnic Chinese and Tibetan insurgents battling China's People's Liberation Army (PLA). Therefore, it was not indifference regarding the target or abandonment of paramilitary methods altogether that led to the change. Rather, it seems that the CIA well understood its blunder and would not repeat it during the next two decades in which China remained a hostile Cold War enemy. Instead of bitterness, Jack Downey expressed sorrow for his immediate boss, whom he was sure carried a terrible burden for having ordered the mission.[5]

* * *

The paramilitary and intelligence operations of the early Korean War were plagued by problems: poorly trained personnel, weak intelligence about mainland China, the manipulation of the U.S. government by anticommunist Chinese citizens who were collaborating with American officials in Asia, and the pressing need to take some action, however risky, during the costly war.

During the war, the United States ran a rather large and secretive program to train Chinese nationals for paramilitary and intelligence missions against the communist regime in mainland China. American officials were stationed in Taiwan, Hong Kong, occupied Japan, Okinawa, and Saipan, a territory seized from Japan at the close of World War II. Several years after an armistice was reached in the Korean War in 1953, the United States would also train and work with Tibetan insurgents fighting PLA forces in the Himalayas from bases in India, Nepal, and Colorado.[6]

These programs, none of which were successful, were rooted in the experiences of World War II. In 1947, the CIA was founded through an act of Congress to partner with the new Department of Defense (which itself was formed from a merger of the Department of War and the Department of the Navy), the new National Security Council (NSC), and the preexisting State Department.[7] The CIA's predecessor was the highly secretive Office of Strategic Services (OSS), which successfully inserted paramilitary and intelligence officers behind enemy lines in Axis territories and wrought damage to the war efforts of Nazi Germany, militarist Japan, and fascist Italy. In 1948, the National Security Council would create the Office of Political Coordination (OPC), a new branch of the CIA that controlled clandestine services and paramilitary intelligence operations against the Soviet Union and its allies. In 1949, as the tide of the Chinese Civil War was turning in favor of the Chinese Communist Party (CCP), the OPC turned its attention to hampering or delaying CCP control of Chinese territory.[8] Downey and Fecteau, college freshmen in the spring of 1948, would join the OPC soon after their graduation in 1951.

On October 1, 1949, Mao Zedong declared victory for the CCP in the war against Chiang Kai-shek's Chinese Nationalist Party (KMT) on the mainland. Mao's speech marked the founding of the PRC, which would be controlled by the CCP. In late 1949, Chiang and many of his fellow nationalists would escape to the island of Taiwan and nearby offshore islands, where they refused to surrender. Instead, they declared that Taipei, Taiwan's capital, was the seat of the government of the Republic of China, the sole legitimate government of all China. The KMT and the CCP labeled each other rogue governments and claimed the other was illegally occupying a part of "one China." But, according to both parties' definitions, this rightfully included both the mainland and Taiwan.[9]

For its part, the United States would continue to recognize the government in Taipei as the sole legitimate Chinese government until 1979, when diplomatic recognition was formally transferred to the PRC and stripped from Taiwan. Chiang had been an ally in World War II against Japan, and his Republic of China was one of the "Big Four" Allied powers in the war: the United States, the United Kingdom, the Soviet Union, and the Republic of China. Like the Americans, Chiang was a staunch anticommunist. Though his popularity in the American press would wane in the years after World War II, he and his Wellesley-educated wife, Soong Mei-ling, were named *Time* magazine's "Man and Woman of the Year" for 1937.[10] Chiang, an anticommunist Christian, was far more appealing to Americans than were the communist atheists in Moscow and Beijing. After July 1949, when Mao Zedong announced that he would "lean to one side" (the Soviet side) in the Cold War and then formed a formal alliance with the USSR in February 1950, there seemed little hope, at least in the near term, of encouraging the PRC to become an independent or anti-Soviet communist force in the vein of Josip Broz Tito's Yugoslavia, which broke with the Soviets in 1948.[11]

Despite their shared aversion to communism, the Truman administration deeply mistrusted and was often annoyed by Chiang and the KMT. As far back as 1946, the administration had urged Chiang to reform his government in ways that might make it more popular and stable, thereby more capable of preventing an outright communist victory in the civil war. Truman even sent over perhaps the greatest statesman of his generation, the WWII military leader and future secretary of state and secretary of defense George C. Marshall, for an entire year to encourage KMT reform and attempt to forge a peace accord between the KMT and the CCP. But at the end of that year Marshall left in frustration. Chiang accepted generous amounts of military and economic assistance from the United States in the late 1940s but very rarely accepted advice on how to govern or how to deal with the CCP. Truman once famously complained about corruption in the KMT and that too much U.S. aid given to Chiang's government ended up in real estate back in the United States.[12] "They're thieves," he said later, "every damn one of them."

The flow of aid to Chiang was guaranteed by his supporters in Congress—the so-called "China lobby"—and because the Truman administration needed to rally sufficient domestic support around a theme of anticommunism for Cold War efforts. When Congress was asked to provide unprecedented peacetime aid to Europe for programs like the Marshall Plan, such aid could not pass without earmarks for Chiang. The administration could not justify big expenses to fight communism elsewhere without also supporting its staunchly anticommunist Chinese former ally, who himself faced a dire threat of communist overthrow. Still, Truman, Marshall, and Dean Acheson, who succeeded Marshall as secretary of state, trusted Chiang less and less. Frank Wisner, the director of the OPC, apparently shared that sentiment.[13] Before the Korean War broke out in June 1950, even though they, like the vast majority of Americans, were sincere in their desire to staunch the spread of communism, they also wanted to extract the United States from the Chinese Civil War, concentrate their efforts in the parts of the world deemed more important to U.S. national security, and perhaps foster an eventual split between the Soviet and Chinese communists.[14]

But that strategy was complicated by the simple fact that Chiang's government not only endured after its defeat on the mainland, but also, since it was ensconced on an island, stayed relatively safe from the Chinese communists' heavily land-based military one hundred nautical miles across the Taiwan Strait. The KMT's personnel were a ready and willing tool with which the Americans could harass the Chinese communists on the mainland. This was true even if, at the same time, few viewed Chiang's goal of recovering the mainland by military force as realistic. It took the CCP a couple of years to consolidate control of the entire mainland, especially in the portions that bordered the Southeast Asian mainland and in Tibet. Just south of the Chinese border in northern Laos and Burma, Chiang's KMT military had a fairly strong presence under General Li Mi. This meant that it would have been difficult and costly for the Truman administration to simply reject the KMT's offers to send agents into mainland China to agitate disgruntled elements of the population and reconnect with former KMT comrades in the civil war. Although they consistently acquiesced both publicly and privately to requests for cooperation from Taiwan to oppose the Chinese communists, the U.S. government still saw Chiang as fatally unpopular on the mainland. Moreover, U.S. officials believed Chiang wanted nothing more than to drag the United States into World War III with China and its Soviet ally so that Chiang could recover mainland China at America's expense.[15]

The Truman administration hoped that a "third force" could congeal in Chinese politics, one that was staunchly anticommunist but not associated with Chiang's failed government. Chiang had sometimes used brutal coercion and payoffs to consolidate his own power on the island, so there was really no viable anticommunist alternative to his leadership. Another option was to collaborate with Chiang's former military officers with whom he had fallen out of favor when the KMT lost the war on the mainland. Such figures met U.S. intelligence agents frequently in Hong Kong, which was neutral ground since it was still a British colony. They argued that only they, not Chiang, could mobilize support on the mainland to reverse the communist victories there. Among these officers, Cai Wenzhi was the most appealing to the Americans. A relatively charismatic general and Chiang's former deputy chief of staff of the army. he claimed to have contacts and agents on the mainland with whom his officers could link up and mobilize potentially hundreds of thousands of disgruntled citizens against the CCP regime. What appealed most to the Americans about the third force leaders was that they had their best connections in southern China, which was near Hong Kong and which the communists only conquered very late in the war. This lent some degree of credibility to their claims.[16]

Of course, Chiang was extremely suspicious of the third force and the U.S. government for supporting it.[17] His biographer, Jay Taylor, writes, "Chiang perceived most Taiwan-related activities by the Truman government as part of a conspiratorial plot to unseat him from power."[18] Chiang's son and security chief, Chiang Ching-kuo, even reportedly ordered assassination attempts on Cai by KMT agents in Hong Kong.[19] The administration worried that Chiang would complain about U.S. cooperation with his anticommunist rivals to his supporters on Capitol Hill and in the American public. One way to undercut that possibility, of course, was to maintain or increase U.S. support for Chiang's own clandestine paramilitary and intelligence-gathering operations on the mainland. So, in essence, the OPC ended up funding and training two rival clandestine Chinese operations against the PRC.

Both groups needed to make themselves appear as valuable as possible. Therefore, perhaps predictably, the United States heard exaggerated claims from both the third force officers and Chiang's deputies about the untapped potential of popular resistance to the ascendant CCP and each group's own special connections on the mainland, which they could mobilize into a fighting force and intelligence apparatus against the CCP.[20] What these entreaties from

Chiang and the third force consciously or unconsciously left out was that the CCP was a skilled Leninist organization, which meant that it was more adept at consolidating control over conquered territory than it was being portrayed. While the new and often brutal revolutionary CCP regime was almost certainly unpopular in segments of Chinese society, this did not mean that it would be easy or even possible to mobilize and arm large-scale resistance groups to oppose it.

For Chiang in particular, the maintenance of American support and the marketing of his government as a useful tool in the Cold War was a matter of long-term survival. Mao's CCP had vowed to "liberate" Taiwan from the KMT and thereby unify China. Moreover, Chiang's stated goal of recovering the mainland from the CCP was essential to the legitimacy of his government on Taiwan itself. That government was full of mainland Chinese, like Chiang himself, with few local connections to this island a hundred miles off the coast. Taiwan had been separated from China as a Japanese colony from 1895 until the end of World War II in 1945. After the KMT killed thousands of local political elites in a mass terror event launched in February 1947, Chiang's main argument for political legitimacy on the island was the notion that Taiwan was part of China and his KMT-led Republic of China was China's sole legitimate government. His expansive dreams of recovering all of China were, therefore, considered essential to the preservation of his much smaller goal of staying safely in power on Taiwan.[21]

After the PRC was formed in 1949, the United States had very weak intelligence about the mainland. It relied heavily on Chiang's intelligence services for assessments of domestic political conditions on the mainland, since Chiang claimed he had active agents planted there.[22] Though the KMT claimed that as many as two million armed rebels existed across the mainland, the CIA downgraded that estimate to about seven hundred thousand as of early 1951.[23] Third force generals, of course, also argued that there were several hundred thousand anticommunist armed holdouts that could weaken if not outright overthrow the CCP, but they also argued that those groups had no loyalties to Chiang's KMT.[24] In the January 1951 National Intelligence Estimate on China, the CIA rejected the notion that there was any purely internal force that could overthrow the communist Chinese. But with the advent of the Korean War, the United States began to lower its standards for paramilitary operations; almost any political trouble that might distract or weaken the Chinese communist war effort became worth it in the OPC's eyes.

Much of American behavior during the early Cold War was dictated by a major national security document drafted in the spring of 1950 called NSC 68. According to NSC 68, the Cold War was an existential struggle of ideas between communist tyranny on one side and freedom on the other. It called for the containment of communism globally rather than just in select geostrategically important locations. Before its drafting, the Truman administration had tried to focus on protecting only those "strongpoints" as defined by Director of Policy Planning George F. Kennan and otherwise avoid getting bogged down in expensive anticommunist struggles in less vital sections of the world.

But in 1950, Kennan's successor, Paul Nitze, drafted NSC 68, a more expansive—and much more expensive—plan for fighting the Cold War. It called not only for global containment of communism but, where possible, a "roll-back" of previous communist advances by undermining and overthrowing communist regimes in the Soviet-led bloc. This new plan was driven in part from the anxious fact that the United States had lost its nuclear monopoly the year before. The Americans could no longer blithely rely on nuclear deterrence to contain the USSR, given the risk of Soviet nuclear retaliation; it would need much more robust and much more expensive conventional military and political options to counter communist expansionism.[25]

Though there was widespread consensus on NSC 68 among international security policy makers within the administration, Truman shelved the plan in April and ordered most copies destroyed. The implied cost of the strategy was deemed too high in the years directly following World War II, a time in which most Americans were not eager to take on such sacrifices for expensive national security policies again, let alone fight in some far-flung corner of the world. And the strategy envisioned in NSC 68 was indeed very expensive. Truman probably worried that any leak of the document to the USSR would be dangerous. It would suggest that the United States' leadership believed it needed massive increases in the defense budget to protect U.S. national interests but could not secure those increases from a wary public and legislature.[26]

NSC 68, while top secret, was unusual for a classified document. In stark and simplistic language, it articulated a struggle of ideas that was designed to prepare the U.S. government for a sweeping and global opposition to communism. The document was not a typical analytical report. It was actually a primer of sorts for public speeches officials could give to explain why the United States was fighting the Cold War and the great sacrifices that would be required to win it. Dean Acheson famously said of the document's unusually moralistic and pedantic language that it was "clearer than truth."[27] Just two months earlier, in February 1950, Senator Joseph McCarthy had launched his notorious campaign against communist infiltration of American institutions; the more moralistic and proactively anticommunist tone of NSC 68 created a useful baseline for officials to defend their preferred policies and evade being targeted by his campaign. For a complex set of bureaucratic reasons that seem hard to imagine today—the OPC, though nominally a CIA entity, received its strategic guidance from Nitze's Office of Policy Planning at the State Department.

Unlike the military buildups necessary to fulfill NSC 68's vision, OPC outreach to both Chiang's government and the third force volunteers for the purpose of harassing and destabilizing the new PRC was relatively cheap. Washington was also hungry for intelligence about the CCP regime, as the American officials had been driven entirely out of the mainland in late 1949 and early 1950 as Mao pledged, in good Leninist style, to "clean the house before inviting guests."[28] Before the outbreak of war in Korea, the OPC operations in the Far East were not only smaller but also much more expertly run. The officers in Taiwan and Hong Kong were highly experienced and linguistically capable. The Hong Kong operation was considered the most important because it involved the so-called third force personnel.[29]

But one major problem for the covert operations against China was that a close ally of the United States, the United Kingdom, had outlawed any paramilitary activities in Hong Kong aimed at the PRC government out of fear that it would provoke a PRC attack on the territory, ending British rule there.[30] Moreover, the U.S. government feared that Hong Kong was penetrated by PRC spies who could compromise the operations. So even though many of the third force operations were aimed at nearby southern China, it was difficult and somewhat risky to train and launch any operations from Hong Kong. In 1950, the United States began moving many of its OPC facilities for Chinese operations to military bases in Japan (which was occupied after its defeat in World War II until 1951), Okinawa, and Saipan, a U.S. territory in the Mariana Islands seized from Japan by the U.S. Marine Corps after a brutal campaign in the summer of 1944.[31]

Then, on June 25, 1950, Kim Il-sung's North Korea crossed the 38th parallel and invaded South Korea in a massive armored assault that was clearly supported by the Soviet Union. Even though the Truman administration had excluded South Korea from the Asian "defense perimeter" six months earlier as part of Kennan's strongpoint approach, Truman ordered U.S. forces into Korea two days later. Those forces operated as part of a multinational United Nations mission to save the imperiled South Korean regime, which was led by its pro-American and Princeton-educated president Syngman Rhee. Elements of the U.S. Navy's Seventh Fleet were deployed in the Taiwan Strait, thus reversing the president's pledge from earlier that year to remove the United States from the Chinese Civil War. But Truman still did not trust Chiang and insisted the navy was there to prevent an attack from either side of the Taiwan Strait.[32]

The outbreak of the Korean War and Mao's fateful decision a few months later to secretly send hundreds of thousands of Chinese troops into the Korean peninsula to attack advancing American, UN, and South Korean forces finally gave Truman the opportunity to mobilize his nation around the active Cold War strategy envisioned in NSC 68. The U.S. defense budget would soon triple from its levels before the Korean War. Most of those resources would not be spent in the Korean theater, which was still not considered as important as Japan, the Middle East, and especially Western Europe, where the NATO alliance had been formed the previous year.

The outbreak of the Korean War and its escalation into a U.S.-PRC proxy war would lead to an even more dramatic expansion of the OPC, especially its activities in Asia. By the fall of 1951, the OPC accounted for 50 percent of the CIA budget and 20 percent of its personnel. The OPC grew from 300 officers in 1949 to more than 2,200 in 1952.[33] The budget grew seventeenfold.[34]

Downey and Fecteau entered into this context in 1951. Their mission was to train former KMT soldiers associated with the third force and prepare them before they were flown into Northeast China to foment rebellion and gather intelligence about the CCP regime and its military wing, the People's Liberation Army.

Neither Downey nor Fecteau knew much about Chinese history, politics, or language. They were both recent college graduates, too young to have had experience in paramilitary operations with the OSS in World War II. Even before they were ordered on the flight that would see them captured, there was something excessively optimistic and strategically shallow about the entire mission. For his part, Downey recognized the incongruity of training battle-hardened soldiers from China in paramilitary operations in their own home country, which he had never even visited. In a 2009 interview with Nicholas Dujmovic, Downey reported in typically humble fashion: "I was in charge of this group of a dozen Chinese. . . . I was one of the teachers, which is appalling since I had no experience of my own and was just feeding them what someone had fed me. . . . These guys all had much more experience in military affairs than I had."[35] Elsewhere, Dujmovic writes that this was hardly an unusual condition for the early years of CIA paramilitary operations, which were characterized by disarray and "learning by doing."[36]

Some young recruits to the expanded Korean War OPC program had more experience in China than Downey and Fecteau. One was Downey's classmate at Yale, James Lilley, who would go on to a legendary career at the CIA, later becoming a senior official at the State Department and the Defense Department, and eventually the only person to head U.S. diplomatic missions on both sides of the Taiwan Strait. Lilley had spent a good part of his childhood in China as the son of an American oil industry executive. But even Lilley was far removed from the China of 1952 when he dutifully started his undercover work in Hong Kong and Taiwan. He had attended prep school in the United States and majored in Russian at Yale. His bosses assumed he would be fluent in Chinese. In his memoir, Lilley writes, "My superiors decided to move me to Taiwan to take advantage of my limited Chinese-language ability. 'But you were born and raised in China,' they protested. Yes, I was, but that just meant that I could speak Chinese like a four-year-old. I had mastered the vocabulary to count, eat, swear, and defecate."[37] In the fall of 1952, CIA Director Walter Beddell Smith said that the difficulties in OPC "stemmed, by and large, from the use of improperly trained personnel."[38] An internal CIA inspection report of the Far East Branch similarly described its operations as "poorly staffed, poorly planned, and poorly executed."[39]

Like the national security establishment in general, the CIA and OPC were largely staffed by white members of European descent, like Downey, Fecteau, and Lilley. The successes of the OSS in Europe in World War II were facilitated by the ready availability of first-generation European Americans who looked like the locals and often had native or near native fluency in French, Italian, Polish, Romanian, Ukrainian, or Serbo-Croatian. They could understand local conditions and operate effectively and safely behind enemy lines. Since they were generally infiltrating countries occupied by the German Nazi regime, they could often link up with resistance fighters who spoke English and wanted nothing more than to rid their countries of foreign invaders. While the original leadership of the smaller pre–Korean War OPC in Asia had tremendous experience in China from before the revolution, younger officers put in places of authority in the OPC after the Korean War surge, like Downey and Fecteau, did not. These nonetheless intelligent and dedicated OPC officers had neither the knowledge nor skills to be as effective as their World War II predecessors in Europe.

But that was not the only glaring difference that explains the relative success of the OSS in World War II and the almost unadulterated failure of Cold War OPC paramilitary operations in Europe and Asia, not just communist China. Communist countries had no organized, sympathetic resistance forces on the ground, and there was only weak potential to create them. An internal CIA history of the OPC lamented that "the communist countries know a great deal about how to deal with their internal security; consequently little resistance by the local population could be found."[40] The communist parties allied with the Soviet Union shared Moscow's Leninist penchant for social control and surveillance, and the CCP was no exception. Moreover, unlike Poland, France, or Ukraine in 1942, PRC China in 1952 was not occupied by a hostile foreign power, even if it might be considered infected with the European ideology of Marxism-Leninism. This meant the potential was much lower for active patriotic resistance that could link up with infiltrating OPC-trained agents than it was for OSS agents operating in Nazi-controlled territories in World War II.

The problems of CIA paramilitary operations in China continued into the next decade. Highly inexperienced U.S. trainers inserted Tibetan freedom fighters into western China, even though those trainers had never been to Tibet and did not know its physical or political geography.[41] At least in that case the Tibetan fighters were entering an environment in which they could more easily blend in with the locals, many of whom viewed the Chinese troops as foreign invaders. Still, no populations were liberated by these operations, and many hundreds of U.S.-trained Tibetans were killed or captured.[42]

During the Korean War, the United States often relied on intelligence about the mainland from captured Chinese soldiers on the peninsula, many of whom were former KMT soldiers fighting with the "Chinese People's Volunteers." They were ordered by the PRC government to support North Korea but had few loyalties to the CCP. They often wanted to defect to Taiwan or at least were persuaded to do so by psychological pressure campaigns in the POW camps. Their relatively high defection rate itself and the general dissatisfaction they expressed with the new government in China must have given the CIA some unfounded hope about the prospect of locating resistance and fomenting turmoil on the mainland. Without enough trained soldiers and civilians fluent in Mandarin Chinese (most Chinese Americans at the time spoke Cantonese or other non-Mandarin dialects), the United States had to rely on KMT interpreters to interrogate Chinese prisoners. The U.S. Air Force tried to fix the shortage of language-capable military personnel by launching a wartime Mandarin Chinese program at Yale, but such training simply took too long to ramp up effectively for a hot war.[43]

KMT agents were also hired to teach "political education" classes to the prisoners. For those prisoners who did not jump at the first opportunity to defect to the enemy during the war but were simply captured, this amounted to anticommunist brainwashing that closely mimicked KMT propaganda about recovering the mainland. Even though the OPC was more interested in creating an anticommunist third force separate from the KMT than simply supporting the KMT's efforts, these education classes at least instilled anticommunism.[44] By the summer of 1951, some twenty-one thousand Chinese POWs were in UN Command's custody, so U.S. forces in Korea had little choice but to rely on Chiang's personnel, which revealed the CIA's connection to all these POW activities. Chinese operatives were often flown behind enemy lines in wartime Korea and China on ostensibly privately owned aircraft belonging to Civil Air Transport (CAT), an airline owned and operated in part by Claire Chennault, the legendary commander of the Flying Tigers, the American volunteer aviators who defended China against Japanese invaders even before Pearl Harbor.[45] Downey and Fecteau were onboard a CAT aircraft when they were shot down and captured in Manchuria. Chennault's CAT airline logged fifteen thousand flights between Taiwan and Korea during the course of the war.[46]

This reliance on nationalist interpreters and "teachers" created danger for the Americans. The nationalist agents spun their intelligence about the mainland to make it more plausible that Chiang could indeed return to the mainland and overthrow the communist regime there. This could thereby shore up the fading prospects that an anticommunist rebellion could be catalyzed by agents in areas of alleged resistance by OPC operations. Since nationalist government agents teaching political education classes lured defectors and other prisoners away from the mainland and to Taiwan to bolster Chiang's own legitimacy there as the true leader of Chinese anticommunism, this arrangement was inconsistent with OPC's goal of creating a credible third force that was neither communist nor nationalist.[47] In late 1951, the CIA assessed that no large organized guerilla movement likely existed in mainland China for either the nationalists or the third force to exploit. Given the press of wartime necessity, however, OPC operations on the mainland continued.[48]

The covert missions involving noncommunist Chinese were almost all unadulterated failures. The only real exception was on the Korean peninsula itself. Koreans were fighting on both sides in the war, as were many foreigners, including hundreds of thousands of Chinese in support of North Korea and a multinational force fighting under a UN flag alongside the South Koreans. Although we do not have some of the fine-grained detail, it seems clear from available open-source histories that CIA operations on the peninsula itself during the Korean War were more successful than any of the operations in which Downey, Fecteau, and Lilley were engaged with third force or KMT operatives in mainland China. In Korea, the clandestine operations may have weakened the North Korean and Chinese war efforts by providing useful intelligence about their troop strengths and movements (commonly referred to as the "order of battle"). Therefore, in Korea, the intelligence gathering operations seemed to perform better than the OPC paramilitary or intelligence-gathering operations on the mainland itself.[49]

According to the historian David Cheng Chang, it appears that even these operations had an enormous toll. One group, called "Unit 8240," comprised two or three hundred former Chinese POWs who had been soldiers in the Chinese People's Volunteers. These prisoners were initially mobilized for—or coerced into—missions in which they were inserted into North Korea and then walked back to the 38th parallel, gathering intelligence on enemy troop dispositions along the way. The vast majority were apparently killed or captured in these operations.[50] But unlike in OPC operations on the mainland during the Korean War, from which apparently no agents returned, at least several dozen of the men of Unit 8240 survived multiple missions and were eventually sent to Taiwan. Still, given the low survival rate it is fair to say that these Korea-focused missions shared one grim quality of the OPC missions on the mainland: a rather callous indifference to the lives of the Chinese collaborators.

But even in wartime, communist China was not the same as battlefield Korea. Political subterfuge is more complicated than simply gathering intelligence on troop dispositions, and even the latter is harder in a stable political environment than in a more fluid war situation. Both the nationalists in Taiwan with whom Lilley cooperated and the third force agents with whom Downey and Fecteau worked simply did not have well-placed or well-organized opposition contacts in China, disgruntled citizens with whom they could collaborate in paramilitary operations or from whom they could gather actionable intelligence about the Chinese war effort in Korea. Downey and Fecteau's third force Chinese team were dropped into Manchuria in July 1952, apparently failed to link up with any alleged local anticommunist warlords, and were captured and turned by the Chinese security forces in the following months. This enabled the November ambush that killed the two American pilots and captured the two CIA officers. For his part, Lilley dispatched his first Taiwan-based team into Manchuria in October 1952 with similarly disappointing results. He wrote, "My team successfully parachuted into Manchuria in October 1952. . . . We hoped that they would be able to give us helpful information on Chinese troop movements on the Chinese-Korean border. They came up once on the radio and then we never heard from them again. We guess that they assimilated into Chinese society or had been caught."[51]

Lilley summarized the problem for the OPC like this: "Contrary to CIA predictions, our missions were unable to locate or exploit the kind of discontent among the Chinese population that could be used to establish intelligence bases in China. The Chinese were not willing to side with outside forces."[52] He continued: "One explanation for our lack of success was that security was so tight in Communist China." Moreover, "our intelligence partners in Taiwan were a defeated and demoralized group. . . . If they once did have good intelligence contacts on the mainland, those sources had eventually dried up."[53]

While frustrated with his charges in Taiwan, Lilley had particular disdain for Downey's third force collaborators, whom he accused of having "swindled" the CIA by inflating their influence and connections and then concocting fabricated intelligence reports based on publicly available newspaper accounts of events on the mainland rather than from clandestine activity.[54] On the occasion of Downey and Fecteau's trial in November 1954, the Chinese government issued statistics on CIA clandestine operations in China from 1951 to 1953. In all, just over two hundred agents had been inserted into the PRC in those two years. About half of them had been killed and the other half captured. According to an American expert chronicling U.S. clandestine activities, these Chinese statistics were not questioned as propagandistic but accepted as factual in internal U.S. government reports.[55] And the more straightforward incursions from Burma by remnant nationalist troops under General Li Mi, themselves backed by the OPC, fared no better. The PLA consistently repelled the invaders in China's southwest without ever greatly hampering China's pursuit of a bloody but limited war on the Korean peninsula.[56] It is hard to imagine a more pure record of failure than this.

3

WHO I AM, WHERE I CAME FROM

ONE OF the first rules in prison is to submerge one's self in whatever routine is imposed. Let the trivia work as a sponge to absorb each day of confinement. Forget the taste of ice cream, a girl's laughter, drinks with friends, Christmas with family. These are the memories to be repressed. But the forgetting must be selective, for the humiliations of prison can be withstood only if one keeps his essential identity. And in prison, I never forgot who I was and where I came from.

I had told the Chinese court that my home was in New Britain because that compact, rugged industrial city was where my mother lived and where I had spent part of my adolescence. But New Britain was just one of the places I thought of as home. The others were Wallingford, Connecticut, the town where the Downey family lived, where I was born, where I spent my most innocent childhood. Then Choate School and Yale University, the campuses where I made the passage to manhood, were the other places I call home.

Wallingford, where my deepest roots are, was the first stop on the rail line running north from New Haven. It was a classic New England combination of factory and farm. The plants belonged to the International Silver Company, the Wallace Silverware Company, and the Backus "Star Brand" Fireworks Company. Even in the Depression, when my younger brother Bill, my sister Joan, and I were growing up, the factories were busy and they gave jobs to many of the town's eleven thousand people. For us kids, our domain was outside of town, the countryside where we could swim in any pond or creek, and there was no water that scared us. In little Wallingford, we had a sense of unbounded space, and we roamed its back roads and woods and pastures for miles on foot and on bicycle. Here was where I started my sense of adventure in life.

The Downeys were farmers who came to Wallingford from Ireland before the American Civil War. My grandfather, Jack F. Downey, left the new family homestead when he was fourteen years old to work in a manufacturing shop in town. Eventually he saved enough money to buy a tavern across the tracks from the railroad station. Although it happened to be the poor side of the tracks, that did not deter him in his political ambitions. In this country which treated him so well, my grandfather became a devout Democrat. He served one term in the state legislature and many years as chairman of the town Democratic party. He saw his sons' successes exceed his own. For a time, the intersection of South Cherry Street and Quinnipiac Street, where his tavern stood, amounted to a Downey enclave. Diagonally opposite the tavern was a grocery store owned by my Uncle Tommy, and on another corner was the main firehouse, where my Uncle Jim was the chief. A few blocks up Center Street was the brick-paved main street of Wallingford, where my grandfather's first son, Jack E. Downey, my father, maintained two offices. My father was the pride and joy of the entire family. He graduated from Catholic University in Washington, DC, in 1920 then graduated from Yale Law School in 1923. My father had one office for his private law practice above a bank; the other was his office for serving as probate judge in the Town Hall. The municipal building stood at the top of the Center Street hill. When I drove with my father down the hill to visit my grandfather, the tires of his big car made a loud humming noise rushing over the brick pavement. I was on top of the world.

My family's prosperity was measured by the houses where we lived. Our first house, the one where I was born, was small and rented. The second house was larger, at a better address on North Main Street, but still rented. From here I was able to enroll in the Putnam School.

This nursery was run by the refined Miss Morgan, who insisted on the benefit one could get from knowing French. I was more enchanted by the nature walks to the nearby Harrison Park looking for stones or digging for worms. After four subsequent years in public schools, I transferred to parochial school, named for the Holy Trinity. By this time my father had saved enough money to buy a lot on the street in the town's best new neighborhood, as noted in the local newspaper. The new house, built by my parents with a circular staircase and seven spacious rooms, was my new castle. It stood on a hill across from the local country club, whose greens and fairways were almost an extension of our front lawn.

The absolute security we had known as beloved children of a prominent Irish family in a small town ended on an autumn day of my eighth year. I was playing with friends a few houses down from my home when my aunt came through the backyards to call me inside and tell me my father was in the hospital. I found out later, reading the local news, that he had an auto accident driving back from seeing a client. His Ford station wagon had run off a quiet country road and hit a tree. No one knew how the accident happened, whether he had been speeding or had swerved to avoid a dog, a deer, or another car. He died at the hospital, never having regained consciousness. I only knew that he was my father and that I loved him, that my future was now going to be different. This loss was so big, I never got over it. I tried to do well in school, always looking for the father figure I had lost. In later years, when I become involved in sports, my coaches became my father figures.

Our outward lives did not change immediately; my mother made sure of that. We stayed in the same big house for awhile, as my mother quietly looked for a job. But the months passed, and money was mentioned more and more often. As the oldest son, I tried to assume some manly responsibilities. Since the golf course clubhouse was directly across the road and I was big and tall for my age, I had no trouble getting a job as a caddie. I kept a careful record of the number of rounds I worked and my earnings, separating tips from fees. As my shortsightedness got worse, I missed finding the balls. One day after I missed two balls, I got no pay, even though I had sweated all day in the tall grass.

We left Wallingford in 1941 when I was eleven. My mother had inherited half ownership in a three-family house in New Britain, where her family had settled and where she still had three living sisters. Since she had taught in this city for twelve years before she married my father, she had no problem finding a teaching job again. With her salary and the sale of the Wallingford house, we had a secure, although a much more modest life. As soon as I settled in New Britain, I found a job as a newspaper boy with a neighbor named Tom Meskill,[1] who was two years my senior. He first hired me then sold me the route for five dollars. I got up early and raced to get my job done. My mother allowed me to keep part of my earnings, and I bought my first volume of an encyclopedia. Once I finished my job, I would climb onto my bed and read my encyclopedia.

I had barely begun to feel at home after three years in New Britain when I was back in Wallingford again, this time as a scholarship student at the preparatory Choate School for boys. Every summer our family spent our vacation along the Connecticut shore. This year I had become friends with a Choate boy, whose mother heard that I was a good student and I had been elected class president at Saint Joseph School. She urged my mother to let me apply to Choate School. At first that was not my mother's plan; as a widow with three children she could not afford to send me to a prep school. But the other mother suggested that I apply for a scholarship from Choate. I had dreamed of going back home to Wallingford since the day I left. I arrived on the Choate campus with a townie's chip on my shoulder, but I soon sloughed it off. I felt more than accepted at Choate; I was part of it. I began spending summers there as a counselor for New York City youths who attended a camp run by the school.

I may have been surprised to find myself at Choate, but by the time I graduated I was not surprised to find myself headed for Yale University. Again I was a scholarship student, and though I lacked the J. Press wardrobes of my richer classmates, I was even happier at Yale than at Choate. By senior year, I was on the varsity football team. There were five of us who played both offense and defense, and we got off only at half time—we considered ourselves the iron men. I also was the captain of Yale's varsity wrestling team. While typical Yalies dressed in ties and blazers, I made a virtue of cultivating a jock image by wearing ragged sweaters and baggy khaki trousers every-where I could. My dress did not keep me from being elected class representative from Timothy Dwight, my undergraduate college at Yale, or being rushed at Saint Anthony Hall, a two-year fraternity, in my junior year.

Even in my Yale years, I did not miss any opportunity for adventure. I rode the bus to Ivy League colleges to play football and wrestled up and down the Northeast. I also rode with my St. A's brother John Kittredge to Smith College for mixers. And I was a blind date for girls who pined for my dashing roommate, Putney Westerfield.

The summer after sophomore year, my poor mother reluctantly agreed to let me join classmate Bayard Fox to tour Europe. We covered France, Spain, England, and Scotland. We found the best way to see the country was by hitchhiking; not only did we get to see more of the countryside, we also got to meet the people, and eat at local eateries. Several times we slept in the park or on a field of a farm. Bayard and I could not have been from more different backgrounds; he was from an upper-class family in the city of Philadelphia, and I was from an Irish family with a widowed teacher mother. But as we had lived and died together in wrestling for Yale University, we felt as close as brothers. Bayard and I also shared the same sense of adventure.

The last summer in college, my Yale buddies Bob Longman, Henry Ott-Hansen, and Bayard Fox and I wanted to make the most of it. We decided to venture to Alaska. Two underclassmen, one of whom had a car, got wind of our plan and joined us. In mid-May 1950, some of us started out of New Haven for our adventure west. Along the way we picked up our group one by one until all six of us were in the old station wagon. The trip to Alaska covered almost five thousand miles of highway. It took us at least eight days of continuous driving. All the way, we followed a simple scheme: three guys sat in the front, three slept in the back, and we made a counter-clockwise rotation every two hours. To break the monotony of driving, we stopped every once in a while at a diner to have a good meal, or we would get washed up and go to a local dance. There were long stretches of driving on flat ground where we saw nothing but cornfields, so we sang to amuse ourselves. A lot of the roads were not paved, and at times the riding could be rough. We certainly learned how wide and open the country was. It all worked out well most of the way, except that the old car broke down once somewhere on the west coast of British Columbia, Canada. We had to wait fourteen long hours for a spare part.

Our last stop was to be Anchorage, Alaska. Once we got there, we were surprised to find that there were hundreds of young guys just like us milling around in town looking for summer jobs. But we were lucky that we accidentally drove into Valdez, which had a thriving shipping business. The cargo ship needed longshoremen, and eventually all six of us were hired. They paid us $2.17 per regular hour, $3.25 per overtime hour. That was good money. But the work load was grueling, and sometimes the overtime went over twenty-four hours straight. The days were long. We had to sleep in daylight. Once the ship was unloaded, we had to wait for the next ship to come ashore. These were the times we ventured to the small downtown of Valdez.

The first time I heard the word "Korea," we were on Main Street in Valdez, the one-block-long, only paved street in town. Some guy ran down the street yelling, "The war broke out in Korea! The war broke out in Korea!" The six of us stopped in our tracks. We looked at each other and asked, "Where the hell is Korea?" None of us knew. And we thought it had nothing to do with us, and soon forgot about it. We went into a bar and had some beer, and we drove around aimlessly. When Bayard went inland for fly fishing, the rest of us went to the beach and dared each other to jump into the icy cold water. While war was going on in Korea, our lives in America were carefree and exuberant, and we knew nothing but happiness.

A couple of months later, Bayard Fox and I were the first ones to leave. We flew to Portland, Oregon, and then decided to hitchhike southward toward San Francisco. This trip down the West Coast of the U.S. was just the extension of our trip in Europe. We stuck out our thumbs by the roadside and got picked up by some nice folks. We talked and laughed while looking out of the windows of a truck. San Francisco was a dreamland for me; the Golden Gate Bridge, Chinatown, the trolley cars gliding down steep hills all seemed so exotic. We attended a few parties arranged by a cousin of Bayard. Then we continued our hitchhiking trip out of San Francisco all the way to Yellowstone Park. Once we got to Wyoming, Bayard went on another fly fishing trip somewhere, and I took a bus back to Connecticut.

As I was the only one on the bus when we were in Connecticut, the bus driver went out of his way to get me closer to my home.

My football training started two weeks before the other students returned to the Yale campus. I was very aware that this was my last year at the University. I needed to make a good showing in my football games; the game depended highly on the five tough guys, we needed to be in top shape. My senior fall season went quickly. We lived on the highs and lows of our football battles. All in all, our football team did well; we had a 6–3 record. The best part of our football results was that we won "The Game" against Harvard on their home turf. That day's weather was terrible, and Cambridge caught the tail of a late November hurricane. It was windy, rainy, and some hail was beating down on us, but we battled to the end and won, 14–6. We were aware this would be a Yale vs. Harvard football record for generations to come.

When the spring term came along, all the seniors had become somebody. Friends of mine would be known as a member of the Whiffenpoofs, a prestigious singing group; a varsity golfer; a varsity wrestler; and a varsity hockey player. Others would be known as members of a certain secret society; an editor of *Yale Daily News;* and a radio broadcaster. I recounted my accomplishments at Yale. By the spring of 1951, I had a sense that my job at Yale was done, and now I was wondering what I would do after graduation. Although we were preoccupied with our senior lives at Yale and on other campuses, we were aware of the changing world outside. The threat of Communism's expansion was in the news almost every day. We heard President Truman's forceful speech against Communism, and we saw short films of Russian Communist army tanks rolling into China. We knew the whole of mainland China had been taken over by Communism, and Generalissimo Chiang Kai-shek had evacuated with his Kuomintang army to Taiwan.

My fraternity brothers would sit around in groups and discuss our future in the new world. We speculated who was going to do what after college. We knew who planned to be married, who would travel abroad, who would go to law school and so on. I had always dreamed of being a lawyer just like my father, and running for political office later. But first I had to earn and save some money.

One day in early spring in the basement bar of Saint Anthony Hall, a brother a year ahead of our class was present. He gave us the story of the newly established Central Intelligence Agency organization (CIA). He told us the CIA was the successor of the Office of Strategic Services (OSS). We all had heard of the glamorous stories of the OSS during World War II. The upperclassman emphasized that now we had our own war in Korea, and our new agency, the CIA. He promised that the CIA would be doing things as exciting as the old OSS. Besides, he added, the CIA was less stuffy than the State Department. Like all seniors at the time, we admired the other seniors in our class who were veterans of World War II. Now it was our turn to contribute. North Korea was obviously the aggressor. It had the backing of Communist China and Russia. South Korea had the backing of the United Nations and the United States. We wanted to stop Communism the way some of our veteran classmates had stopped Nazism.

One night a St. A's, a brother named Reg ran into the basement bar. He announced with excitement that the CIA had sent a recruiter to the Yale campus. The next evening there was going to be a gathering at the residence of Professor Arnold Wolfers from the Political Science department. At least two dozen seniors were at that meeting. An undistinguished CIA representative spoke fluently of the new organization and its mission. There were plans to organize the resistance fighters and to parachute behind enemy lines. It all sounded irresistibly adventurous to young men like us. At the end of the talk, I was among those who submitted our names and credentials. In those days, the students at Yale knew of another political science professor named Sherman Kent who went down to Washington, DC, almost every weekend. There surely were more campus recruiting meetings going on, as I later learned.[2]

That evening I was told to come back the next day for a one-on-one initial interview. When I went back the next day, the recruiter noticed that my major was English, my foreign language was Spanish, and I played several sports. A few weeks later, I received an application form from Washington in a disguised envelope. I filled out the form and took it with me when I went to Washington by train for the official interview. To my disappointment, the interview was held at an area known as Foggy Bottom, a dismal name. The offices were in a two-story barracks-style temporary building. At the end of the interview, the officer told me that, if I were to be accepted, I would be notified by telephone. I went home and had my twenty-first birthday while anxiously waiting to hear from the CIA. When the phone call finally came, it also went individually to everyone who had been accepted. The calls were made the same evening through the same main Yale switchboard. The names of those selected were quickly common knowledge on campus. So much for the high-level clandestine operations! We were told to be in Washington the next day for proceedings. The short notice seemed rather arbitrary. The only way to make it on time was to fly from New York City to Washington. It was outlandish but rather exciting as well. Much to my delight, among my twenty-one St. A's brothers of the class of '51, seven had made it. Among our four roommates at Timothy Dwight College at Yale, two made it.[3]

Suddenly, my life had a purpose. I was to join the movement to stop the evil advance of Communism. I no longer wondered what I was going to do after graduation. Also the CIA payment was good; it was about three times the teacher salary of my mother. I could save it all for law school. Besides, I could travel to Asia. I had been fascinated by Asia since I was a young boy. I remember during the Second World War, as kids, we collected pennies to save the starving children in China. During my second year at Yale, I thought I was going to China to teach English through the Yale-in-China program. Communism ended that dream for me. Now the new Communist China had become our new enemy in the Korean War. But I was sure we were the good guys, and we were to save the world from the oppression of Communism.

In the meantime, there were a lot of senior parties to attend, both at Yale and at Smith College. I continued to hitch a ride with John Kittredge to go up to Smith College to meet with our gals. The question of what I was going to do after college kept coming up with my mother and my friends. I had to make evasive answers, not characteristic of me. The more I tried to avoid the question, the more suspicious I seemed. Once Nancy said jokingly, "I hope you are not going to be an international spy or something." I almost fell out of my chair. She had no idea how close she had gotten.

The weekend before our Yale graduation, my fraternity brother John Kittredge got married to his longtime sweetheart from Smith College. It was an idealistic wedding of established New England families. The reception was in a beautiful family garden. The handsome young couple was surrounded by well-dressed handsome Yale guys and beautiful young ladies from Smith College. The hilltop garden seemed to be humming with harmonious songs of peace and prosperity. The newlyweds were to fly to Bermuda for their honeymoon. In the back of my mind, I knew this would be my last hurrah before I left these dear people and peaceful places behind. I would soon march into the front line of a war. I might never be back again. I was intoxicated by my imagined scene in Casablanca, so "Play it again, Sam!" I got roaring drunk. I don't remember how I got home that night. I do remember that I missed my graduation ceremony the next morning, much to my mother's disappointment. But since I was going to war, the graduation ceremony seemed meaningless.

The CIA training classes were held in Washington, D.C. I found in my class of thirty-five, that there were two of my fraternity brothers, and five classmates from Yale, Bayard Fox among them. There were also four from Harvard, and seven from Princeton. Ben McAlpin was one from Princeton, who was also from Connecticut. To be sure there were men from other colleges, but the tone of those 1951 classes was distinctively Ivied. Many of my rivals from other colleges soon became my closest friends. As the training classes in Clandestine Operations began, it seemed an extension of my college days. By July, we were transferred to Fort Benning, Georgia to start three months of military training. Here it was more like a college summer camp. At Fort Benning, our class was joined by young officers from all three armed services, which brought our total number in the class up to seventy-five. Now the atmosphere was really getting serious. We continued our training in field craft and the use of weapons and explosives. We slogged through the swamps and pine woods of southern Georgia. We college students had never gotten as down and dirty as this. But we gritted our teeth and put on brave faces to tough it out. We did not lose our high spirit at all. On free weekends, we piled into cars and drove for hours to visit exotic Southern cities, one after another. In Phoenix City, Alabama, a tawdry town famous for its vice, we hung around bars and reveled in our carefully nurtured sophistication. When the time came for parachute jump school, we were more than ready to prove how robust we were; we jogged everywhere we went. We made sure that none of our guys balked on any jump, whether it was from a 150-foot high practice tower or from any of the five real jumps we made from airplanes. I was a heavyweight; when I jumped, I went down fast and landed like a ton of bricks, while the lighter guys came down like a feather and landed on their feet.

In mid-October, we returned to the Washington area again for a final six weeks of clandestine methods instruction. We studied at a safe house situated in a non-descript place in Maryland. It was here we received our first real assignments. Members of our class who had prized academic specialties tended to draw missions in Europe. Bayard Fox, who spoke French, was assigned to Europe. The rest of us were assigned to Asia and the war zone in Korea.

After the Korean war had raged back and forth in the Korean peninsula for more than a year, the fighting stabilized at the 38th parallel. Most of us in our training class wanted to get to the war zone before the fighting was over. Before I left Washington, I wrote to my mother and my girlfriend and paid a last visit to the Lincoln Memorial. Under the giant statue, I was spellbound; there was so much good one person could do if he had the courage to stand up. I squared my shoulders and walked away telling myself it was time for me to take on my share of duty for my country.

The three of us, Ben McAlpin, Joe E. from Georgetown, and I were flying out of Washington together. Our first stop was San Francisco. We stayed overnight in a hotel on a hilltop overlooking the glistening San Francisco Bay with the suspended Golden Gate Bridge. The hotel had a pool of water and a live mermaid, and we could not take our eyes off of her. The next day, we boarded a commercial airline for our next stop in Hawaii. In the '50s, Northwest Orient aircraft had two levels; the lower level had seats that could turn into bunk beds, and the upper level was a bar with a lounge. For whatever reason, I had fallen into a sound sleep, and my comrades were unable to wake me up. Eventually the two guys literally picked me up, lifted me out of the bunk, and carried me up to the lounge. There was a boisterous party going on with the other soldiers who were heading to the front line.

We landed in Honolulu at the crack of dawn. We decided to check into the luxurious Moana Hotel for the day, and we quickly changed into swimming trunks and headed for Waikiki Beach. The sounds and sights were mesmerizing. We lingered on the beach almost the whole day. As evening came, we suited up and took the plane for the last leg of our trip to Japan. The plane stopped on Midway Island in the North Pacific Ocean to refuel and continued onward. We three arrived at Atsugi Naval Air Station the next morning. Immediately Ben and Joe were assigned to go to the front line in South Korea, and I was assigned a desk job at the base. I protested that I should be going to South Korea with my buddies. It was no consolation to me to be told that the reason for my special assignment was due to my peers in my class rating me higher in the class in leadership abilities. Deepening my irritation was the fact that I had packed few civilian clothes, expecting to wear military issues at the front line. I saw Ben and Joe off, ashamed to have let them down. For the first time, I realized that my fate was no longer in my hands. I must obey orders from my superiors.

4

THE KOREAN WATERSHED

The Cold War Begins for Downey and America

Thomas J. Christensen

N MAY 1950, Jack Downey was a carefree rising senior at Yale, seemingly destined to follow his late father's career in law and then public service. His future was bright. Even at an elite institution like Yale, he was a leader among leaders, captain of his wrestling team, and a key offensive and defensive player on the varsity football team. Although he was an Irish Catholic from a single-parent home—hardly the norm for Yale at the time—he had attended the Choate School on scholarship. In classrooms and university clubs, he mingled with America's aristocracy, like his good friend Bayard Fox from Philadelphia.

The United States was also on top of the world. Five years earlier, America and its allies had defeated fascism, demanding and receiving unconditional surrender from Germany, Japan, and Italy. But unlike its allies, the United States had not been crippled by the war. The industrial wartime economy that developed had pulled the United States out of the Great Depression and built a foundation for decades of uncontested American leadership. Downey was riding the immediate, large, and rather happy wave of his immediate elders, later dubbed the Greatest Generation, who had fought in the war; some of them then returned to attend college at places like Yale.

Downey's own college life would become, in a sense, a metaphor for the nation. On June 25, 1950, events in a country of which Downey claims he had never heard would change the direction of his own life and the course of American foreign policy. North Korean military forces crossed an international boundary between North and South Korea that had been drawn by the young United Nations. Kim Il-sung's government threatened to unify the peninsula under communist rule. The United States correctly saw the conflict as not just a civil war but as communist expansionism backed by the Soviet Union and the People's Republic of China (PRC). President Truman had seen in the late 1930s how future U.S. allies in Europe naively attempted and failed to appease Hitler's Germany. With that bitter lesson in mind, he ordered U.S. forces to enter the conflict under the flag of the United Nations. Their goal was to save the South Korean regime of Syngman Rhee and in so doing halt the growth of communism.[1]

Downey heard about the outbreak of war while traveling to Alaska during summer break with his college roommates. After returning for his senior year at Yale, a hotbed of recruitment for the young CIA, Downey and other Yalies—among them James Lilley, also from the Class of '51—were brought to the front line of the increasingly hot Cold War.[2]

The Korean War was the first major conflict of the Cold War for the United States. But it was much more than that. The fighting on the Korean peninsula, particularly after it escalated into a Sino-American conflict there in late 1950, mobilized the United States for the decades-long struggle with the Soviet Union and its allies. From 1950 to 1951, the defense budget tripled. Most of the resources absorbed by the federal government for national security purposes during the Korean War would not be devoted to Korea but to places like Western Europe, the Middle East, and Japan. The North Atlantic Treaty Organization (NATO) was not quite a year old when the Korean War broke out, and though it may be difficult to imagine today, the United States had not yet stationed many troops in allied Europe. The first six months of the Korean War changed all that. In a nutshell, the Korean War moved America to fight the Cold War in earnest.[3]

As mentioned in chapter 2, the escalation of the Korean War in the second half of 1950 allowed the Truman administration to pull NSC 68 off the shelf and fund the expensive national security strategy it envisioned. This massive mobilization included a 200-percent increase in the defense budget by early 1951 and the incredible expansion of the CIA and its clandestine service, the Office of Policy Coordination (OPC), in which Downey would eventually serve.[4] In Downey's own telling, he flags the drafting of NSC 68 in April 1950, about which he could not have known in real time, and the outbreak of the Korean War a few months later as the pivotal moments of that year.[5]

The Cold War had begun before the North Korean invasion. But despite some notable and bold exceptions—the launching of the Marshall Plan for reconstructing Europe in 1948 and the formation of NATO in 1949—the United States was not yet fully committed to countering the spread of international communism in Europe and Asia. This was mostly because of domestic politics. After victory over the Axis powers in 1945, Americans were eager to bring their soldiers home and return to normal life and were reluctant to support foreign entanglements that might yield another world war. Although public opinion was not as isolationist as it was during the Great Depression, Americans resisted the high costs of national security objectives in what was ostensibly peacetime, and huge budget deficits had not yet become normal. Congress was inundated with mail that included the baby shoes of children who had never met their fathers, attached to notes that said "Bring Daddy Home."[6]

In early 1947, with some help from Winston Churchill's famous 1946 Iron Curtain speech, the Truman administration began to draw public attention to the threats posed by the Soviets. A crisis in Greece and Turkey threatened the stability of those anticommunist governments. These two countries straddle the straits connecting the Mediterranean Sea and the Black Sea, and the survival of friendly governments there limited the Soviet navy's movements, protecting the democracies of Western Europe. In February, in a speech dubbed the Truman Doctrine, President Truman convinced Congress to pass an unprecedented peacetime aid package for those countries and then, the next year, to provide funds for the much larger Marshall Plan assistance program for the future NATO allies. Truman did so by using crusading rhetoric: "The seeds of totalitarian regimes are nurtured by misery and want. They spread and grow in the evil soil of poverty and strife. They reach their full growth when the hope of a people for a better life has died. We must keep that hope alive." His speech called for the United States to defend "free peoples" everywhere from the scourge of communism. He knew he was being hyperbolic, but the Republican senator Arthur Vandenberg had advised him to "scare hell out of the American people."[7] By historic standards, Truman was relatively successful. He secured a large peacetime national security budget that included about 5 percent of GNP for defense and about 2 percent of GNP for foreign economic and military aid from 1948 to 1950. Such expenditures for national security had no peacetime precedent in American history.[8] By comparison, today such security expenditures constitute about half that percentage of GNP, and the U.S. economy is much larger, so the marginal cost to the average citizen is much lower than it was in the spring of 1950.

Foreign policy experts knew, however, that even this was not enough to match Truman's speeches' universalistic approach to anticommunism. So, contra the public globalist rhetoric, from 1947 to 1950, the Truman administration focused national security resources on bolstering the economies and security portfolios of a select group of friendly states. They looked especially toward states with industrial potential, like Europe and Japan, states with natural resources, like those in the Middle East, and states in important geopolitical locations, like Greece and Turkey. In the thinking of Truman's influential director of policy planning, George Kennan, preventing communist advances in these "strongpoints" was far more important than doing so in places like mainland China, Taiwan, and the Korean peninsula.[9] In a speech in January 1950, just six months before the outbreak of the Korean War, Secretary of State Dean Acheson explained that the strongpoint strategy of containing the Soviet Union in Asia did not include mainland China, Taiwan, or South Korea in the U.S. "defense perimeter." A week earlier, Truman himself said the United States had no intention of getting involved in the civil war between mainland China and Taiwan.[10]

The strongpoint strategy was controversial. Many Americans resented the expense and the risks involved in binding security commitments in Europe. Others wanted to do more, to invest in places like China, which was excluded from the list of strongpoints but was in the very process of falling to communism. As some of his advisers feared during the drafting of the Truman Doctrine speech, the president was often accused of hypocrisy and even racism for defending only a select group of targets while claiming communism threatened all humanity. Some of those holding the president to his word sincerely wanted the United States to oppose the Chinese communists more actively. Others, later dubbed the "Asialationists," wanted only to point out the contradiction between Truman's Eurocentric strategy and his globalist rhetoric. Their real goal was to undercut support for the expensive and potentially risky Cold War approaches in Europe, not to stimulate even more spending and foreign entanglements.[11]

Truman and his advisers had to take both challenges seriously. They responded by providing economic and military assistance to Chiang Kai-shek whenever controversial bills were raised in Congress regarding Europe. This frustrated George Kennan, who complained, "My specialty was the defense of the United States' interests against others, not against our own representatives."[12] But George Marshall and Acheson were wise to ignore Kennan on this score. Without such additions to the pristine strongpoint logic, the domestic consensus around controversial and expensive policies that were deemed essential to national security—like the seventeen-billion-dollar Marshall Plan, the creation of NATO, and the granting of large military aid packages to the new allies—would be impossible to sustain.[13] When Senator Joseph McCarthy launched his domestic anticommunism campaign in February 1950, this put further pressure on government officials to remain staunch in their anticommunist stance around the world.

Still, before the Korean War, the United States did not intervene directly in the Chinese Civil War, even as the Chinese Communist Party (CCP) consolidated its control over the mainland and threatened Chiang's Republic of China on Taiwan. Most U.S. forces in South Korea that had been deployed since the end of WWII were withdrawn in the spring of 1949. Remaining military aid to South Korea was intentionally limited not only to save resources but also because Washington correctly believed that South Korean president Syngman Rhee stood ready to invade the North—in violation of United Nations resolutions—if he only had the wherewithal to do so.[14] Communists did not have a monopoly on revisionist strategies, as both Chiang and Rhee demonstrated.

The Truman administration's thinking about Cold War strategy was already changing in the months just before the Korean War, as demonstrated by the drafting of NSC 68 by Kennan's successor at the Policy Planning Staff, Paul Nitze. But we cannot point the finger at domestic political forces like McCarthyism for this. It was instead a series of international shocks in the previous two years that changed the Cold War. The first was the consolidation of Soviet control over Eastern Europe. The second was the fall of China to communism. And the third was the successful Soviet testing of a nuclear bomb in August 1949, just one month after the formation of NATO. These three events conspired to create the strong impression that the anticommunist coalition—known in shorthand as the Free World—might lose this new Cold War.[15]

The Soviet breaking of the American nuclear monopoly was particularly important because it called into question the preferred strategy of many fiscal conservatives who wanted to oppose communism expansion in principle but did not like the high costs of large conventional militaries, entangling alliances like NATO, or expensive foreign aid programs. Before 1950, they preferred to simply threaten the Soviet Union with nuclear annihilation if it acted aggressively.[16] However effective or ineffective that might have been—and it was never Truman's preferred approach—relying so heavily on nuclear deterrence suddenly looked much riskier when the Soviets entered the nuclear realm. By the spring of 1950, most national security elites believed the United States needed more conventional military options to credibly deter communist aggression directed by a nuclear Soviet Union. And there was a more general sense expressed in NSC 68 that communist victories in places that might have been less critical to U.S. national security than the strongpoints still harmed the morale of the Free World.[17] Coaches in sporting events talk about the importance of momentum in competition. The communists seemed to have it, and the anticommunist coalition seemed to be sitting back on their heels.

While hardly objecting to NSC 68 on strategic grounds, Truman paid careful attention to what the domestic political environment would bear in sacrifices for national security. Because of this, he initially sided with fiscal conservatives and strategists in his administration who opposed adopting NSC 68 and sent the initial report back for further study and consideration. Even under Kennan's more limited strongpoint strategy from 1947 to 1950, Truman had been asking citizens to sacrifice a lot. He knew that, while McCarthy's hearings might have made American citizens worried about communist spies infiltrating Hollywood, academia, and the government itself, the public was not yet prepared to shoulder the burden of the sweeping anticommunist foreign policy envisioned in NSC 68. Searching for communists under one's bed and in one's closet was relatively cheap. Deploying troops around the world during perceived peacetime would be significantly more expensive.

Everything changed because of what can only be called a gigantic strategic blunder by Joseph Stalin and Mao Zedong. They misread the signals sent by the United States toward its future allies in Seoul and Taipei and approved Kim Il-sung's plan to invade South Korea. The shock of the invasion and its similarity to Nazi blitzkriegs in the early days of World War II led Truman to reverse his decisions on Korea and Taiwan.[18] On June 27, 1950, he decided simultaneously to defend South Korea with U.S. forces under a UN flag and also to protect Taiwan from the CCP with the navy. Acheson's defense perimeter had been expanded.

The new perimeter cut Mao off from Taiwan but not Korea. After General Douglas MacArthur's brilliant amphibious landing behind enemy lines at Inchon in September cut North Korean forces in two, Mao decided to intervene if the Americans were to push into North Korea. The disarray in the North Korean forces afforded the United States and other allied UN forces the opportunity to drive north across the 38th parallel toward the Yalu River to finish off the North Korean regime. In the words of NSC 68, the United States had an opportunity to "roll back" communism in Korea by unifying the peninsula under South Korean leadership. But Mao did not want to see a fellow communist party destroyed, and he certainly did not want American troops on the PRC's northeast border with Korea.[19]

The shock of the invasion had removed much of the American public's reluctance to send American troops abroad in peacetime to halt the spread of communism. It also revived Chiang's previously waning popularity in America. In an internal government public opinion poll conducted in July, a majority of Americans believed that the government *should* risk war not just with the PRC but even the Soviet Union if that was what it took to protect Taiwan.[20] The defense budget in the United States increased from about fifteen billion dollars in June to about twenty-two billion by the end of the summer. China's surprise entrance into the war in late 1950 truly mobilized the United States for the Cold War; the defense budget jumped to just over fifty billion dollars, mostly apportioned to places other than Korea to counter the Soviet Union.[21]

Just as Tojo's Japan had woken a sleeping giant with the attack on Pearl Harbor in December 1941, so too had Stalin and his junior Asian allies created a fully committed enemy in the United States. He did so by arming North Korea, approving its invasion of South Korea, and then manipulating Mao's China into approving the invasion by doing what bad parents do, telling Kim that an invasion was fine with him as long as it was acceptable to Mao. After U.S. forces crossed the 38th parallel, Stalin persuaded Mao that he must save North Korea from destruction. Stalin argued that if the United States unified the Korean peninsula, China would lose Taiwan permanently and face an emboldened United States and a remilitarized and aggressive Japan.[22] Mao was eager to demonstrate to Stalin that he was a true revolutionary internationalist and a loyal member of the international communist movement, so he was reluctant to refuse Kim Il-sung's request for permission for the initial invasion of South Korea. For this reason and for straightforward national security concerns of U.S. forces on his northeast border, Mao did not want to see Kim's regime fall after that initial invasion failed.

For its part, the United States government also misread signals from the PRC. It ignored warnings from the Chinese in early October 1950 against moving U.S. forces into North Korea following the Inchon landing. Those warnings had been passed through an untrusted third party, the Indian ambassador to Beijing, and so the Americans generally dismissed them. American intelligence wrongly believed that if Mao had the necessary resolve to participate in the Korean War, he would have joined in the summer, before

Inchon, when the UN forces were penned into a small southeast-ern area of South Korea near Pusan, the so-called Pusan Perimeter. That's when Chinese troops, they surmised, likely would have pro-vided North Korea a decisive edge in its initial invasion, and their absence must have meant that Mao had no intention to join the war in force.[23]

American intelligence estimation on this score was logical but fatally flawed. It assumed that the PRC and the North Korean regime were tightly coordinated at the time of the initial invasion and that Mao knew the details of Kim's operations fully. In the spring of 1950, Mao had indeed approved of Kim's plan to drive south. At the most general level, then, the United States government was not wrong to think Mao supported Kim's aggression. But the Korean and Chinese communist parties distrusted each other, and this doubt precluded tight coordination in the military sphere early in the war. Beijing was not involved in the prewar planning. Mao found out about the June invasion from the news, and Kim did not invite the PRC to enter the war until MacArthur's troops were about to cross the 38th parallel in early October and Kim was desperate for Chinese help.[24]

The PRC failed to deter the American push north across the 38th parallel in October, so Mao and his colleagues were confronted with a torturous decision. Should they send Chinese troops into Korea or let North Korea fall to the Americans? Stalin pressured and cajoled the Chinese to intervene. Mao eventually resolved to do so in tremen-dous numbers. He sent hundreds of thousands of Chinese troops into Korea, surprising MacArthur's advancing troops and driving them back below the 38th parallel in what would be the greatest retreat in U.S. military history outside of the American Civil War. In December, Seoul would fall to the communists for a second time, only to be rescued again by UN forces the next month. By the spring of 1951, the war settled into an attritional affair along a blood-soaked but relatively stable geographic line close to where it had started less than a year before. The fighting would drag on for two more years until the United States and the communist states would finally reach an agreement on the sticky issue of how to manage the exchange of tens of thousands of prisoners of war.[25] By the time of the July 1953 Korea War armistice at Panmunjom, Stalin was dead and Truman had retired. Millions of Koreans had died in the war. China had suffered 260,000 dead, including Mao's son, and around three quarters of a million wounded. The United States casualties counted 36,000 dead and 92,000 wounded. And Jack Downey and Richard Fecteau had been captured and detained in Chinese Communist jails, now serving the first year of their sentences.

* * *

In their respective memoirs, Jack Downey and his Yale classmate James Lilley both spoke of their respect for their older Yale classmates who had fought in World War II and their reverence for the Office of Strategic Services.[26] And why not? Their classmates saved the world from fascism, and OSS officers performed bravely and brilliantly behind enemy lines. Both talked of how joining the CIA's Office of Policy Coordination, not yet three years old, seemed like their generation's OSS.

But the strategic environment of 1951 was very different than it had been in 1941. The communist domination of Eastern Europe and Northeast Asia was not the same as the Nazi and Japanese occupation of foreign countries in WWII. Those differences alone posed enormous, almost insurmountable challenges for the OPC. But there was another important general difference between the budding Cold War and World War II, one that would become evident in places like Korea, Vietnam, and Afghanistan and would have strong implications for OSS-style tactics in the Cold War. That difference is the distinction between a total war and a limited war. The Soviet and American superpowers had reason to avoid wide-scale direct confrontations in part because, after 1949, they ran the risk of cataclysmic escalation to nuclear war. The superpowers instead fought each other through proxies in what are called limited wars, often in what might otherwise be viewed as peripheral parts of the world. Since these limited wars were generally not death struggles among the great powers, clandestine operations behind enemy lines could not carry the same strategic punch that they did in a total war like WWII, in which anything one could do to weaken the enemy's military effort anywhere would contribute to the ultimate goal of total victory.

From both the North Korean and South Korean perspectives, of course, the civil war between them *was*, at least at first, an all-out struggle for survival in the same way that the Axis and Allied powers were in a mortal death struggle in World War II. It was simply the failure of Pyongyang's initial invasion in June 1950 and then the failure of the U.S. and South Korean counteroffensive north in October 1950 that led to a stalemate back at the 38th parallel and turned the conflict into a grinding limited war. But the United States, the Soviet Union, and the PRC always intended the Korean War to be limited.[27] They always sought to contain the war on the Korean peninsula, not launch a broader regional or global conflagration. This meant that Downey's OPC operation inside of China, which, even if it had been more successful than it was, could hardly have prevented the PRC from supporting North Korea in its grinding limited war against UN forces.

From the outset, even the Soviet Union wanted a limited war in Korea. Moscow always tried its best to keep Soviet fingerprints off the North Korean war effort, even though anyone who knew anything about military affairs could see that the Soviets must have equipped and trained the North Koreans for the massive initial invasion of South Korea. Later in the war, when the UN forces under MacArthur's command successfully drove north, heavily advantaged by their air superiority, Stalin enlisted Mao's China to bail the North Koreans out on the ground in lieu of Soviet troops, again demonstrating his desire to limit the chance of escalating the Korea proxy war into a direct U.S.-Soviet conflict. But the Chinese and North Korean ground forces needed Soviet air power to protect them from U.S. bombing runs. Neither China nor North Korea had an air force of which to speak at the time. So the Soviets painted their fighter jets with North Korean and Chinese markings before challenging the U.S. bombers over North Korea. The Soviet pilots were instructed to speak over the radio in Korean or Chinese, using language flash cards they kept on their laps. But unsurprisingly, in the heat of battle, they often resorted to Russian.[28]

The United States also tried to limit escalation of the war. Pilots were warned under threat of court martial not to reveal that they were flying against Soviet pilots. Truman feared that if the American public found out that Soviet pilots were shooting down Americans, they would demand a new war against the Soviet Union, an escalation he feared would begin World War III.[29] Amazingly, the secret held until the 1990s, when the Cold War was over and retired Russian and U.S. pilots began to talk.

Truman also tried to limit the chance of a broader war with China. He stiff-armed MacArthur's recommendation for a broad bombing campaign against China. More limited violations of Chinese sovereignty in the airspace over the Yalu River did, however, occur. Fighter pilots sometimes chased communist MIG-15s over the Chinese border if they were already in hot pursuit over Korean airspace. But it is very clear that the United States generally took great pains to avoid escalating the conflict with either the Soviet Union or the PRC.

The effort to limit the scope of the war started very early. When Truman sent the U.S. Navy Seventh Fleet into the Taiwan Strait on June 27, 1950, he said he did so to prevent hostilities from *either* side of the strait. This was not just a politically correct peacekeeping posture. Chiang's KMT had been bombing Chinese coastal cities like Shanghai earlier in the year, mostly using planes with remnant U.S. markings. Officials in the U.S. State Department believed this was part of Chiang's effort to drag the United States into war with the mainland, which might allow the KMT to recover mainland China at great American expense.[30] For similar reasons, the Truman administration consistently declined Chiang's many offers to send KMT troops into battle with UN forces in Korea.

For his part, Mao ordered hundreds of thousands of Chinese troops into Korea to push back the Americans with the initial intention of saving North Korea and driving the U.S. and UN forces into the sea, unifying the peninsula under Pyongyang's leadership. He accepted the risk of U.S. escalation to general war with China, even a war that included the bombing of Chinese cities, perhaps even with nuclear weapons. So there was little the United States could have done to deter Chinese entry into the war once UN forces crossed the 38th parallel into North Korea in October.[31] But Mao still tried to limit the likelihood of escalation to the degree he could by sending in the troops under the false flag of the Chinese People's Volunteer Army (CPV), as if 360,000 Chinese citizens concerned about the safety of a neighboring country could spontaneously organize themselves into an effective fighting force to repel the nearby superpower invaders.

After four campaigns against the United States, Republic of Korea, and UN allied forces, it became clear that no quick victory was in sight. In the spring of 1951, Mao launched a fifth campaign designed to kill so many American forces that Washington might decide to withdraw, but this too failed, and the CPV forces were the ones decimated and exhausted. Mao then decided to settle into a two-year pattern of fighting and negotiating, abandoning grander war aims for the revised goals of saving North Korea as a sovereign state and securing some face-saving method for the exchange of prisoners of war. By mid-1951, Mao would resist North Korean entreaties to escalate the war in the hopes of seeking total victory on the peninsula. By the time Downey and Fecteau entered the scene in Manchuria in late 1952, all the major combatants with the possible exception of Syngman Rhee had accepted that the war would remain limited until a peace was negotiated.

The political scientist Morton Halperin may have been the first to analyze the Korean War as fundamentally different from the absolute wars in Europe and the Pacific that preceded it. Those wars were all-out struggles for survival. The goal was to destroy or strangle the enemy into "unconditional surrender." Such wars precluded subtle negotiations. For Halperin and contemporary strategic theorists like Thomas Schelling, the Korean War, especially after it settled into stalemate at the 38th parallel, was a more typical example of what Prussian general and theorist Carl von Clausewitz called the continuation of "politics by other means." It was an example of coercive diplomacy, in which the goal was to make continuing the war too painful for the enemy, which provided leverage to reach an acceptable negotiated settlement. But that rarely leads to full-scale enemy surrender and total victory.[32]

This distinction between World War II as a total war and the Korean War as a limited war underscores a crucial difference between the OSS's role in Europe and the OPC's role in Korea and China. The goal against Nazi Germany was to destroy the Third Reich, so anything the Allies could do anywhere to weaken the overall power of Germany as a nation served that purpose. This meant that OSS efforts to raise costs to Nazi forces in the Balkans worked toward that goal even if the main thrust of the American plan was to attack Germany on land from the direction of France and Belgium. As long as the costs of OSS operations to Germany outstripped the costs to the United States, these efforts became an important part of the calculation for victory in the war. But in Korea, after the first attempt to unify the peninsula under UN control in late 1950 failed, the United States no longer sought to exploit temporary military advantages to change the territorial status quo. Instead it sought a negotiated settlement and fought for leverage in that negotiation. The notion that the former Chinese nationalist soldiers working with Jack Downey would "overthrow" the CCP regime in China—which, according to Downey, was the main OPC goal in Manchurian operations—was always fantastical. In an all-out war between China and the United States, however, any resources that China used to roll up the inserted insurgents would still count toward the overall cause of weakening the enemy as long as the costs to the United States of inserting them did not exceed the costs to China of countering them. This is much less true in a limited war like the one in Korea. China was extremely unlikely to suffer a severe enough loss from the insertion of a small number of insurgents to reconsider the wisdom of supporting North Korea to hold out for better terms.

Theoretically, one could say that by raising the costs to China, the OPC operations could have raised the overall pain of the war for China and thereby improved the U.S.'s negotiating position. But even this is a stretch. Such a marginal difference in the overall war costs to China could hardly have proven decisive in the negotiating process. A year before Downey and Fecteau's mission, the United States itself had settled into the mindset of a limited war, in which it would not exploit temporary weaknesses to seek significant changes to the territorial status quo. We now know that by mid-1952, Mao and Stalin were more committed to sustaining the war than even North Korea was. Stalin considered the attritional Korean War a useful way to sap overall U.S. power, especially when China and North Korea were shouldering much of the burden. For his part, Mao refused to accept the humiliating U.S. conditions for prisoner swaps because he thought it would undercut the prestige and legitimacy of his new regime on the international stage. Kim Il-sung wanted to pursue total victory only into the second half of 1951. In mid-1951, Stalin and Mao were the voices of restraint, as they did not want to trigger major escalation by the United States. But once Kim had given up hope of unifying the peninsula in the near term under his leadership, he became the major force for compromise in the communist camp, as his nation paid the heaviest costs of the war. Even once U.S. and allied UN forces were all safely below the 38th parallel, they continued to attack North Korea mercilessly from the air.[33]

In fact, Mao's China was the last of the three communist actors to accept the idea of a negotiated settlement that would require Chinese concessions on prisoner-of-war exchanges. Mao only changed course when, at Stalin's funeral in March 1953, the successor Soviet leaders expressed to Premier Zhou Enlai a desire to end the Korean War. The Soviets now urged the PRC to compromise further in the negotiations than Beijing had previously been willing to do. Zhou was frustrated by the Soviet about-face, but Mao could hardly refuse. Within four months the two opposing camps reached an agreement on POW disposition and an armistice.[34] Even if the OPC operations against China had been more successful in raising significant costs to the PRC than they were, it is difficult to see how they would have changed the outcome of this limited war in the decisive way that other factors did, like North Korean war fatigue under aerial bombardment and Stalin's death.

5

THE MAKING OF A MISSION

THE MISSION began soon after I arrived at Atsugi Naval Air Station in Japan. I reported directly to Joe Kiyonaga, the Chief of Operations who was under the Chief of Station, John Mason. I was to work closely with Jim Reilly,[1] the Base Deputy for Operations.

Atsugi was a rude collection of barracks and hangars constructed as imaginatively as a flight authorization form. Its importance, to the war and to me, had to do with its location. It was only a few hours flying time across the Korea Strait to Seoul, making it a busy support base. And it was a short hour's drive from Tokyo, a city of many diversions. Working from Atsugi, Reilly, who was a few years older than I, was under agency orders to establish operations in northeast China, an area about the size of Alaska. When it was conquered by Genghis Khan in the twelfth century, the local culture was already thousands of years old. The size and age of this designated territory did not seem to deter the CIA nor Reilly. The problem was that the Communists, in the few years since their revolution, had gained firm control over the whole country. There were few dissidents to contact and no guerrillas to smuggle arms to.

Reilly was under orders to carry out such a covert operation. He and I flew over to Saipan, went through the records of the Chinese recruits, and picked twelve to bring back to Japan. Their files showed most of them were the sons of small landlords, part of a social class the Communists would call petty exploiters.

The twelve agents arrived in Japan in April 1952, a bloody stalemate still prevailed in Korea. Most of the Chinese agents had the copper skin common to Chinese peasants. An army lieutenant and I were put in charge of these ex-soldiers who would soon become undercover operatives. We took them down the coast about fifteen miles to a town called Chigasaki. There the Agency had acquired a lovely residential compound as a safe-house.

The countryside surrounding Chigasaki and the safe-house was given over to rice farming. The farmers lived in thatched-roof cottages that were two or three centuries old, and their venerability was underlined by the even older rhythms of planting and harvesting. We saw the annual cherry blossom festival and the children's holiday on which the youngest children dressed in elaborate kimonos. Tradition was not uniformly intact, however. In town, many of the young people wore Western-style clothes. One could see a country and western band playing to teenagers wearing cowboy hats.

Against this backdrop, the lieutenant and I began training our agents. Since Reilly was hatching his plan one step at a time, the agents had to be kept busy until he could figure out where inside China to put them and how to get them there. So we began a program of physical conditioning and set up classes in clandestine operations. In Saipan, the Chinese already had been instructed in using explosives and American weapons. So we taught them textbook espionage. They learned how to choose locations for message drops, how to maintain secrecy around safe-houses, and how to set up cutouts. A cutout was an intermediary who passed messages between two agents. The agents themselves never met, so if either were caught, each could not reveal the identity of the other. We gave the Chinese theoretical mission problems and asked them to solve them as a group. It reminded me of case studies in college. I sometimes wondered what I was doing, a twenty-two-year-old just out of college, teaching Chinese soldiers twice my age, asking them to follow our orders to infiltrate their own country. I was aware that the Chinese had survived centuries of invasions simply by swallowing up the invaders.

The agents and I did not even speak a common language. All our talking was done through interpreters, and vigorous, if crude, sign language. It was hard to know how the Chinese felt about us, but I doubted we were inspiring much confidence, given the mistakes we made. For instance, we used agency evaluation techniques to identify potential group leaders. Among the candidates was a middle-aged colonel who smiled all the time and seemed very willing and bright. We had begun giving him extra responsibility, such as leading exercises and problem solving sessions. The only Manchu was young and amiable but he surprised us by saying he could accept anyone as a leader except the colonel whom we were grooming for the job. What we saw as a cooperative and eager personality the Chinese saw as opportunistic and hypocritical. When we informed Reilly of the dissension, he quickly began devising a special assignment for the disliked colonel, one that he could carry out in solitude. Not long after we discovered that error, we made a potentially more dangerous mistake. Regardless of what Reilly decided he would have the Chinese do once they got there, we knew they would need drop zones on the mainland. Photographic reconnaissance missions had been flown, and we pored over maps looking for safe landing areas. Finally, we settled on what our maps showed to be the most remote mountain in a rugged, little populated area. When we showed our carefully selected site to the Chinese, they were speechless. Then they laughed. Our remote mountain, they informed us, was a sacred peak inhabited by Buddhist monks and visited by thousands of pilgrims a year.

Despite such embarrassments, I managed to establish a degree of friendship with these Chinese. I ate with them regularly, and they accepted this as a sign of respect. As part of their survival training, they did their own cooking. Except for a memorable dish of snake soup, I found the food they made good, and I acquired a reputation for using an extraordinary amount of soy sauce. I also earned their favor by joining them in songfests in the evenings. I bought a record player and played my Western music to entertain them. They were mesmerized by the record player.

I had only one antagonist among the Chinese. He was the biggest of them, just under six feet tall, with the sloping shoulders and the expressionless facial features of an oaf. He said he was the son of a general, and he was always looking for a way to make work easier. We were jogging one day as part of our exercise regimen when I came up behind him, grabbed the seat of his pants and hustled him along a few steps. He picked up the pace without uttering a word, but his scowl told me I had made an enemy. What I intended as a good natured reprimand, he saw as a deep affront. He had lost face. Judged by Western standards, this hulking agent was very naive. He told us how, as a youth, he had gone to the docks of the city where he was living to see a visiting American warship. When a Black sailor appeared, he ran away in fright. It was the first Black man he had ever seen. When we gave all the agents a lie detector test, this big fellow's graph read unnaturally flat. No question triggered any kind of reaction. We knew he loved apples, so just to get some sort of reading, we asked him, "Do you like apples?" His reaction was so strong that the stylus nearly went off the chart.

We had used the polygraph because one of the Chinese had lingered in China for several months after the Communist takeover. We wondered whether he had been sent out as a double-agent. We debated for days about how to broach the test with the Chinese; we were sure they would regard it as an insult. Again we were surprised. They plunged eagerly into the test and everyone, including the suspected agent, passed with flying colors.

By late spring, Reilly had refined his planning enough that we were ready to implement it. It was my job to explain the mission to the Chinese agent. I told them, the plan was to parachute them into PRC, and asked them to find guerrilla troops, and build up an uprising to overthrow the Communist government. Right away, the Chinese agents were upset and made a strong protest; they refused to go. They knew it was an impossible scheme to carry out, and they knew they could not survive it. In Saipan, these men were under General Wu's command. Reilly brought General Wu over from Saipan and pressured him to order these soldiers to cooperate with the Americans. The general was aware he was sending them on a suicide mission, and he looked at them as dead men. But the soldiers obeyed the order from the general.

Reilly's plan was to divide the agents into two teams: the first four would parachute into a mountain area with the goal of proving they could survive inside China without being captured or starving to death; the second team of five would follow the first by a few weeks into the same remote region and have the added task of contacting a former Kuomintang general who had made an uneasy peace with the Communists. The team would set up a base camp and a lone agent would be dispatched to find the general. This was the job Reilly had found for the disliked colonel. Except for the colonel who would have to brief us on his meeting with the general, we had no firm plans for extracting the rest of the agents. If they could not find support among the local people, their only realistic hope for survival would be for the war to spread north over the Korean border. Then, perhaps, they could sneak or fight their way through enemy lines and rejoin friendly United Nations forces. Both scenarios were unlikely and the Chinese knew it. They were brave men; we asked them to tak a huge risk for their homeland.

Chosen as leader of the first team was a young agent who had been an officer in the Kwangtung Army, the puppet army organized by the Japanese during their occupation of Manchuria. He was held in faint contempt by the other agents who had been officers in the Kuomintang, the regular nationalist army of Chiang Kai-shek. The young agent's cleverness, however, was recognized by everyone. He embarrassed us at times in classes by asking apparently innocent questions, and exposing the inadequacy of our instruction. He was small and slender, and his mouth was so sharply down-turned that it formed an inverted U that gave him a perpetually cruel look.

The leader of the second team was a grizzled Kuomintang colonel who looked ancient to me. I thought he must have been at least forty-five. He bore a crescent scar across one cheek, and it made him look fierce. Among all the agents, he objected most strongly to a mission that demanded secretiveness rather than fighting. All the Chinese were proud soldiers, and he was the proudest of them all. As part of their training, we had asked the Chinese to do a self-analysis, listing their virtues and vices. At the head of the latter list, the scar-faced colonel had written "lack Christian spirit; like to kill." He had asked not to be sent to the Peking area because the Communists had labeled him a war criminal. During the Civil War he had been ordered to dispose of a group of Communist prisoners. It was winter, and he had the prisoners chop holes in a frozen river. Then he pushed them through those holes.

The last of the team members to arrive were the radio operators. They were trained separately, and they would work independently of the team leaders. When messages were to be transmitted, the operator would be the one in command. All operators had distinctive sending patterns that identified them as precisely as fingerprints. Theoretically, these unique patterns alone would prevent the Communists from sending false messages back to us if either team was captured. Our operators added several layers of precaution to this. Any deviation from this prearranged pattern would be a warning of trouble.

By early July, the first team was ready. We had finally decided on a drop zone in the Chang P'ai (Forever White) Mountains, about twenty-five miles north of the Korean border. The maps showed the region to be rugged and densely forested. A few days before the full moon at the end of the month, Reilly took them up to the K-16 airbase outside Seoul. K-16 was well behind the front lines, and most of its traffic was for either supply transport or evacuating the wounded to Japan. Two nights in succession the team took off in a C-47, a sturdy, twin-engine plane, then almost as common to air travel as the Model-T had been to car travel forty years before. On both nights, the team was forced back by bad weather at the drop zone. By the third night the Chinese were refusing to go. They claimed the first two flights must have alerted people on the ground and that Communist soldiers would be waiting for them next time. No one worried about the Chinese Air Force, which was nearly non-existent, we thought. What worried us most was the moon. If the jump were delayed another day or two, the needed light of the full moon would be lost and the team would have to wait until late August to try again. And that would put off the second team's jump to late September. In the mountains where the agents would make camp, severe and bitterly cold weather often came early and if forced to wait until September, the second team could end up trapped in the climate. Reilly shamed these agents into going for the third time. This time the weather held and the plane came back empty.

The next weeks passed quickly as we prepared the second team. They would be dropped in the same mountains about thirty miles northeast of the first team. The second group, which included the apple-loving general's son, was anxious and so were we. We had not heard a word from the first team. That should have been a serious warning sign, but Reilly charged ahead; nothing was going to stop him. Again a few days before the full moon, we flew from Atsugi to K-16. This time I accompanied the agents. And again, bad weather forced the team back on its first two attempts.

"It's all a wild dream. We are all going to be killed," cried the general's son, and no one argued with him. Whatever influence I had with the Chinese had been exhausted convincing them to go the second night. I could not persuade them to fly the third night. So we returned to Japan. Soon Reilly placed an urgent call to their leader, General Wu. Wu came reluctantly and exhorted his men to have courage. I had the feeling Wu looked upon them as dead men, but if the agents themselves detected Wu's pessimism, they did not show it. They waited for the next full moon, and this time they jumped. Soon they were sending back messages that were typical of men in the field; they were full of complaints. We knew all was well.

With the agents gone, my own morale fell to where it had been before they arrived in April. Now I went back to a boring desk job, with very little to do, and I considered it a big waste of my time. Whenever I encountered a buddy assigned to Korea, he never failed to mention an adventure in the combat zone and how peaceful Japan was by comparison. I knew he exaggerated, but still I longed to be closer to the action. I began to think about quitting the agency and joining the Marines. What stopped me was the contract I signed with the agency specified that if I resigned in the first twelve months, I would have to pay for my own transportation home. The restlessness led me to volunteer for a resupply flight at the end of October. Our first team still had not been heard from, but the second team had kept in regular contact. Now, they needed more food, and with cold weather settling in, more gear and clothing. In the same way we had dropped off the agents, the resupply flight now would be flown by two American pilots who were working for the Civil Air Transport (CAT). Getting the pilots was no problem, but a Chinese agent had to be brought over from Taiwan to act as drop master. His job was to ride in the back of the C-47 and push the supply bundle out the cargo door at the proper moment. I saw my chance to go along when I overheard the Air Force colonel in charge of the mission worry out loud about what would happen if the Chinese agent could not manage the supply bundle alone. The gear, packed on a wooden pallet covered with a tarpaulin, made a package about the size of an office desk. I told the colonel I would be happy to assist, since I would be helping to load the plane anyway. The colonel approved of my offer, but he warned me that I could never reveal his complicity if anything went wrong. Agency policy clearly stated that case officers were forbidden to fly over hostile territory. But nothing did go wrong. The only fire we saw was the signal flares our agents lit to mark the drop zone. I helped the Chinese drop master shoulder the supply bundle out the cargo door and watched the chute open, then disappear into darkness.

Back at Atsugi, I was delighted to see Reilly's barely concealed envy at my adventure. I knew he wished he had made the trip. He was very competitive, the sort who kept track of the number of parachute jumps that everyone at the station had made. He always wanted to have the most. My one adventure did not sustain me for long, though; the routine of desk work soon reasserted itself. Reilly quickly moved on to another assignment. As a gesture of sympathy, my boss assigned me to carry the monthly message pouch to Hong Kong. The courier not only got out of Atsugi, but he also got to spend a few days in that mysterious and pleasure-packed British colony. My trip was scheduled for Monday, December 1. I was happily planning my itinerary when on Thursday, November 27, I got a surprise new order to go to Seoul. A radio message had come in from our second team. The smiling colonel had located the anti-Communist general and had boasted he had much to report. He was waiting for us to fly in and pick him up. The pickup was scheduled for Saturday night, the night of another full moon.

6

THE FLIGHT OVER CHINA

ARRIVED IN Seoul dressed in Army fatigue coveralls over my Yale varsity sweater. I had barely stepped off the plane when an Army major I knew, "Jumping" Jack Singlaub,[1] stopped me and ripped into me for being out of uniform. It wasn't the first time my penchant for wearing a mixture of uniforms and civilian clothes had gotten me into trouble. Most often I drew glares or reproaches from officers who wondered why I failed to salute them. Singlaub, who had a reputation for toughness, probably would have me shot on the spot had he seen the big Y on the sweater. Fortunately, I had taken the precaution of wearing the sweater backwards, so the Y was covered by my overcoat.

Dick Fecteau, who had arrived at Atsugi a few weeks before, met me. We both were needed to replace two American civilians who had been recruited to operate the winch which would haul the lone Chinese agent into the plane. With Dick as their overseer, they had begun rehearsing the pickup several days before. They had volunteered on the vague understanding that they would be making a flight over North Korea and serving their country. When they learned they would be flying at night over Red China to pick up a guerrilla, they were having second and third thoughts about the mission. They must have called to the headquarters in Japan, refusing to make the trip. The suggestion to use two Nationalists from Taiwan was rejected, due to their lack of security clearance. That was when Dick Fecteau and I were assigned to take their place. Our superiors were concerned more about security clearance than the rule against putting CIA case officers on the front line.* In addition the Chiefs had ignored the fact that we never heard from the first team of four who were air-dropped into China in July.

The decision suited me fine. I was going to get into real action. I began training with Fecteau. I had not had a chance to get to know him well, but he had impressed me as a tough, energetic fellow. I knew little about his background, though later I learned that Dick had joined the Merchant Marines out of high school. He served a few years, then went to Boston University on a football scholarship, joining the Agency after he graduated. He had twin daughters by a first wife, and he had remarried shortly before being sent overseas. In fact, his new wife was scheduled to arrive in Japan that very weekend.

Since Fecteau already had been introduced to the winch, he got the job of tending it. It was powered by an electric motor and it vibrated violently once started. The piece of equipment I had to use was simpler. It was a long wooden pole with a self-closing hook on one end. It wasn't much more complicated than the poles my elementary school teachers had employed to open and close the high windows. Now I would be wielding such a pole while leaning out the cargo door of a C-47. My job was to ram the pole into a metal sleeve that ran parallel to the fuselage. The pole and the sleeve were designed so that one quick twist would lock the pole in place. We would make two passes over the pickup zone. On the first run, our job was to deliver supplies: food and gear for the Chinese who would remain behind as well as the pickup apparatus for the colonel. The pickup bundle included two aluminum poles, a chest harness, and a long nylon rope. The colonel would need to set himself up between the poles so that we could snatch him on our second run. As far as we knew, the apparatus had never been used

---

* The CIA historian Nicholas Dujmovic believes that it was actually the two American civilians who were pulled off the mission for lacking security clearance, after which Jack Downey and Dick Fecteau were assigned to the mission.

to pick up an agent in operations before. It was so new, the Air Force sergeant who showed us how to use it had no name for it.

Fecteau warned me to treat the sergeant with deference. The sergeant was so possessive of his pickup device, he would have preferred that no one else touch it. He probably thought the less anyone knew about it, the better. Our two pilots were more cooperative. Both were CAT regulars, so they had security clearance. One was Robert "Bob" Snoddy, a tall, slender former Navy pilot, and the other was Norman Schwartz, a short, compact former Marine pilot. They may have been physical opposites, but both were quiet, easy-going, and capable of flying a C-47 between two poles as easily as they might land on a runway.

We began rehearsing together at first light on Friday. We took off from K-16 and flew out over the Nan River. In late autumn, the river ran fast and low through a wide, dry floodplain. At one point the river passed an enormous sandbar, and it was there that the sergeant had erected his pickup device. I had seen the device used only once before, in a training film in which the guinea pig on the ground was an Air Force captain who kept a cigar clenched in his teeth throughout the pickup. The nylon rope tended to stretch when it was first hooked, then snap back like an elastic. The result was that the person on the ground was as much slung into the air as he was pulled by the plane. Nevertheless, Snoddy and Schwartz had to be prepared to open the engines full throttle and climb steeply at the instant of contact or risk bouncing the man in harness along the ground. Fecteau reminded me to brace for the sudden upward surge. I did. But on my first run, the acceleration against gravity forced me to my knees.

Without the benefit of the cavalier Air Force captain, we practiced with a dummy built to simulate the weight of the Chinese agent. Again and again, we made runs at the pickup device. Snoddy and Schwartz would turn, straighten their approach, and throttle back. Fecteau would yank the winch motor to life, and I would thrust my pole home. The line would catch, and the plane would jerk upward. We circled and banked so much that the world began to seem permanently tilted. So when Fecteau jabbed me in the shoulder and pointed across the dry flood plain, I momentarily could not believe my eyes. A mile or so away, I saw puppet-sized figures of men suspended from open parachutes. Some were coming down on land, some on sandbars, and some in the river itself. My heart turned to lead. I had jumped enough myself to know the parachutist's fear of landing in water. Even in a still lake, the jumper can get tangled in his lines and be dragged under by the weight of the chute. In the fast flowing, freezing water of the river, these jumpers had no chance at all. When we got back to K-16, we learned they were Korean recruits on a training jump for an army intelligence unit. The first man had hesitated in the door only a few seconds, but that was long enough to permit the plane to overrun its drop zone before the last men had jumped. When they did jump, they were over the river. Three who came down in the current were drowned. The irony was that the land was open for miles on either side of the river. They had all the room in God's world to come down safely. Of course, it was wartime and stories of death were everywhere.

When in Seoul, we stayed at a second-rate hotel that had been converted into a military billet. Before I met up with my Harvard buddy Tucker for dinner, other acquaintances had induced me to join a card game I had never played. Beginner's luck was with me, and by the time Tucker arrived, I had won many hands, much to the chagrin of those who had asked me to play. Sweeping up my winnings with a great flourish and heading for the door, I passed a slot machine. I dropped a quarter in, pulled the handle, and watched the jackpot come up. I was riding on a wave of luck.

When I thought about the mission scheduled for the next night, it was more with anticipation than fear. For nearly a year, I had been a rear-echelon drone in the eyes of my buddies in Korea. Now our roles were reversed. I was going far behind enemy lines, and I enjoyed the deference they paid me. I got so carried away with myself that I thought briefly of writing "eve of battle" letters to my family and my girl back home. Only once or twice did I worry about the risk of the mission, but not enough to keep me from a sound sleep. I was in bed by midnight.

The next day passed without incident. I arose late, lounged around headquarters, and went over the flight plan again. We were scheduled to leave at nine in the evening and reach the drop zone at midnight. We would drop the supplies and the colonel's pickup apparatus then make a forty-five minute loop while the apparatus was assembled on the ground. If all went according to plan, we would arrive back at K-16 at about four-thirty in the morning. The weather was cold, and I dressed as warmly as I could in my usual mixture of civilian and military garments. I wore long underwear belonging to another case officer (our laundry had been mixed up) and Army fatigues. Over those I put on a hooded Air Force flight suit. I pulled on my new jump boots and carried my fleece-lined articles under my arm. We rode by jeep to the airfield, where we all ate together in a mess hall. Besides Fecteau and me, there was Major Scott, the sergeant who was our driver; the Air Force sergeant in charge of the pickup device who wanted to be with his device until the last possible moment; and Sam, the Chinese-American who had acted as our interpreter from the time the Chinese agents arrived in April.

After supper, Sam wrote a note in Chinese and stuffed it in the supply bundle. "Jack himself is flying in this plane," said the note. Sam intended it as encouragement to the men on the ground. It did not occur to me to worry about what would happen if it fell into enemy hands. Our cover story was flimsy enough. If captured, we were to claim we were on a mission to drop propaganda leaflets over North Korea and had strayed off course. Following agency procedure, I stripped myself of all personal belongings, anything that might identify me as John Downey, and turned them over to Sam. Just as we were about to board, an Air Force captain who had joined us pulled out a .38-caliber revolver complete with shoulder holster and handed it to me. He said I might need it. I was not a marksman, and I doubted the revolver would offer much protection if we happened to crash behind enemy lines. Still, I took the captain's .38. It had a more reassuring heft than the puny .22-caliber pistol each of us carried in the survival vests we wore over our flight suits.

We were on board, the engines idling, when the sergeant who instructed us in the use of the pickup device called out that he would be there waiting when we returned. I think he was more anxious about his precious device than he was about us. In the years to come, I often imagined him, consumed with irritation in the predawn hours, his growing puzzlement as the minutes passed, then the sky lightening, and, with it, the deadening realization that we were not coming back.

7

INTERROGATION DAYS IN SHENYANG

"**Y**OU ARE JACK,**"** said the Chinese officer standing over me. It was half question and half accusation. He wanted me to confirm what he already knew. "Tell the truth and your future will be bright; lie and your future will be dark," he said. I wondered how dark a future his threat implied, but I shook my head and stuck by my cover story. I was a Department of Defense Army civilian on a leaflet-dropping mission over North Korea. I wasn't Jack, I was John. It was a lame distinction, but I thought it might confuse my questioner. "You are Jack," he repeated patiently, almost kindly.

I could barely see his features. I was sitting on a low mud bed in a large room inside what I took to be a farmhouse. Hot coals were spread under the bed to provide heat. My glasses were half fogged over and with my hands tied, I couldn't remove them to wipe the lenses clear. I was conscious of Dick nearby. Across the room, through my steamed-up glasses and smoke from the fires, I thought I saw the colonel we had tried to pick up.

We had hiked to the farmhouse directly from the crash site. We marched single file, with several soldiers separating Fecteau and me so we couldn't communicate. Despite the thin crust of snow on the ground, walking was not difficult. The terrain was hardly the rugged mountain our reconnaissance had indicated. In the early morning darkness, the countryside appeared mostly open or covered with thin trees and bushes that were evidently second growth. It took more than an hour to reach the farmhouse. But it wasn't until I sat down that I became aware of how much my feet hurt in my tight jump boots.

During what remained of the night, my interrogator seemed content to repeat his "You are Jack" question in several variations. He told me he knew I was Jack because I had a record player; he knew I was Jack because I liked soy sauce. I knew right away there was no denying that they knew exactly who I was. Obviously, the agents had been captured days before and had been questioned extensively before our flight to pick up the colonel. They had a lot to say about their American friend Jack. I wondered why the radio operator had failed to warn us of any trouble; he could easily have sent his array of signals. I finally concluded that once the Communists had learned our mission included the retrieval of the colonel, they could have threatened the radio man and held him responsible for our arrival at the appointed hour. If there was anyone relieved to hear the sound of our C-47's engine that night, it must have been the radio operator.

At dawn, we were led from the farmhouse and ordered into waiting trucks. Fecteau and I were put in different vehicles. The colonel I thought I had seen across the room in the farmhouse was nowhere to be seen. The country we drove through was open and confirmed my impression that it was more suited to farming than hiding guerrillas. In mid-morning we arrived in a small town and were taken to a train station. The town apparently was a railroad final stop because the tracks stopped a short distance beyond the station.

Inside the station, a nurse, who also wore a military uniform, examined Fecteau and me for injuries. Fecteau had a large bump on his head, so the nurse checked his pupils for signs of concussion. When it was my turn, she put salve on a burn on my cheek and sucked in her breath when she removed my boots and saw the raw blisters on both feet. Her sympathetic gasp lifted my spirits a little. My image of the new Communist China was as a godless police state, the dire images only reinforced by the outbreak of the Korean War and the newspaper reports of human waves of assault troops so numerous that their generals could concede the deaths of thousands and still claim victory. I had been in the war zone long enough to hear too many tales of Communist brutality to assume their soldiers were capable of any kind of compassion. So when the nurse felt the hurt I felt, I hoped for a second that the Communists were not the heartless ideologues I assumed they were.

While still at the train station, we had a confrontation. When they had searched us at the crash site, they found maps packed in our survival vests which showed the region where we had dropped the two teams of agents. Luckily, someone back at K-16 had mistakenly packed the wrong map. Instead of the map of the second drop zone, they had packed the map of the first drop zone. This mistake gave Fecteau and me another excuse to act innocent and confused. When they told us we were in the People's Republic of China, we turned to each other and acted out an elaborate charade of surprise. If it were not deadly serious, it would have been comical.

Soon a train steamed into the station. It had European-style cars with closed passenger compartments. Again Fecteau and I were separated. Inside my compartment, the guards untied my hands and through the window, I watched the bleak winter landscape rush past. I had been awake more than twenty-four hours, yet I was not sleepy. In midafternoon, the countryside yielded to the gray jumble of dwellings on the outskirts of what proved to be a large city. Later I would learn it was Shenyang, a metropolis of more than two million people, which had been developed industrially by the Japanese during their occupation of Manchuria in the years preceding World War II. Shenyang was the capital of Manchuria, known to the Western world as Mukden. Its buildings were more functional than graceful, and its air was grimy with soot from the thousands of coal-burning stoves and boilers that heated the city. From the train station, I was driven a short distance to a building compound of faded elegance. Surrounded by high walls of stone and cement, the compound appeared to be a former foreign consulate now occupied by Communist government officers. A courtyard of beaten dirt led to the main building, which was several stories high. Wrought-iron grillwork covered the windows and edged the steps that led up to the main entrance.

I had no time to acquaint myself with the interior of the building before I was taken out again and driven across the city to what must have been the main train station. I had not seen Fecteau since we boarded the train that morning. Still alone, I was taken to the upper level of this large station and into a large hall that extended most of the building's width and length. Standing along the walls were at least a hundred Chinese wearing uniforms that identified them as party functionaries and military officers; cadres they were called. At the far end of the hall hung huge likenesses of Marx, Engels, Lenin, Stalin, and Chairman Mao. Beneath these heroes of communism sat three stern-looking military officers at a table covered with plain red cloth. They were on a low stage, and I was brought before them. An interpreter stood at my side.

With great formality, they repeated the same questions that I had been asked in the farmhouse the night before. Just as I had then, I recited my cover story. My inquisitors were not amused. "You are Jack. You are in China!" they informed me again. But the audience of cadres was amused, especially when I asked to see the Swiss chargé d'affaires. Mine was not a case for the Swiss, I was told. The cadres seemed to be bursting with pride and pleasure at the big American imperialist who appeared so foolish before the people's tribunal. I wondered if the entire hearing had been staged for their entertainment.

Once they had finished listing my crimes—consorting with guerrillas, spreading imperialism, seeking the overthrow of The People's Republic—I scoffed nervously at their falseness. Then I was driven back to the consulate. I was taken downstairs to a complex of rooms just below ground level. Guards approached carrying black iron shackles. They fitted the heavy, hinged bands around my ankles and sealed them by hammering metal spikes through interlocking rings. A length of hemp rope was attached to the chain that joined the bands of iron. The guards handed me the loose end. I soon discovered that to move without tripping on the chain, I had to pull up the rope. Even so, movement was possible only in a stiff-legged shuffle. So shuffling now, I was led into a small room where a heavy wooden door shut behind me. I lay down on a low cot against one wall. A bare, bright light bulb glared from the center of the ceiling. For the first time since being captured, I was alone with time to think. I did not shake from fear or weep from self-pity. The fear and sorrow I felt were frozen inside me. I knew the last forty-eight hours had carried me much further than from Seoul to Shenyang. I had been transported from my world to a world that belonged to others, and now I belonged to them. Whatever was going to happen to me would be determined by someone on the other side of the wooden door. That made me a prisoner of an enemy country. I fell asleep staring at the door.

The rapid ringing of an electric bell awoke me at dawn. Guards came to the door and handed me a bowl of gruel and a fist-sized loaf of soft-crusted white bread. I studied the cell. The chipped, white-washed walls were covered with graffiti written in Chinese characters. The door was of heavy oak, and inset at eye level was a small window the guards could open to survey the cell interior. The cot I slept on was covered by a thin straw mattress. A steam pipe ran low along the back wall. A window in the wall opposite the door was covered with wrought iron bars, and through them I could look out into the dirt courtyard. Below the window stood a simple wooden desk with a single drawer and a straight-backed wooden chair. In one corner was a chamber pot, a cylindrical clay jar capped by a wooden lid. The lid had a long handle so that it could be lifted without stooping. As the day passed, I had nothing to distract me from my worries. Since my cell was sunken, I saw the outside world of people from the waist down.

I strained to decipher sounds coming from the other side of my door. I heard Fecteau speak a few words, and I knew he was nearby, probably in a cell like mine. In my short time outside, I had seen several other heavy wooden doors with peepholes that suggested they opened into other cells. Guards brought me lunch and dinner of boiled vegetables garnished with a few shreds of meat. They showed no hint of sadism or maliciousness, and instead presented a mask of sternness and reserve. Twice I was taken out of my cell and down the corridor to a water-closet. I was escorted by a guard armed with a sub-machine gun. He watched me impassively while I squatted over the fixture to relieve myself. He was young with split eyebrows that gave a cast of surprise to his otherwise expressionless face. His insistence on watching me was irritating and unsettling. Did he expect me to bolt away, shackled, with my pants down?

About ten in the evening, another bell sounded, signaling time to sleep. The cell, which had been cold during the day, was now stifling;

apparently the heat was turned on only at night. Shackled, I could not remove my flight suit, so I pushed it down around my ankles. The bare light bulb remained lit, and I turned my head away from it, shielding my eyes from its glare as best I could. I was just beginning to doze off when the door opened. Guards entered and gestured for me to stand and follow them. I fished up my pants and pulled up the shackles and waddled after them. My ankles began rubbing against the shackle irons as I went down the corridor and up two flights of stairs to a sparsely furnished room. Large windows in one wall opened onto a balcony. Two men and a woman, all uniformed, sat at a table in the center of another wall. Behind them hung the standard pictures of Marx, Engels, Lenin, Stalin, and Mao. The room was a small-scale replica of the scene the night before in the train station. The woman was buxom for a Chinese, and she smoked cigarettes. I was told to sit facing them in a plain wooden chair. Guards stood behind me and an interpreter stood by the chair. He was a pudgy, soft-spoken -aged man, with a brush mustache and a mop of black hair. He was much too timid for the task ahead of him.

My interrogation began with the warning refrain that if I spoke the truth, my future would be bright and that if not, my future would be dark. They asked me who I was, where I had come from, who had sent me, and who my collaborators were. They operated in classic police fashion, sometimes angry and threatening, sometimes sympathetic and cajoling. I answered each question with a lie, and each answer led to another question and another lie. Soon I was struggling to remember the details of my own fabrications. By the time the questioning ended, four hours later, my head was spinning. I was taken back to my cell. I wondered how long I could resist them, and I assumed that prolonged resistance would lead to physical abuse. But I fell asleep out of exhaustion.

The electric bell woke me at dawn. Again there was gruel and bread for breakfast. The guards warned me not to lie down; during the day I had to stand or sit. I could find no diversion in the cell, and I could not even pace without inflicting pain on myself. I sat at the desk, and when I fell asleep sitting there, the guards banged on the door to wake me. With the heat off, I shivered through the day. After two meals of boiled vegetables, I looked forward to sleep. But again, twenty minutes into a sound sleep, the door opened and I retraced my steps of the night before, up the stairs to another interrogation session. Again I was warned about the futures bright and dark. Again the questioning lasted for four hours; again I lied. Again I was returned to my cell in the predawn hours, and again I was awakened at dawn. Now I understood their pattern, and I tried to steel myself against it. In the days that followed my interrogator gave two shreds of hope that I might beat them. I was wearing another case officer's clothing with his name, Ben McAlpin, stenciled inside the coveralls' collar. The Chinese failure to notice this discrepancy, especially since they never tired of telling me "You are Jack," suggested they were not the most meticulous inquisitors. More encouraging to me was the cessation of interrogation on Sunday. We had been shot down about one in the morning on a Sunday. The interrogation had begun in earnest on Monday night in Shenyang. As the week passed, I grew increasingly tired and confused, but I was able to keep track of the number of nights I had been called upstairs—six. On the seventh night, the night bell rang and I slid under the cover, waiting for the arrival of the guards. The usual twenty minutes passed, then thirty, then an hour. I became elated. I realized they took Sunday off, just like people in my world. Questioning me was their job, and now I imagined that after each night's work they went home to their families and maybe complained about the hard time the American devil was giving them. I found this vision of domesticity momentarily reassuring.

But my euphoria at the Chinese lapses was exactly as extreme as my fears about my captivity. In agency training we had been taught that every captured agent could be made to talk, and that they would talk eventually. What counted was how long the agent could delay before exchanging the cover story for the truth. Every fact held back, every day of stalling, would give the agency time to take measures to protect the mission or the lives of others that could otherwise be jeopardized. Even if confession did not directly endanger another agent's life, just the mention of a name could dilute his effectiveness for the rest of his career.

I began to measure my honor and my courage in the number of hours and days I stuck by my cover story and the lies I embroidered on top of it. How tough was I? I was afraid to find out my limits.

I wondered if I should answer the interrogators with silence. I knew that would be foolhardy, yet no stance seemed the correct one. If I defied the Communists and refused to talk at all, I was sure they would torture me until I did talk and then kill me to conceal the torture. If I confessed everything, I thought they might kill me because they would have no further use for me. If I continued lying, they might distrust when I did begin to tell the truth and persist in questioning me for months after I had told them everything I knew. This last scenario proved to be less far-fetched than I thought.

But I had a greater fear than discovering myself weak-willed, or even of dying. It was a fear of losing myself, and the Chinese nurtured it unwittingly. I had resisted their direct threats easily. Two women interrogators were particularly fond of shouting "Do you want the court martial?" and menacing me with angry stares. They meant to imply execution, but the threat lost its bite in translation, especially when it was conveyed by the timid interpreter who seemed to be more upset by their venom than I was. Once one of them grew so enraged, she decided to vilify me directly. She raised her voice, then began to sputter, "mixed egg, turtle egg, baby rabbit." I found her creative curses almost amusing. She got even more enraged when she couldn't find a strong enough epithet in her limited English vocabulary. Finally she spit out "Bastard." I had been called worse things in greater anger by opposing linemen at the Yale Bowl. It was when the Chinese were being patient and sympathetic that I was in real trouble.

"We don't kill lightly," one of the men would say in a calm voice. "You are a young boy, a victim of your imperialist government. We don't blame you for what you did. Later, when you learn the truth, you will be glad you came to China."

At other times, they would wearily inform me that it was futile to withhold the truth from them. "If a prisoner pretends to be crazy, we give him his stool to eat," went the standard lecture. "If a prisoner is stubborn, we teach him to cooperate. You are like a cow at milking time. We squeeze and pull and you give some milk, but you are not cooperating."

More than threats, their certainty that I would eventually talk gnawed at me. And then, after I had told them my truth and lost all reason for resistance, I feared they would begin to fill me with their truth. They expected me to confess and then embrace them. What the Communists wanted was my soul. One night in my cell, after an interrogation session, I dreamed of being on a sea of black water. The water's surface was smooth as a millpond's. I was on a ship sliding away from the shore, but the shore was where I wanted to be. I stood at the stern and watched the shore recede and strained toward it, but the ship kept gliding away. And I woke up sweating.

As the interrogation continued each night, my confusion and worry deepened. The specificity of the questions told me that Fecteau was being interrogated too, and that our cover stories had become hopelessly divergent as we embellished them to satisfy the Chinese demand for details. They asked me the name of the air base where I had been stationed. Instead of telling them Atsugi, I gave them the name of another base in Japan that I had never visited. Then they asked me to draw a diagram of the base. It was a purely creative exercise and by the time I finished, my sketch looked like an asterisk. Repeatedly I was caught with one lie contradicting another. I admitted that I was scared and confused. I asked that somehow my family be notified that I was still alive. Sitting idle in my cell, I was consumed by the anguish I knew my mother must have begun to suffer once she had been notified of my disappearance. In fact, interrogation was a relief from the uncontrollable worries that overcame me during the day. At night before my questioners, I used every ounce of concentration to do battle with them. As for my fears about my future, the Chinese expressed sympathy and said there was no need for fear if I told them the truth. My family, they said, would be contacted "later."

Finally, on the twelfth night of questioning, I abandoned my first cover story about being on an errant leaflet-dropping mission and offered instead that I was a civilian government employee on a supply mission to agents in North Korea. The new lie was told through tears. I tried to pretend they were tears of remorse for having deceived them. In fact, they flowed from the realization, certain now, that I would eventually talk and that I was not the iron man I had hoped I was.

On the sixteenth night, I admitted I was a CIA agent. The confession was almost a relief. It gave me a kind of second wind. I resolved to answer each of their questions truthfully from that point on but to give no more information than the question required. More than before, I began to use the language barrier as a defense. The timid interpreter's English was a comical patchwork of mixed tenses and misused idioms. I asked to have questions repeated. I gave answers that I knew were ambiguous then pretended I had misunderstood the question. It was a controlled retreat and each time I took a step back, revealing another piece of the truth, my self-respect fell another notch. Also, I began to discover that my earlier fear that the Chinese would not believe the truth when I finally began to tell it was being realized. I was made to explain dozens of things over and over simply because the facts were beyond the Chinese's frame of reference. I had told them about the CIA and a separate intelligence force operated by the Army. But they could not comprehend why a government should have more than one intelligence service. Later they asked me to describe the National Security Council and who in the White House had given me my orders. They could not believe no one in the White House knew who John Downey was, nor what my mission had been. To them, I was a master spy sent directly by the president to overthrow the Communist regime.

As long as the questioning persisted, I got only a few hours of sleep each night. After the guards caught me several more times dozing at my desk, they turned the table around so that I sat facing the doorway. I concocted escape plans that I knew were impossible even as I plotted the details. I thought of overpowering the guard when I was taken to the toilet. But I knew from my trips to the second-floor interrogation room that I would also have to get by a second guard, also armed with a submachine gun, who stood at the landing at the top of the first flight of stairs. I thought of bolting from the interrogation room and jumping from its balcony. I had no idea how I would shed my shackles. In preparation for an escape, I began to squirrel away bits of food, slipping peanuts that were sometimes served at breakfast and crusts of bread into my desk drawer. Within a day or two, the bread turned gray and rock hard. The Chinese considered the possibility of my escape so remote that when they discovered my food cache they suspected nothing. They merely told me to make sure I ate everything that was served. Occasionally, I conjured up suicide, but it was an escape I could not take seriously. I had been raised to believe suicide was the ultimate sin, and I knew the impulse for me was juvenile. And there was my mother. How could I abandon her after knowing what I meant to her? I knew she would rather have me alive.

Despite the poor food and enforced wakefulness during the day, I knew the guards considered me an important prisoner and for that reason alone they cared about my well-being. For instance, by the end of the first week in Shenyang, the shackles had rubbed my ankles raw. A uniformed guard patrolled the corridor between Fecteau's cell and mine in forty-five-second circuits. My keeper was a middle-aged civilian who wore a black Mao suit. He examined my ankles often and wrapped the shackles in gauze to soften their abrasiveness. It was of little help. The gauze quickly bunched in strips, exposing the iron edges. My skin had as little chance to restore itself as the grass in the dirt courtyard outside my window. A burning itch in my groin led to the embarrassing discovery of an infestation of lice, a gift apparently left in the cell's straw mattress by its previous occupant. When I scratched to relieve the itch, the guards gestured for me to stop. The Chinese, I was discovering, were sexual puritans and they disapproved of a man fondling himself. To establish my innocence and get some help, I trapped a couple of my insect tormentors and held them up at the peephole for the guards to see. The message was clear and they understood immediately. They gave me a crystal powder that stung worse than the lice, but it drove them off.

My infestation was just one indication among many that though the Chinese civilization was many times older than the American, the Chinese were far behind when it came to sanitation. All water had to be boiled before it could be drunk, and few toilets were connected to sewers. Spittoons were distributed in every hallway and stairway. The Chinese, it seemed, were flamboyant hackers and spit experts. They may have been trying to purge themselves of the pervasive dust and coal soot.

I knew Fecteau was nearby because I heard his cough occasionally and had come to recognize the sound of his shuffle when he was taken from his cell to the toilet. Also, only Fecteau could have been the source of some startling messages delivered by one of the guards. He was no more than twenty, a couple of years younger than I, and was eager to communicate. Once when I finished my rice bowl, he collected the empty bowl. But he asked me a question in Chinese, "Gou bu gou?" I was starved to make a conversation. I knew he was asking if I wanted more rice, so I took a chance and answered, "Bu gou." I thought I said "No more." But to my surprise, he handed me another full bowl of rice. After three full bowls of rice, he peeked through the opening on the door, I puffed up my cheeks, and used my hands' motion to indicate an overstuffed stomach. He laughed and said, "Gou la!" That was how I learned to say my first Chinese word: "Enough!"

This young guard made a game of teasing me. He reenacted my capture, pointing an imaginary rifle at me with a ferocious look on his face then turned around and took my part, throwing his hands over his head and looking dejected. He enjoyed such charades immensely and when done would laugh at his own wit. Stung, I began to answer him back, beating my chest and gesturing that I wanted to fight him one on one. I flicked ten fingers at him to show him how outnumbered I had been. Our relationship became pictorial when he brought me paper and pencil and somehow indicated he wanted to see scenes from my life. I drew stick pictures of my family, mother, brother, sister. I drew pictures of soccer players and wrestlers. He was delighted despite the crudeness of the style. Eventually, his superiors put a stop to this fraternization. But before they did, he taught me a few Chinese words. It was apparent that they were derogatory and that he was trying to get me to insult myself. I retaliated by instructing him in English profanities. Fecteau must have been getting the same treatment, for one day the young guard threw open the peephole in my cell door and yelled "Eat shit!" Then he smiled in a friendly fashion. I had not taught him that particular phrase. I was startled until I realized it was Fecteau's handiwork.

The walls of my cell were thick, and the single window looking out to the courtyard was deeply inset. A thick layer of dust covered the lower surface of the wide casement, which was tiled. I had been in captivity three weeks, and I knew Christmas was approaching. In the windowsill dust, I traced a "Merry Christmas" to myself. The dust was so heavy and the underlying tile so white, the greeting was clearly visible from some feet away. Whether the Chinese saw it and could read it, or whether they were watching the calendar themselves, I didn't know. But on December 25, they brought me a larger than normal meal. Instead of shreds of meat, there was an actual hunk of pork that took several bites to consume.

I enjoyed the meal, but I soon discovered it was given less in the Christmas spirit than in the spirit of psychological warfare. They were trying to soften me up. Soon after I was done eating, I was taken upstairs for an interrogation session, where I got a warning adjusted to the session.

"Better than gifts from the Christmas Old Man is that you tell the truth," they told me.

The interrogation persisted into the new year. I continued to answer precisely, volunteering no more information than was necessary, confusing issues whenever I could. One day the guards entered my cell with the interpreter. He informed me that I was being moved to a more peaceful cell where my memory might improve. I was surprised to find my throat suddenly dry and my heart pounding. It took me a few minutes to realize I was afraid of leaving my cell; it had become my anchor. I counted on being returned to it after interrogation sessions. I knew its meager furnishings. I needed to be able to hear Fecteau a few doors away. It was nothing, but it was everything. That my jailers could take it away so abruptly reminded me how little control I had over my existence.

My new cell turned out to be elsewhere in the basement of the consulate and larger than the one I had left. Interrogation sessions grew less intense and less frequent. The Chinese's new attitude seemed to be patience; they would wait for me to become cooperative. "Take your time. There is no hurry," they would say with infuriating confidence. "If we don't get what we want today, we will get it tomorrow."

So I was ignored. Once or twice I was taken outside to a small courtyard for fresh air. My shackles remained on. I was given a propaganda pamphlet printed in English to read now and then. One was by a Ceylonese politician who wrote glowingly about his ten-day tour of China. As fatuous as it was, I read the pamphlet over and over again. It was better than nothing, which is what I had had.

Then in early April, the interpreter came to my cell and announced that I was "going to another place." I was still wearing the clothes I was captured in. A small tear in the leg of my fatigues had extended from the thigh to the knee. My underwear was filthy and seemed to chafe almost as much as my shackles. I had washed my face and neck and hands each morning with a small ration of hot water brought to my cell with breakfast. Now I was allowed to bathe for the first time in four months. I stood in a shallow tub and splashed water over myself. The skin was pale where dirt came away. After the bath, I was given new clothes, a cadre suit that consisted of simple black trousers and black tunic, and a short-brimmed Lenin cap.

These preparations made it clear that the trip this time would be further than to another cell. In the evening, I was taken outside and helped into a covered jeep, still in shackles. I could see little of the streets we drove through, though once I glimpsed the neon lights of a movie theater. We stopped at the train station and immediately boarded a new passenger car, its compartments paneled in blond wood. No one gave any hint of our destination. Such was my ignorance of my fate that I could have as easily been on my way to freedom as to a new prison. I dreaded the possibility I might be going to the Soviet Union. I considered Chinese Communism an ill-guided copy of Russia's. The Soviet Union was the real heart of Communist darkness. If being a prisoner of the People's Republic of China was bad, being a prisoner of the KGB would be worse.

8

OF SOLDIERS AND SPIES

Thomas J. Christensen

JACK DOWNEY considered himself a soldier and, thus, a prisoner of war. When he had joined up, he felt he was following in the footsteps of his predecessors at Yale who had joined the OSS during World War II. He trained for military combat at Fort Benning, Georgia, where elite forces still train to this day, and he felt a certain esprit de corps with the Marines who lived alongside him on bases in the Asia Pacific. He was not wrong to feel this way. Even in his final mission, flying deep into enemy territory during a hot war, he accepted physical risks rarely experienced by most uniformed military personnel, even in wartime. The two pilots on that expedition were killed when the plane was shot down.

So his treatment by the People's Republic of China as something other than a soldier frustrated him. But the CCP's distinction between soldier and spy, and his designation in the latter category, was much more important to his own fate than he could have realized from his prison cell in China. And it was not just the PRC who made that distinction in consequential ways—so too did the U.S. government and the United Nations Secretary General's Office. The one thing on which all of these actors agreed was that Downey and Fecteau were not wartime combatants, and they could not be treated as such.

For the Chinese communists, spies like Downey and the former KMT soldiers he dispatched into China posed a different and more serious threat than the non-Chinese soldiers who met their army on the battlefield in Korea. In Leninist states, regime security is more important than national security. The best single piece of evidence for this is that the People's Liberation Army (PLA) is not a Chinese national army but rather the military wing of the Chinese Communist Party. It is a party military, not a national military. Its mission is to protect the CCP from all enemies, foreign and domestic. CCP civilian leaders have reminded the PLA of this fact on many occasions, not least in June 1989, when top leader Deng Xiaoping and Premier Li Peng ordered the PLA to enter the center of Beijing and crush pro-democracy protests. The image of a Chinese man standing in front of a heavy tank near Tiananmen Square is seared into the world's collective memory. After the massacre, the CCP leadership decided to peel off a big section of the existing military and create the People's Armed Police, a giant paramilitary organization designed to "maintain stability" and defend one-party rule. President Xi Jinping often says that the idea of a professional, national military without political affiliation is a poisonous "Western" idea that should never come to China.[1]

The argument that an apolitical military is a foundation of a democracy with free elections is not wrong, although it is hardly purely a Western phenomenon. Such national militaries exist all around the PRC's Asian periphery: South Korea, Japan, Taiwan, the Philippines, and India. Most people would consider it a good thing. But none of this holds for the PRC. The CCP was particularly challenged in the 1990s when Taiwan's military—which previously had been the party army of the KMT—became a national military. This was part of Taiwan's democratization, a broader process that poses ideological challenges for the authoritarian mainland, which claims that Taiwan is still part of China.

For the same reasons that China has no national military, China also has no courts independent of party control. Even though the existing court system is fully dominated by the party, much punishment is still handled outside normal state channels, purely by internal party disciplinary organs. This practice has become frequent in the past several years under Xi Jinping's rule and his massive anticorruption drive. Many of the hundreds of thousands of targets in the party's most recent anticorruption drive were investigated and punished in extralegal internal party disciplinary channels rather than by state police or judges.[2]

More evidence that the CCP prioritizes domestic regime security over national security is found in Beijing's national budget expenditures. The PLA has been modernizing rapidly since the 1990s, and China has now developed impressive capabilities to challenge forward deployed U.S. forces in East Asia, their bases in allied countries, and those allied countries' homelands. It is widely reported that despite decades of fast-paced increases in the military budget, the PRC still spends more on domestic security than on international security.[3] Under Xi Jinping, China has increased the party's control of society by attacking foreign NGOs and insisting that a CCP member—a political commissar, if you will—sit on the board of all major companies, whether or not those companies are state-owned. In the PRC, there really is no civil society as we might find in the United States.[4] The only societal organizations that are permitted to exist, including religious organizations, must report to the Chinese state and include a controlling party member in their leadership. This insistence on monopoly political control over society comes out of its foundation in 1921 as a revolutionary party that would soon find itself in a civil war death struggle with the ruling KMT in what was then the Republic of China. Such obsession with internal control is a signature aspect of Leninist parties around the world and explains why the OPC had so much trouble effectively penetrating its communist-controlled target nations.

The CCP is assisted here by a quirk in the Chinese language, which uses the same two characters (*guojia* 国家) for "state" and for "nation." When one adds the two characters for security (*anquan* 安全) on the tail end of these two characters, "state security" (read: CCP security) and "national security" become one in the same. The CCP not only refuses to clear up this linguistic conflation but fosters it. Foreigners who criticize the CCP's form of rule at home are labeled "anti-China forces" (*fanhua shili* 反华势力) or "hostile foreign forces" (*guowai didui shili* 国外敌对势力). The equating of the CCP state with the nation allows the CCP to use nationalism to bolster regime security. And when the CCP created a "National Security Council" to coordinate policies across agencies, it seemed even more focused on internal security problems than problems abroad. Beijing's obsession with regime security also explains why it reacted so harshly to speeches by Trump administration officials like Secretary of State Mike Pompeo and Deputy National Security Adviser Matthew Pottinger that explicitly make the distinction between the Chinese people (good) and the CCP's authoritarian rule (bad) under which they live.[5]

With this knowledge, we can understand why Downey and Fecteau received such harsh sentences as captured spies—threats to the CCP's regime security—as opposed to prisoners of war, threats to China's national security. As Downey reports, their mission was explicitly designed to sow political trouble for the regime, to use the CCP's civil war enemies from the KMT military to undermine CCP rule in Manchuria. Much more so than soldiers captured on the battlefield by Chinese forces in Korea, who only challenged China's "national security" by endangering a neighboring ally of the PRC, North Korea, Downey and Fecteau posed a direct threat to the Chinese communists' state security at home. And by their own admission they were civilians, not soldiers.

It is also in this context that we might understand the relatively harsh treatment of the crew of the USAF B-29 commanded by Colonel John Arnold that was downed in January 1953 near the North Korean border and was being held in the same prison as Downey and Fecteau in late 1954. These were unusual POWs in part because the Chinese claimed that they had been shot down over Chinese, not North Korean, airspace. The members of the B-29 crew who survived the ensuing crash insisted that they were flying over North Korea near the Yalu River border with China distributing political leaflets in Chinese and Korean when they were attacked by MiG-15s. Downey reports that they had indeed crashed on the Chinese side of the Yalu border. Whatever the truth about their final flight path, the Chinese claim that they came down in China, and this made them different than those captured on the Korean peninsula, most of whom had already been repatriated soon after the negotiated Korean Armistice Agreement in July 1953.

But what is more important than where they landed is who the Chinese believed they were. They suspected the B-29 crew were not simply combatants but instead part of an American spying effort that inserted agents into communist-controlled areas and established radio communications with them. According to an exposé in the *Los Angeles Times* in 1998, the Chinese were correct that Arnold's B-29 crew was part of a larger Air Force group that ran intelligence and subversion operations for the CIA out of the Philippines. But the crew in question apparently had not yet carried out such missions and was indeed simply dropping leaflets over enemy locations in northernmost North Korea when the plane was shot down. All of these facts are confirmed in Downey's account. Of course, the distribution of political leaflets to communist troops itself was consistent with the OPC mission of destabilization of communist regimes. Moreover, we know that Downey's initial cover story to his Chinese captors, before he confessed a couple of weeks later to being a CIA officer (as discussed in chapter 7), was that he was a civilian working for the Army who was distributing leaflets over North Korea in a plane that had flown off course. Since the B-29 was shot down early the next year, their Chinese captors must have been very skeptical of their story regarding leaflet distribution over Korea. Whatever their internal logic, in November 1954 the CCP tried and convicted Arnold and his crew of "plotting to undermine the state" and initially sentenced them harshly to as many as ten years in prison. Like Downey and Fecteau, they were not being treated simply as prisoners of war.[6]

Downey reports in his memoir that Arnold was tortured, which has been confirmed in published reports of the crew's twenty-two-month detention. Under duress, Arnold apparently confessed that he was indeed associated with units that undertook activities like those conducted by the OPC but that he was unaware of any operational details and had not actually conducted any such activities to date. Even though the CCP interrogators had reason to doubt his confession, in retrospect the crew's claim that they dropped propaganda leaflets in Korean and Chinese over North Korea seems fully credible. This became a somewhat common practice during the Korean War.[7] In the waning period of hostilities, a few months after Arnold and his crew were shot down, the United States launched Operation Moolah, in which U.S. bombers dropped leaflets in Russian, Chinese, and Korean over communist air bases to try to bribe fighter pilots to defect with intact Soviet-built MiG-15 fighter jets. The Americans were eager to study the strengths and weaknesses of the enemy force's aircraft. It is unclear that this effort was any more successful than the OPC subversion efforts. There was no such defection until after the armistice and the North Korean pilot claimed that he did not know about the bribes in any case and was only interested in political asylum. Still, he was apparently paid the promised $100,000 (USD) for being the first pilot to so defect with his aircraft.[8]

During a visit to Beijing in early January 1955, Dag Hammarskjöld, the secretary general of the United Nations, under whose flag U.S. forces had been fighting in Korea, began negotiating the release of the B-29 crew and four other detained fighter pilots who had been shot down over Chinese territory.[9] The visit followed a UN General Assembly action initiated by the United States calling on him to

Jack Downey (*back, facing forward*), Dick Fecteau
(*standing at table, right*), and members of the B-29 crew, 1954–1955.

engage the Chinese communists in reaction to the criminal sentencing of the B-29 crew in November. Unlike Downey and Fecteau, the
B-29 crew were considered POWs in the United States, and their treatment as criminals was widely seen as unjust, an affront to the UN,
and a violation of the Korean War armistice signed two years earlier.
Hammarskjöld argued to Premier Zhou Enlai that the B-29 crew were
indeed POWs—uniformed military personnel—and not spies. They
should therefore be treated in the same way as the rest of the POWs
exchanged after the armistice. He pointed out that they could not
be spies because they did not even speak Chinese.[10] Of course, the
Chinese knew that Downey and Fecteau also did not speak Chinese
and were indeed plotting to undermine their state. And, like Arnold,
Downey had already confessed.

Upon his return to New York, Hammarskjöld told Henry Cabot
Lodge, the U.S. ambassador to the UN, that Zhou had raised the
cases of Downey and Fecteau in their conversations. Zhou said that
they had been caught in flagrant acts of espionage and that a death
sentence would be warranted in their case, but he also hinted that
they someday might "return home" to the United States.[11] But there
was another link made between the B-29 crew and Downey and Fecteau that complicated Hammarskjöld's mission. Ambassador U.
Alexis Johnson represented the United States at the negotiations of
an Indo-China peace accord in Geneva in June 1954, where he met
his PRC counterpart, Ambassador Wang Bingnan, on the sidelines
of the deliberations to discuss prisoner exchange, including some
sixty Americans who were being held in Chinese prisons. After the
sentencing of the B-29 crew and Downey and Fecteau in November 1954, there was a brief set of lower-level bilateral talks between
PRC and U.S. consuls general in Geneva on repatriating civilians,
but this too produced no results.[12] In June, Johnson included the
B-29 crew and four fighter pilots captured as POWs in the Korean
War who were being held by China in violation of the Korean War
armistice. The Chinese delegation admitted that the PRC was holding these airmen. According to Hammarskjöld, the omission of the
names of Downey and Fecteau from the U.S. list of POWs at Geneva
made Zhou suspicious. He suspected that the United States would
deny and cover up its subversion operations in China, and this only

sharpened his suspicions about the nature of the B-29 crew's mission.[13] Of course, the U.S. government had presumed Downey and Fecteau dead until the PRC announced their imprisonment, trial, and conviction in November 1954.[14] Moreover, they were civilians. So it would have been extremely unusual if they had been included on a list of POWs and MIAs.

Despite these challenges, Hammarskjöld left Beijing rather optimistic but still uncertain that his mission would produce results. His optimism and his caution both proved warranted.[15] The B-29 crew would spend nearly another eight months in Chinese prisons before their release to U.S. officials in Hong Kong on July 31, 1955. But Downey and Fecteau were left behind. It is difficult to see how Hammarskjöld could have achieved anything else. The U.S. government itself did not recognize the two CIA officers as prisoners of war either. Instead, the United States simply denied the Chinese claim that they were captured spies, which Beijing had publicized around the world after the trial and Downey's 1954 confessions. In fact, the U.S. government did its best to hide the two officers' clandestine mission from the public, which would become a great source of frustration for the Downey family over time as they came to believe that an apology to Beijing by the U.S. government was needed to gain the spies' release.[16] The U.S. government knew it was covering up the real nature of their mission, but what is perhaps more important, it knew that the PRC knew the nature of their mission. A sufficiently detailed summary of Downey's prison confession had been published in a Japanese newspaper in early January 1955 and translated by U.S. Air Force intelligence.[17]

But Hammarskjöld's case for the release of the B-29 crew as uniformed military detainees could not credibly apply to civilians like Downey and Fecteau. There's no evidence that the government even asked him to raise their cases. Nicholas Dujmovic, an official CIA historian, explains how CIA leaders were frustrated by their omission from the initial U.S. lists presented at the United Nations in 1954–1955, but State Department officials argued that "If the same line were adopted for military and civilian personnel, Beijing might then deny the prisoner of war status of the former, and all would remain in captivity."[18]

One can surmise that even if the United States had known that Downey and Fecteau were alive during the Korean War, they likely would have been excluded in the armistice negotiations. To add two spies—whom the United States would not even recognize as spies until 1971—might have simply complicated already fraught negotiations.

From 1951 to 1953, the main sticking point in the negotiations was the dispensation of prisoners of war. Because the countries could not agree on this issue, many thousands of soldiers on all sides were killed in the prolonged fighting along the 38th parallel. The war raged on for two extra years with terrible costs, including for the North Korean population, which suffered from persistent air strikes. In those negotiations, the communists, and, in particular, the Chinese communists, were asked to make major concessions, accepting the return of only a fraction of their compatriots captured during the hostilities on the peninsula. The United States, on the other hand, insisted on the return of every one of its imprisoned service members. The UN offered to return 80 percent of captured North Koreans and only 32 percent of captured Chinese.[19] The Chinese communists, who in any case did not view the two CIA agents as soldiers but as spies and political saboteurs, were not going to voluntarily add the two men to the negotiations, even if they had been willing to tell the Americans earlier than they did that they were alive and being detained in China.

The United States claimed that many of the Chinese soldiers captured in Korea did not want to return to China and should be allowed to choose which jurisdiction they were released to at war's end. This was a principled position on which neither Truman nor his successor, Dwight D. Eisenhower, would waver. The Truman administration had mobilized the nation for the Cold War under the principle of protecting "free peoples" from the scourge of communism. How, then, could Truman intentionally turn over prisoners to live under a communist regime when they did not want to return home? His many critics had a ready answer to that question: He should have sacrificed the freedom of those Chinese citizens to free American prisoners of war sooner and stop the bloody fighting in Korea. But Truman and Eisenhower stuck to this position to the tremendous frustration of the Chinese communists and with the great cost of prolonging the war for two more years.[20]

Many of the captured Chinese troops had fought for the KMT in the Chinese civil war and were sent to the Korean War front lines by the communists as part of the Chinese People's Volunteers. At least some of them had even allowed themselves to be captured as a way to be free from communism and seek refuge with their former KMT colleagues now in Taiwan. Others had simply been captured on the battlefield and had decided their future would be better outside the PRC than inside it, particularly if they had expressed anticommunist views during their captivity as POWs. They had a ready alternative landing spot in Taiwan, which the KMT and its supporters in the United States were calling "Free China." The KMT government exploited the Korean War prisoner issue to its advantage on the international stage to emphasize the superiority of the KMT to the CCP as a legitimate governing force for Chinese citizens. So Chinese POWs being held in U.S.-run camps in South Korea were enthusiastically offered asylum in Taiwan by Chiang Kai-shek's government there and, in the end, two-thirds of them would go there.[21]

The Taiwan option was much more than a simple choice for many of the Chinese prisoners. Once captured, they were interrogated and also subject to "political education," which was intended to teach them the evils of communism and the virtues of the anticommunist coalition in the young Cold War. The U.S. military and its government did not have sufficient expertise on China, and too few U.S. personnel spoke Mandarin Chinese, which made the interrogation and reeducation of the tens of thousands of Chinese prisoners especially difficult. (There were more than twenty-one thousand Chinese held captive in the last two years of the war.) So they turned to Chiang Kai-shek's government in Taiwan to provide personnel. The use of Taiwan agents almost certainly affected the flavor of the information about the PRC drawn from the interrogations, and the presence of pro-KMT instructors also influenced the degree of pressure put on prisoners to choose Taiwan over the mainland. The KMT agents sent to Korea for this purpose often collaborated with pro-KMT prisoners to harass and pressure the CCP loyalists in the camps. In many cases, such political reeducation could easily be equated with brainwashing, especially since coercion was often used against resistant pro-communist prisoners.[22]

The U.S. government had multiple and sometimes contradictory views of the Chinese POWs under their control. The education program in the camps was intended to plant anticommunist political ideas in the heads of the prisoners so that those who still chose to return to China might create a kind of ideological fifth column within the PRC. This policy was fully consistent with the OPC's rather quixotic mission to insert former KMT soldiers into mainland China and promote subversion, but it seemed callously indifferent to the fate of the prisoners themselves. If a prisoner's political psychology was transformed in the camp or even if CCP officials perceived that this might be the case, the historian David Cheng Chang argues, then the prisoner was more likely in danger upon his return to the PRC.[23] The prisoners themselves realized this, and many of them—both the diehard anticommunists and the converted—chose Taiwan over the mainland. The great number of such converted prisoners complicated U.S. negotiations with the Chinese communists at Panmunjom because it meant the UN Command now had fewer returned prisoners to offer the PRC. How could such a psychological warfare policy, Chang asks, sit comfortably beside a policy that insisted on only voluntary repatriation out of concern for the human rights of the individual prisoner?[24] And to complicate things further, many of the most diehard anticommunist Chinese, the kind who did not need to be "educated" in the camps, were later recruited by U.S. intelligence agencies for generally unsuccessful wartime missions in North Korea, with very high attrition rates for the participants.[25]

The negotiations were held up for two years and the war raged on while China and the United States haggled over what percentage of the Chinese and North Korean prisoners would be returned to their home countries. Twelve thousand Americans would die over this time, and three thousand U.S. and nine thousand non-American UN troops were held prisoner during the negotiation period.[26] The sticking point was the Chinese prisoners, some of whom did not want to go back to the mainland because of their sincere anticommunist views, others because Taiwan seemed a more attractive option for other reasons, and others simply because they believed, correctly, that they would be persecuted as bad political elements by the communists upon their repatriation. Perhaps this persecution came because they had surrendered rather than fight to the death like many of their compatriots. Or perhaps it was because the CCP suspected they had become ideologically polluted by the anticommunist forces who had imprisoned them. Readers will recall that the main reason OPC missions in Manchuria seemed so ill-advised is that Leninists took internal security so seriously. Mao was no exception, and in the first two decades of the PRC this often took the form of widespread repression against "bad societal elements" with potentially subversive political views, a practice that placed Korean War prisoners of war in a particularly precarious state.

It is an open question, a historical counterfactual, if you will, whether the prisoners would have received less harsh treatment in China upon their return if they had not received political education in the camps. And Chang describes how even some of the most steadfast pro-communist prisoners suffered discrimination, hardship, and even death upon their return to Mao's China, a nation plagued by often paranoid political campaigns against "reactionaries" and "bad class elements" in Chinese society.[27] It would be difficult to pin blame for that harsh treatment on U.S. indoctrination efforts in Korea.

Chang estimates that only three thousand of the fourteen thousand Chinese POWs who refused repatriation were true anticommunists before entering the camps.[28] While the U.S. principle of voluntary return was steadfast, this came with a high cost. Moreover, only returned prisoners could play their intended role as subversive elements within the PRC, and few if any prisoners who became sincere anticommunists in the camps would choose to return to mainland China. Washington needed to maximize the number of Chinese prisoners they could offer back to Beijing without violating this principle of only voluntary repatriation. As the historian William Stueck writes, despite the best efforts of the UN Command to persuade prisoners to return to China, the vast majority of them were opposed, often violently, to the idea.[29] This had become the crux of armistice negotiations and, all things being equal, the United States wanted to end the hostilities at the 38th parallel. When the reeducated prisoners chose Taiwan over the mainland in droves, this only exaggerated the asymmetric negotiations, the very point on which Mao and Stalin convinced a war-weary Kim Il-sung that he must keep fighting. Since the second half of 1951, Kim had wanted the war to end, and he made this point emphatically to Mao in February 1952.[30]

And of course this was all even further complicated by the KMT agents in the camps, who had a very different incentive structure than their American bosses. From Chiang's perspective, the more Chinese who refused to return to the mainland and instead chose Taiwan, the better. Nothing amplified his message about the relative legitimacy of the KMT over the Chinese communists than mainland soldiers defecting. So KMT agents in the camps in South Korea worked to achieve this. They used persuasion, direct coercion, and indirect coercion via the pro-KMT gangs to convince prisoners to choose Taiwan over the mainland, and they silenced pro-communist prisoners who were trying to maintain loyalty to the PRC among the prisoner population. This made it harder for the Americans to promise credibly in negotiations that they could return a large percentage of the Chinese prisoners to China.

China was the last holdout among the communist powers in the Panmunjom negotiations. Because Beijing was only promised a minority of its prisoners of war and because many seemed likely to choose Taiwan anyway, Chinese generals and diplomats urged the Soviets and the North Koreans to support a prolonged war in Korea until an arrangement more consistent with international laws and norms could be secured by the Chinese communists. In other words, the PRC believed the negotiations would hurt its reputation. While he was alive, Stalin fully agreed with the Chinese position and aided Mao in stiff-arming North Korean pleas to end the war through a speedy armistice.[31]

But Stalin would die in March 1953, and his successors did not share his desire to prolong a conflict in Korea with the United States in an attempt to sap its strength. The costs of the war to the communist camp were also high, and the risk of escalation to a broader war, always a prospect, seemed an even greater one after January 1953, when the relatively hawkish President Dwight D. Eisenhower and Secretary of State John Foster Dulles took office. It was only at Stalin's funeral, which Zhou Enlai attended as Mao's emissary, that the Soviets urged the CCP to accept the deal offered by the Americans. That deal included third-party vetting of the prisoners by relatively neutral actors like India, who would determine what each prisoner actually wanted.[32] This arrangement saved some face for the communist camp because at least their enemies in Washington, Seoul, and Taipei were not directly determining the prisoners' decisions. Zhou complained bitterly about the Soviet reversal at the funeral ceremonies, citing the righteousness of the PRC position on POW exchange; but his boss, Mao Zedong, and the young PRC could hardly sustain even a limited war in Korea without Soviet support.[33]

In the summer of 1953, as the Panmunjom armistice negotiations were concluding, Jack Downey was still awaiting trial. He wondered whether he would be treated as a spy or as a soldier. He could not have known how consequential the distinction would be. If the Chinese communists had treated him as a prisoner of the Korean War, he might have been sent back to America in late 1953 after the signing of the armistice. But the Chinese communists did *not* view Downey and Fecteau as soldiers. And even if the U.S. government had known the two were alive, they would have had genuine reasons not to complicate the negotiations over prisoners by demanding the release of two civilians caught spying alongside the thousands of soldiers held in communist camps. In fact, long after the war and long after the CCP made public their detention and November 1954 conviction, the United States refused to even recognize them as spies, placing a clumsy fig leaf over the covert CIA operations in the communist world.

9

A MAN IN A BOX

T HE TRAIN'S slow sway disappeared as it gathered speed, leaving behind the lights of Shenyang and entering the darkness of the countryside. A winter had come and gone since I arrived in the city, and now there was no snow on the ground to catch the moonlight. In my compartment window, I saw only my own reflection and the reflections of my silent guards. I tried to judge the direction of travel. It seemed to be southward, away from the Soviet border. When I asked to use the toilet, the guards took me from the compartment and down the narrow, shifting corridor. For once the miniature proportions of a train lavatory proved a blessing; the guards could not follow me in, so they removed my handcuffs and watched anxiously as I squeezed through the door and closed it behind me. I noticed a small window that immediately teased me with the possibility of escape. I gauged the dimensions of the window and wondered if I could smash it and pull myself through before the guards could react. One look at my shackled legs convinced me otherwise.

By the time the train penetrated a very large city and stopped at a bustling station, dawn had come and the day had established itself as sunny and pleasant. Wherever we were, it wasn't in the Soviet Union, which was evident from the jumble of signs and posters I could see from the train window, all of them covered with rows of Chinese characters that to me looked like so many mutant Pi symbols. The city's name was probably plainly visible, if only I could read Chinese. The guards gave no hint of where we were. They waited until all the other train passengers had disembarked before we made our move.

Off the train, each guard took an arm and hustled me to a waiting truck. Before it began to move, they slipped a pair of oversized goggles on my face. They were similar to a welder's safety goggles, closed on the sides, but with opaque plastic. Looking ahead or to the sides, I could see nothing but blurry shapes in diffused light. I could see clearly only by looking down at my feet. The ride was short, and when we stopped, I was led a few paces to what I sensed to be a wide door set high in a stone wall. We halted. Four pairs of hands took hold of me at the legs and shoulders. My feet were pulled upward, my shoulders were tilted back, and I found my body being carried. I made myself go limp, and with some satisfaction heard my four bearers grunt under the dead weight and swear. Even though I estimated I had lost fifteen pounds on my Shenyang diet of peanuts and vegetables, I was still a Gulliver by Chinese standards. I felt myself being lifted over thresholds and being turned down corridors. I heard metal gates opened and shut.

In a whitewashed cell with walls of stone, I was returned to an upright position and relieved of my goggles. The floor was cement; its width could be covered in three unshackled strides, its length in five. The door was made of heavy wood, sheathed in metal, and was secured from the outside by a sliding bolt, which in turn was pad-locked. There were two windows. One was on the same wall as the door and opened onto the corridor, or would have if its lower half were not covered with cheesecloth. The other window was identical and set in the opposite wall. The view the cheesecloth blocked was of a small courtyard.

The furnishings consisted of a bed, a chamber pot, and a light bulb. The bed was made of wooden planks nailed together and laid across a pair of nine-inch-high sawhorses. A cotton sack stuffed with rice husks served as a pillow. The light bulb hung in an opening cut high in a side wall so that it could illuminate two cells at once with its fifteen watts.

The new clothes that had been given me to wear for the journey from Shenyang now were taken away. In their place I was handed rough cotton underwear, a shapeless pair of drawstring trousers, a pair of fabric slippers, and a tunic with one cloth button at the throat and another that pulled to one side on the chest, "a grannie suit" used by old Chinese women. Of my own clothes, the fatigues were beyond mending, and the flight suit and oversized articles were not returned. But the guard gave me back my long underwear, which they allowed me to put on before they fitted me with new shackles. These shackles were of a more modern construction, lighter in weight and chrome plated. They would have been an improvement, except that the interior surface of the bands had corroded, creating a sand-paper surface that made them even more abrasive than the heavier iron shackles. To make matters worse, the new shackles had a shorter chain, so my gait, which had been reduced from a walk to a shuffle, now became a mincing, penguin-like waddle.

Before the guard left the cell, he ordered me to sit on the plank bed. Whenever I reclined against the wall, they would tell me to sit up straight. Almost as soon as the door was bolted and padlocked, one of them appeared at the corridor window, holding aside the cheesecloth curtain. He stayed there staring at me then left, only to be replaced by another watcher. His passive unwavering gaze soon transformed from an unsettling intrusion to an act of aggression and a challenge. I began staring back. It was a fight I won and lost at the same time, when the guard broke his stare and barked at me to direct my eyes elsewhere. Then I changed my strategy; I stared at a spot that they could not see from where they were. I twisted my face into a bewildered expression. I stayed that way until the guard could not resist the bait and walked into my cell to examine the spot. When he found there was nothing there to warrant my expression, he walked out embarrassed. I fooled him; I won this round.

When night came, the guard instructed me in the correct prison sleeping position: arms outside the blankets, lying on my back with my head straight up so my face was always visible. For some reason, the guards wanted to be able to see my face at all times, even while I was sleeping. In the morning, my breakfast consisted of gruel and steamed bread. The guard told me to resume my seat on the low bed and did not permit pacing. By afternoon, my legs and back ached unbearably from sitting so long on a low bed. Too sore to care,

I waved my arm at the bed and scowled in protest. The guard on duty grinned and without speaking managed to indicate I had foolishly misinterpreted his orders. His amused casual expression seemed to say "Of course you can lean back against the wall; we Communists do not abuse our prisoners."

Days went by, and there were no interrogation sessions. Even the visits from an interpreter were infrequent. When the guards tried to communicate with me, they did so with sharp strings of single syllables and gestures. In Shenyang, I had been a prisoner, but Shenyang had not been a prison, either in design or in practice. In Shenyang, I had a window through which I had seen many signs of communal life. There my captors may have been stern and sometimes hostile, but they were also concerned for my well-being, if only to keep me healthy for questioning. But here in Peking, I soon learned I was in a real prison, and to the guard I was at best a burden, at worst an object of scorn. More than once, I was jabbed on my shoulder and was shouted at to return to the prescribed sleeping position.

To ask a guard for anything out of turn produced only frustration for me and, even worse, refusal. Each prisoner was on a schedule, set by the guards, to go to the toilet, which was often at odds with the prisoner's digestive natural needs. Any request to use the toilet out of turn was granted with reluctance, irritation, or not at all. One guard chose to ration toilet paper to save the Chinese people's resources. Many times we were reduced to arguing or begging for an extra piece of toilet paper; the degradation one felt was complete.

In the heat, I wore my winter underwear down around my ankles in an attempt to keep cool. I did not know whether they refused to let me get rid of the underwear because they didn't want to bother or because they were afraid to take any action not approved by a superior. Most guards were low-ranking soldiers or public security workers who doggedly followed their simple notion of what they understood to be the rules. So I sat sweltering in my boxer shorts, my long johns lumped over my ankles.

With not even a propaganda leaflet for diversion, I quickly grew attuned to the elements of the Peking prison. In the morning, the rising order was a clapping hand-rung bell. Guards brought me my glasses, washbasin, toothbrush, and tooth powder, all of which they took away each night. I was given a ration of water and did my ablutions. Then the same breakfast, lunch, and dinner. The new items were beehive-shaped lumps of coarse bread made of corn flour or sorghum. The vegetables followed the season. Because Chinese cabbage lasts, it never lost popularity. A green vegetable usually followed the season's produce. In carrot season, we were served boiled carrots, carrot soup, and carrot bread at lunch and dinner. Twice a month, there were strips of meat with our vegetables. This diet made me realize the food I had in Shenyang had been generous.

The vegetables in Peking arrived at the cell corridor in large wooden vats that did double duty as water carriers. The water was ladled into a pint-sized enamel cup fitted with a lid. The cup held the heat and was a comfort I cradled for hours when the weather turned cold. The vats were suspended from a pole borne by two guards. It was not uncommon to get water that tasted of the vegetable soup served the day before. No cold water was ever provided, since all drinking water had to be boiled and there was no refrigeration.

I continued to lose weight and I began to take a hostile pride in my haggard appearance. I was gaunt and pale. My ankles had permanent running sores. The same clippers were used once a week for my face and every other week for my head. My toes became infected and would not heal, despite the administrations of a woman doctor. Following the example of the guard who rationed toilet paper, the nurse used only salvaged cotton on my toe. When the woman doctor came back from a maternity leave and saw my inflamed toes, she was furious. She scolded the nurse and the guard sharply. Later I encountered the guard in the infirmary where he had been transferred to learn proper hygiene. The Communists' zealous reform policy sent intellectuals to farms to learn physical labor, and sent farmers to take care of patients in cities. When a barefoot "doctor" saw my infected toe, he announced "Cee-pha-lis." I laughed to myself at my situation, now that I was declared to have venereal disease in a sterile Chinese prison all by myself. After care by the woman doctor, my toe finally healed.

Sore toes and ankle shackles, bad food and ignorant guards aside, my greatest tormentors in those first months in Peking were time present—empty hours with nothing to fill them—and time future—a featureless void as blank as the whitewashed walls of my cell.

I had not even Fecteau's proximity to reassure me; I had not heard or seen him since I was taken from Shenyang. I was not allowed to have any contact with the Chinese prisoners on my corridor. So to pass the hours between waking and sleep, I visited the past. I remembered football games and wrestling matches from my Choate School days and from my Yale University days. I reconstructed them play by play, period by period. I relived a college summer touring Europe and another summer working in Alaska on the docks. I sang songs to myself. I whistled the tunes under my breath. I created albums of college songs, Latin American songs, pop songs, and I went through album by album, song by song.

What little I could see through the cell windows, I watched for hours. The cheesecloth covered only the lower half of the windows, so from the vantage of my low bed, I was afforded the best diagonal line of vision for looking up and out. The exterior window showed a patch of sky, and as spring turned to summer, the leafy tip of a tree branch. I had seen the sky turn "apple green," as I once read in a book. I also noticed the inhabitants of the sky, the clouds and birds, which offered varieties to the blue. Once I stuck a few grains of rice in the window screen, hoping to attract some birds, but none came. In summer, though, flies swarmed on the screen. From their number and the odor wafting in, I guessed the window was above an outdoor latrine.

The window opening to the corridor was more entertaining. My excursions to the toilet had revealed that the corridor itself was two stories high with a peaked roof, while the cells arranged along either side were one story high with flat roofs. Rows of transom windows ran high along both corridor walls and made the interior light and airy. I could not help thinking of a crude cathedral, flanked by the dark, cramped cells of monks. From my bed, I could look up through my cell window through the transom on the opposite wall and into the center of the prison complex. I could see edges of other roofs and sometimes cats stalking on roofs in search of sun or birds. I could see a round tower so large it resembled a fortress turret. A guard shelter rested on the top of the tower and a catwalk surrounded it. Along the catwalk railing, a monkey kept by the guards sometimes did acrobatics. I adopted the monkey as a pet I could not hold. One day I noticed a guard beating the monkey for no reason that I could comprehend, and my lack of power to stop the cruelty made the protective rage in me ready to explode.

I sat in the same position on my bed for so long through the summer heat that I left a stained spot on the wall. In the morning, there was the predictable clatter of prisoners carrying their full chamber pots to the toilet. The day progressed with three routine tasteless meals. In the evening, the walls took on a warm, rosy glow from the ceiling's one weak light bulb. Then it was time for the guards to bolt the doors; during these hours before sleep, the silence became palpable. As at Shenyang, the light bulb burned through the night.

These days and nights were notable for their emptiness and for their unrelieved tension. Except for the Chinese's specific demands for information and their cryptic hints about teaching me the truth, I had no clue what they intended to do with me. As far as I knew, they had kept my capture a secret. I imagined back in Japan that I would be considered missing in action. I had no notion of Fecteau's fate. I didn't know whether he was still in Shenyang, elsewhere in the Peking prison, or whether he was dead or alive. Certainly, I was vulnerable to execution, for I had led guerrilla warfare against Communist China. But since my arrival in Peking months before, the Chinese government officials had barely spoken to me. If they did regard me as a spy, they had given no signs of preparing for a trial. Neither did there seem to be any indication they were treating me as a prisoner of war, which was a status I would have preferred. I wondered if they had conducted a trial with me, the defendant, in absentia. Or if I could have been sentenced, and the sentence was being withheld from me. I had heard of such things happening in police states. I had been kept in the dark day after day; it was only blind faith that allowed me to believe that my life would not end in a Chinese prison.

Stamped on all clothing and bedding in the prison was an insignia that showed an upside-down *Y* in a square. This symbol of a person in a box is literally the Chinese letter for a prisoner. But I was a proud Yale man, so I wore that letter upside-down. In my mind, I played the battles in sports at Yale to remind me who I was. I played my last football game in my head over and over. I was particularly proud that it was a stormy day and how hard our team battled all the way and beat Harvard 14–6 at their stadium.

10

THE LONG CONFESSION

B Y MIDSUMMER of 1953, I reminded myself of the approaching first anniversary of our ill-fated mission. I was dismayed to realize how my life had changed in such a short time. However, two events occurred that changed my perspective of my destitute and unsettling life for the better.

For brief periods, I was taken from my cell to a small courtyard for exercise. To reach the courtyard, guards led me down the cell corridor through a folding metal gate to a rotunda, where there was a guard station. The rotunda was apparently the hub of the prison. There were two other folding metal gates leading to two other corridors like mine. The rotunda opened to a triangle courtyard; it was accessible to the other corridors as well. At the center of the courtyard was a flower bed, without blossoms. In my shackles, I shuffled around the flower bed. I continued as long as my need to move was greater than the pain the shackles caused.

On one of these outings, I passed under a cell window that attracted no more of my attention than any of the other identical windows along my exercise route. But this time I heard two words that were at once familiar and strange: "New Britain." The name of my last home was unmistakable. I knew immediately what it meant: it was Fecteau who had been here in the prison with me all along.

I flushed with excitement and hope. For the first time, I knew I was not alone in Peking. But hearing the words scared me, too. To have seen me, Fecteau must have broken the rule against looking out the windows, and to have dared to speak to me would increase his risk of being caught. My own dignity had been abused so many times by the unspeakable degradation of prison that I had to follow all their rules meticulously out of the desire to eliminate chances for further abuses. For the same reason, to limit any chances for the guards to exercise control over me, I refused to ask for any special treatment. If my ankles were sore and bleeding, I would let them stay sore and bleeding. If my drinking water tasted of yesterday's cabbage soup, I would not ask for anything better. It was a form of passive resistance that made me sensitive to any deviation in prison routine. Now because my ears had received those forbidden words, "New Britain," I felt as nervous as a plotter in an escape attempt. I shuffled away from the window without acknowledging his words. I tried to keep my outward expression unchanged, while my insides jangled with adrenaline, and I plotted how to communicate with Fecteau. Years later, Fecteau told me I looked so dejected shuffling around the tiny courtyard in my shackles that he had taken the risk of speaking to me in order to buck me up.

Not long after I learned of Fecteau's presence, my interrogation began again. It took place in a small office in a corridor across the rotunda. The route soon became familiar, imprinted by the pain of stepping over several thresholds in shackles. These interrogations were conducted during daytime working hours. I sat facing an interrogator, an interpreter, a guard, and a scribe; each of them had alternates every four hours. One of the interpreters was a pudgy young woman with a fierce revolutionary demeanor who blamed all her translation errors on me. At most sessions, though, the interpreter was a soft-spoken, handsome young man who in the aftermath of World War II had worked for an Air Force colonel attached to the OSS in Manchuria. His English was excellent, marred only by the stereotypical difficulty with *R*s. He was never arrogant, nor threatening, and whether his compassion was illusory or genuine, I felt reassured whenever he was on duty.

The interrogators themselves also changed from one session to the next. Once a fat man wearing a military uniform, but who was obviously an intellectual and not a career soldier, questioned me about technical details of takeoff procedures at the airbases in Korea. I disappointed him with my ignorance, yet his questions were more evidence that the Chinese officials considered me a mastermind of American intelligence operations. The interrogator I feared the most was a man of indeterminate age, with the body of a knife. He had a long, gaunt face and a drooping mustache. Unlike the other interrogators, whose threats most often came across as bluster, the thin man burned with unrelenting malice, and he showed more character and authority.

From the first, the thin interrogator made it clear he knew that I was withholding information and my cooperation was a pretense. When I protested, his glare made me feel more stupid than clever. Nevertheless, I persisted in giving half-truth answers to his questions. Then, one day in August, my ninth month in captivity, he let me know that no more resistance would be tolerated.

"We have been patient with you," he said. "You have told us some things, but you have not told us everything. Our patience is growing short. Tell the truth and your future will be bright. If you do not tell the truth, your future will be dark. Do you understand? Now go back to your cell and think about what I have said."

I did think. His threat was the same one I had heard since my time in Shenyang, but this time it was delivered most convincingly. He knew I had much more to tell, and I knew that if I didn't appear to confess everything, they would question me until I did, or perhaps begin physical torture. Thinking back to a couple years before, while I was in training school, a CIA instructor uttered these haunting words, "You'll talk. You'll talk." His voice seemed to come from decades ago instead of a couple of years. He was as sure then of an inevitability of confession as my interrogator was now.

Next time I faced the thin man, I said, "It's hopeless. I've told you everything." Without knowing it, I had resolved not to yield, even at the expense of an embarrassing plea for pity. "I've told you everything," I said again. "Look at me. I've told you the truth, yet here I am in chains and filthy. I've told the truth, and what do I get in return?"

While I spoke, the thin man had been staring down at his desk. When I finished, he looked up and impatiently snapped his fingers.

"We can improve your conditions," he said, as a guard approached from somewhere and began to unlock my shackles. The chains fell away and suddenly my legs were my own again. Without taking a step, I could feel their lightness; my whole body felt the freedom and the sigh of release.

"Do you see what we can do?" he asked. "You must decide if you want your conditions to improve, or not," he said, ordering me back to my cell to think things over again.

I walked freely for the first time in nine months, yet back in my cell I could not enjoy my restored ambulatory powers. I was battling to control the psychic turmoil imposed by the interrogator's ultimatum. I knew the Communist officials anticipated a formal and full confession and that they were now out of patience. I had no doubt that my captors were prepared to use abusive methods, physical or psychological, to make me talk. I also knew that my own resolve had been weakened by the months of exhausting dueling with interrogators and the unrelenting fear and uncertainty about what would be done with me once the questioning stopped. Whatever little bravado I could muster now would be a pathetic display.

I had given my agency 250 days to prepare for what I might confess once I was caught. I could not see how continuing my resistance for another month or another year would help them. The agency should have made any needed adjustment by now. One by one my defenses had been breached, and now I was at my wits' end. Still . . . still . . . was there some way I could win more time, I wondered. If only to postpone the moment of my surrender would be helpful to my agency. For two days and nights, such thoughts possessed me. I slept fitfully or not at all. Then I hit upon a plan.

If I had been grudgingly responsive to my interrogators before, now I would bury them in details, irrelevancies, and trivia. For them to sort out the useful information from the useless could take months. It meant that I could continue my delaying tactics even in the course of the confession process. It gave me the strength I needed for what I was about to do. On the third day, when the thin interrogator called me back to his room, I was ready. I agreed to make a full confession. It was to be written, not oral, I offered. And he agreed.

A low stool, some sheets of thin paper, a simple pen, and a bottle of ink were brought to my cell. I was to write sitting on the edge of my plank bed, the stool as my desk. I started with the story of my life, beginning with my birth and proceeding slowly through my childhood and days at Choate School and at Yale University. Many pages and many days later when I finally got to CIA matters, I dwelt on the insignificant. If I mentioned someone's name, I recounted all my contacts with that person, to the point of reporting drinking sessions. I wrote in an indiscriminate stream of consciousness. "I spoke to X again on Wednesday, or was it Thursday? No, it was Wednesday," was a representative construction.

After receiving the first few installments of my narrative, the interpreter visited my cell and scolded me. "You're writing too much nonsense," he said.

I replied that since I could not know what information was important to them, I had decided to write everything I knew, especially since I didn't want to be accused of concealing anything. I doubted they accepted the sincerity of my explanation, but perhaps they too were worn down because they let me continue in my ruminating style.

The Chinese had hinted my future would grow brighter if I cooperated, and there were some small improvements in my lot. The shackles were not returned, but the rule against pacing in the cell remained in force. I was given a bath, the first time since leaving Shenyang, which washed away the grime and stench of a Peking summer. But the food was still gruel and boiled vegetables twice a day. Sporadically, I was given something to read, propaganda pamphlets and a Soviet polemical novel called *Far from Moscow* that was stultifying even to my deprived senses. I thought my "confession" had more artistic merit. One of the pamphlets contained a map of China, and I made a game of memorizing the names of all the provinces. I got an abstract written by Pettis Perry, a Black American communist who had been convicted for a Smith Act violation. It was the single bit of news I had gotten from home since my capture. But my own confession occupied most of my time.

I wrote all day long, breaking only for meals. I wrote as summer turned to fall and fall to winter. Sundays were a day of rest when we were served a late lunch and an early dinner. On most Sundays, music was played over the prison loudspeaker system. Usually the program was the strident singsong of Peking opera, a highly stylized musical form, whose appeal to the Chinese had not lessened under the Communists, despite its feudal intellectual heritage. On some Sundays, though, the loudspeakers broadcast western classical music. Sitting in my bare cell, dressed in a Chinese "granny suit," I was nurtured by the strains of Strauss waltzes and Tchaikovsky's "Nutcracker Suite." Once someone must have made a mistake while turning the radio dial to the music channel; a U.S. Armed Forces station with the swelling sounds of the "Star-Spangled Banner" filled the prison for a few moments before someone recognized the tune and switched it off. When I heard it, I straightened my back and felt my eyes and nose sting with emotion. Inside I felt a mixture of homesickness and national pride. I was delighted at my captors' chagrin and felt pure pleasure at the stirring sound of the American national anthem.

In November, while I was still in my light summer clothes, winter came to Peking. The only heat in my cell came from a stovepipe that ran across the ceiling. For days I shivered, though somewhat less after I was issued the bulky quilted pants and jacket that are common winter wear in northern China. The Peking winter was long, cold, and dry. The prison, which was blessedly well ventilated for summer heat, stood open to blasts of frigid air that blew out of the middle of the Asian continent. Windstorms carrying dust from the Gobi Desert lasted three or four days at a time, and the whole world, inside and outside, turned sepia. I sat huddled on my plank bed, my hands jammed "Confucian-style" into the opposite sleeve and my head pulled as far inside as my collar allowed. I sat still in the form of a sleeping turtle.

On all but such days as those when the whole prison hunkered down against a storm, I continued my confession chronicle. I wrote so voluminously, sometimes as many as twenty pages of cramped script a day, that the guard in charge of numbering them and keeping them in order for translators often mixed up the pages. When I detected an error, I would call his attention to it by gesturing, savoring his loss of face as a small triumph over my captors. By April, in a total of eight months, the written confession was finally finished and the guard was spared further embarrassment. He had numbered more than three thousand pages.

11

THE TRIAL

B Y MY second spring in captivity, the interrogation had reached its end. With my confession done, I marked the passage into summer by watching the greening of the few trees and flowers visible from the courtyard where I was taken for exercise. My meals had changed from winter cabbage to fresh vegetables. The odor deepened from the outdoor lavatory. Several times I went outdoors for exercise. I passed Fecteau's window hoping to hear words from him, but I never did. I was sure he would see me, now free of ankle shackles. I don't know whether Fecteau knew the deal I had made with my captors. He might notice that I was now more at ease as I walked in this yard. For a time I expected that once I made a full confession, a trial would follow, or at least I would get a summary sentencing. When weeks went by with no hint of either, I assumed that they had to labor over the mountains of information in my three thousand pages of creation. The delay was of my own making, and I stopped expecting that a formal trial would come any time soon. I went back to my daily speculations about a diplomatically arranged prisoner exchange or release with the end of the Korean War.

Then, one evening in October, a guard came to my cell and motioned me to follow him. We crossed the rotunda at the end of my corridor and turned down another where I had never been before. We stopped at a small office. Inside were three military officers seated at a table covered with red cloth. They pushed a thin sheet of paper toward me. The writing was in English, typewritten and double-spaced. It was my indictment. The officers told me to sign a receipt for it, handing me the same kind of simple pen I had used to write my confession. The receipt was on paper so flimsy, and my hand was so shaky, that the sheet tore when I signed my name. Next to my signature, I noticed the date, October 11, 1954. In the uncertain mental calendar I had kept since my capture, I had somehow lost eleven days. I had thought it was the waning days of September or the beginning of October at the latest.

With the copy of the indictment in my hand, I was taken across the corridor to another office where a smiling Chinese civilian greeted me cordially. He was middle-aged and conducted himself in the manner of the educated class. He was my lawyer. He assured me that everyone accused of a crime against the People's Republic of China was entitled to a legal defense. Then he exhorted me to make a good showing at my trial. It was to begin that very evening, six hundred and eighty-one days after my capture.

The consultations with the lawyer lasted only a few minutes before I was taken back to my cell and told to review the indictment. It was half a dozen pages long and recounted, in the grandiose language typical of the Communists, my CIA training and the events surrounding the guerrilla mission. The first quick reading showed me the Communists considered me, or had chosen to cast me, as an archvillain. In each of the specific charges of the indictment, the same message was implicit. It was John Downey who had recruited the Chinese agents; it was John Downey who had trained them; it was John Downey who had planned their clandestine aggression. This exaggeration exasperated me, and I feared it could only result in a more severe sentence.

I had finished reading the indictment a second time when the guard demanded its return. Moments later other guards came to the cell and reintroduced me to handcuffs and shackles. Then I was taken outside the prison to a canvas-topped jeep. It was now midevening, about eight-thirty or nine o'clock. Little more than an hour had passed since I had been informed of my trial. We drove through the still bustling streets and stopped in front of a formidable stone building. We climbed a wide, curving staircase to the second floor where I was put in a small room. Though there were one or two chairs against the walls, I was told to sit on the floor.

Soon my lawyer entered with an interpreter. "Did you have any questions?" the lawyer asked, still smiling. When I told him the indictment contained mistakes, his cordial mask was washed away by a new expression of desperate fear. He managed to collect himself and mumbled that I should elaborate. I listed five specific errors, but I was now certain my defense counsel had no appetite for any real confrontation with the prosecution. But before he could respond, the interpreter put the conversation back on the preordained track. I did not deny I was guilty, did I? I said no. I wasn't renouncing my confession, was I? I said no. Then they both left, the lawyer looking only half restored to his equanimity.

They were replaced by two guards, who were both armed and both tense. They removed my handcuffs and each grasped one of my arms. They led me out of the room and across a stairway landing to another room. This room was much larger and filled with people. One of the guards unconsciously tightened his grip to a painful pinch. As in Shenyang, again it was a showcase for them, a hundred or so cadres seated in the spectators' section on the left. Each face I focused on seemed to be wearing a grin of triumph; evidently, they were pleased to be the privileged guests at a judicial extravaganza. I noticed several photographers and even an artist with a sketch pad. Against the opposite wall, the unsmiling military officers looked down from a high rostrum. Between this tribunal and the spectators were tables for our defense lawyers and the government's prosecutor. I was now before the Procurator-General of the Supreme People's Court of the People's Republic of China.

I was asked my name and address. I stood at attention and with an act of will responded in a loud voice, "John Downey, 433 Monroe Street, New Britain, Connecticut, United States of America."

The long answer, particularly the trilling syllables of Connecticut, made the interpreter hesitate and finally settle for an abbreviated version.

Then the indictment was read and I was asked if it were true. I said, "Yes." I felt the pressure of a guard's hand pulling me and I backed away, my ankle chains clanking.

There was a general rustling in the crowd, and before I could wonder what would happen next, the courtroom door opened and Fecteau was led in. Though I had had no contact with him since those
furtive words, "New Britain," I was not surprised to see him. It made
sense that we would be tried together. He looked about as I expected,
thinner, pale, with chopped hair, and at that moment, fiery-eyed.
"Who's your tailor?" he asked out of the side of his mouth as soon
as he was positioned next to me. It took me a few seconds to absorb
the wisecrack and remembered the baggy Chinese prison uniforms
we were both wearing. I almost smiled, but the guard's stony glare
stopped me, and I kept my silence.

After Fecteau had given his name and heard his indictment read,
the door opened again. Our nine Chinese agents trooped in, including the two group leaders and the colonel we had tried to pick up. I
had no time to study their faces or exchange glances with them before
they were arranged in a row next to Fecteau and me. We stood side by
side facing the judges. Only by turning our heads and leaning out of
line could we get a good look at one another, and it was evident we
were expected to give our full attention to the court. By now, a guard
stood behind each of us, turning us bodily to direct our gaze at whoever was speaking.

Fecteau and I shared the same lawyer, and each team of agents
had its own lawyers. The two men were middle-aged, but the woman
who represented one of the teams was younger and more animated.
All three were old enough, however, to have had their legal training
under the Western-influenced law schools of the Nationalist government. I was convinced they were hiding some shame at the pretense
of defense they were acting out. The prosecutor, unfortunately, was
the most impressive lawyer in the courtroom. He was in his thir-
ties, also old enough to have gone to a Nationalist law school, and he
looked trim and efficient in his military uniform. He went about his
business briskly, resisting what must have been a strong temptation
toward histrionics.

Only the parts of the proceedings that pertained to Fecteau and me
were repeated in English. Our lawyer's defense amounted to a plea
for mercy. "He is so young," he said several times, referring to me and
trying to suggest it was my youthful innocence that had permitted

me to become the imperialists' dupe. On Fecteau's behalf, our lawyer argued that he had joined the mission only by chance in its last stages and had not participated in its diabolic planning.

When he finished and stepped back to our table, I fixed him with an angry stare that silently reminded him of his charade and his failure to mention the indictment's errors I had objected to. The woman lawyer outdid her male colleagues with the passion of her defense. She spoke for some minutes, and after I heard *Fe-ke-toe* and *Tahn-nye* mentioned several times, I knew she was trying to convince the court that the agents had been our reluctant allies and victims.

In his remarks, the prosecutor declared we had received training in inciting armed riots at "Guerrilla Warfare School" at Fort Benning. We had trained at Fort Benning for combat, but his deliberate ignorance of the apparent contradiction in his statement incensed me. I thought he must recognize the difference between guerrilla action undertaken in wartime and noncombat espionage training. He was painting our mission in the most negative light possible.

Then it was our turn to address the court. Earlier in the evening, when my lawyer had urged me to make a good showing at the trial, I knew he was advising me to give the judges the show of contrition they expected. Admitting my crimes was not enough for the Communists; I had to prove my shame to my righteous accusers. In the tens of thousands of "Thought Reform" groups in Communist China, self-criticism had been part of their daily life. And in my interrogation session, I had learned enough of the reform group dynamics to know that proper self-criticism could save a fellow a lot of trouble. But to me, even standing before the tribunal, there was nothing that could persuade me to flail myself as a misguided agent of imperialism, even if my life were on the line.

"Do you have anything to say?" asked one of the tribunal.

"No," I said firmly.

"Nothing?" he asked, giving me a second chance.

"Guilty as charged," I said, then I stood silent.

"You have nothing to say about all that has been presented?" asked the judge again, now on the verge of being disappointed that his court would produce no juicy denunciation by a reformed American devil that could be reported to the masses.

Making a conscious effort to sound sincere, and hoping the sincerity would drive home the sarcasm I really meant, I said, "No, my attorney has spoken for me."

I heard titters and amused gasps spread through the spectators' gallery, and it became louder when Fecteau topped my remark by adding, "And I thought he spoke well."

Despite our satire, the Chinese found our act of limited entertainment value, and we gave way to the Chinese agents. What they said was not translated for us, but only a few engaged in speech lengthy enough to satisfy the requirements of self-criticism. One who did was the first team leader, the young major who had served in the Japanese occupation army and who had been so clever during our training sessions at Chigasaki.

When the agents were done, we all pivoted in our chains and were marched out of the courtroom. I had no chance to say anything to Fecteau before we were separated. I was returned to the small room where I had awaited the start of the trial, and I was again told to sit on the floor. This time I was joined by the smiling colonel, the one no one trusted. His smile was gone now, and he looked totally defeated. With a guard standing over us, we dared not speak. The colonel sat with his head down, moaning to himself, "Ai-ya, ai-ya." It was a Chinese lament I had heard many times coming from cells on my corridor. Once or twice the colonel looked up and we exchanged sympathetic glances. I saw no reproach in his eyes for the trouble we had gotten him into, only sorrow. In the jeep ride back to the prison, I pressed his arm to show support.

It was near midnight when a guard bolted the door shut behind me in my cell. I lay down, too agitated to sleep. I had stopped expecting a trial, but now that I had had one, I assumed I would be sentenced and probably soon, perhaps the next day. The indictment and the prosecutor had portrayed my offenses as extremely serious. I was certain I would not be treated as a prisoner of war. I tried to guess the minimum sentence I might get. Anything beyond ten years was unthinkable, and ten years seemed like death itself.

The next morning I awoke with the same desperate speculations running through my head, but no interpreter came to my cell to summon me to court. Days passed, each day a copy of the one before in its blankness. I stopped guessing numbers and returned to my old plotting of less finite scenarios of release. Perhaps I would not be told my sentence at all, but instead I would be held indefinitely as a pawn in a political chess match whose progress and players were kept secret from me. The United States and China did not have diplomatic relations. As far as the United States was concerned, China had moved to an island called Taiwan. The United States did not acknowledge the existence of the hundreds of millions of Chinese who remained in mainland China or their government as a legitimate entity. I imagined my fate and Fecteau's would have to be discussed secretly in neutral embassies. If the Chinese communists acknowledged our capture to the world, based on the evidence available to me, my release the next day was entirely as likely as my execution. No matter how optimistic or pessimistic my constructions, each was equally unfounded in empirical fact.

My ignorance ended on November 23, a week before the second anniversary of our capture. A jailer wearing his military uniform for the first time appeared in the evening. He gave me a new suit of pants and a tunic to put on. He was tense and I immediately became just as tense. I was going somewhere. When he scraped my wrists hurriedly, clapping on handcuffs, he sucked in his breath in apology but did not pause to examine the damage. He signaled for me to follow him out of the cell then stopped, looking with concern at my bare head. He told me to wait and he ran back to the cell. A few seconds later I heard a cell door down the corridor being unbolted then quickly shut again. The jailer reappeared carrying a quilted skull cap, which must be a part of a required dress code; he must have appropriated it from another prisoner.

Outside, instead of a covered jeep or a light truck, was an ordinary bus. I climbed in and walked down the aisle until a guard gestured for me to sit. I started to slide onto the nearest seat when he gestured again. I hesitated before realizing he was pointing at the floor between the seats, not at the seat. I guessed they did not want me to see the streets we would drive through, or they did not want people on the streets to see me. I squeezed myself onto the floor in the narrow leg area and soon heard others climb on board. I looked over the tops of the seats to see Fecteau and the nine Chinese agents. They all took their own spots on the floor.

We drove to the same stone building where we had been tried. Inside we were separated and I was again placed alone in a small antechamber. I had been there only a few minutes when I was called out and taken across the landing to the courtroom. The tribunal of judges gazed again from their rostrum, and if the faces in the spectators' gallery were not the same, they were all grinning just as they had six weeks ago at the trial. Fecteau and the Chinese agents were led in. No one had told me that we were to be sentenced, but I was sure that was what was happening. Instinctively trying to prepare myself for the worst, I began thinking about ten more years in prison.

The court was called to order, and each of us—the nine agents, Fecteau and I—stepped forward to give our names. There were very few preliminaries before the judges began their devastating pronouncements of life and death. Now my former fears of a ten-year sentence seemed a silly dream. "Life" was the word the judge declared for me.

I had gone through five months of intensive interrogation in Shenyang and four months of waiting in a solitary cell in Peking—nine months of leg shackles. Then eight months of writing a confession. Then another six months of waiting in a solitary cell. Two years of purgatory finally ended, and now I got a life sentence in a communist prison.

That night I wrestled with the image of an old man who remembered nothing of life but prison. I swore and prayed that I would not become that old man.

12

B-29 CREW WERE RELEASED FROM CHINA

I N THE DAYS following my sentence, life in prison went on as before, with no visible sign of change. Had my family been told I was alive? I did not know. Was my government in touch with my captor? I did not know. The inner turmoil stirred by the trial subsided, and I was left to cope with the routine mix of boredom, fear, and uncertainty.

Then, two weeks later, in early December 1954, a guard entered my cell and told me to collect my possessions. I was wearing most of them and the rest—my bedding, my enamel cup, my washbasin, and my toothbrush—I gathered up in my arms. By now I had learned to conceal the trauma I felt each time I was led away from the familiar walls of my cell. Still, it was with quickened senses that I followed the guard down the corridor, through the rotunda, and down more corridors. We walked far enough to reach an entirely different wing of the prison, and we stopped outside of a cell that appeared just like the one I had left. The guard unbolted the heavy door and directed me inside.

But this cell was not empty. The walls were lined with low plank beds, and standing in the remaining floor space were five or six people, all dressed in black prison uniforms and all surprisingly large in stature. It took me a few moments to realize that they were not

Chinese. I was no more prepared to see people in the cell, people with Western features, than I had been prepared to hear the words "New Britain" whispered from that cell window months before. We gawked at each other in mutual bewilderment. Then one of them spoke, in English. I had no trouble recognizing the accent. It was American; they were all Americans.

They rushed over to shake hands with me and introduce themselves. The only thing that registered in those first minutes with me was that they were officers from a B-29 crew that had been shot down more than a year before, near the Korean border. The enlisted members of the crew were across the corridor in another cell. I told them my name, wondering how to describe myself. I had no rank, and the mission that had put me in that cell with them was too complex to explain in the half sentences our excitement allowed us.

We heard voices calling from across the corridor. We crowded around the peephole and began calling to the enlisted men. No guards moved to stop us. "Hey, Jack!" It was Fecteau! A few moments later, both cell doors were opened and we swarmed into the corridor, milling about, Fecteau and I pumping hands, pounding each other on the back. We exchanged confused introductions with the crew members. Except for the few words Fecteau and I had stolen at our trial and sentencing, I had not spoken to anyone in friendship in two years. My dialogue with the Chinese had been so guarded and infrequent that now I felt I was ending a verbal fast. We talked about our missions, our families, our imprisonment. The crew had been receiving mail from home, and they informed me the Korean Armistice had been signed eighteen months before. They had had no inkling of my capture, and they reacted with amused disbelief when we compared the circumstances of our crashes. Their plane had been brought down from about twenty-two thousand feet in the air by MiGs; ours had been shot down at about thirty feet aboveground by machine guns and rifles.[1]

We kept talking right through dinner, which for me seemed like a feast, carrots and pork fried in oil. I kept talking even after everyone else had gone to bed, and I stopped only from exhaustion. The next morning the door to our cell was opened and left unlocked again, and we could mingle just as the day before. Fecteau was still staying with the enlisted men. The Chinese, who were obsessed with proper form and order, had concluded, wrongly, that Fecteau was my junior in rank and so had barred him from the officers' cell. They might have realized their error when we began pounding each other on the back like long-lost brothers. Now for the first time we were free to talk. We had been in the same prisons all along and our descriptions of interpreters and interrogators seemed to match. We both had particularly vivid memories of a chubby interpreter with a sad face. We were not surprised to discover our captors had regularly compared our stories to catch discrepancies, and the discrepancies had been extreme, especially in the first months when we were both giving wildly creative accounts of our activities. As best as we could judge, however, it seemed my interrogation had gone on longer, in keeping with the Communists' perception of me as the mission leader. Like me, Fecteau had never been physically assaulted. But he had been forced to stand at one point for twenty-four hours straight. I remembered the excruciating stiffness from my enforced sitting posture in my first days in Peking, and I winced to imagine the pain Fecteau must have felt.

We both learned the B-29 crew also had been in Shenyang when we were there. They called it the Peanut Palace since peanuts had been served with so many meals. They had been in the Philippines with a unit assigned to airlift guerrillas behind enemy lines. As a training mission in January 1953, they were to make a leaflet drop over North Korea. On board as observers were extra officers, including their section commander, Colonel Arnold. Their navigator insisted they were six miles south of the Chinese border when they were attacked by MiGs. Regardless of whether the navigator was right or wrong, they crashed on the north side of the Yalu River, which was Chinese territory. Several crewmen were killed; the most seriously injured survivor was an observing officer, Major Baumer, who had just completed a double tour of duty and one hundred combat missions, and had volunteered to make this last flight before returning home. Baumer had been wounded in the air attack, lay in the snow for hours after the crash, and had become severely frostbitten. He lost all his fingers except one thumb and one little finger. He also lost the front half of his right foot.

The fliers had not seen their commander, Colonel Arnold, since Shenyang; when I entered the cell, they at first thought that I was he. They had been in Peking more than a year. They too had been bolstered by the mistaken broadcast of "The Star-Spangled Banner." Despite his painful foot, Baumer had jumped to attention when he heard our national anthem. Chinese doctors had amputated only the frostbitten portion, leaving him with a constantly tender nub of flesh at the end of his leg.[2] He had no crutches, so he hopped about. Once going down the corridor to the toilet, he slipped on a patch of ice and banged the maimed foot. He could not stifle a scream of pain. Fecteau became enraged and cursed at the guards, but they did nothing.

Fecteau and I had been with the B-29 crew only a day when an interpreter instructed our group to elect a "president" and organize ourselves as if we were in a prisoner-of-war camp. Baumer was the unanimous choice. A guard stationed midway down the corridor sealed off our "compound" of cells, which we were required to keep clean. I felt only a small twinge of guilt when one of the crew members had to finish the chores assigned to me. My appetite for talk was so insatiable that I couldn't sweep out a cell without drifting off into a conversation. Our treatment improved, beginning with daily rations of meat and access to a shower that we were allowed to use once a week. A ping-pong table was installed in the corridor and a volleyball net was strung up in the exercise yard. We laughed at ourselves when we discovered how awkward we had become from months of confinement. We were surprised, too, by eruptions of temper. Our jailers had given us a set of boxing gloves with the stipulation that there be no blows to the head. It was a rule that was observed more often in the breach, as contests intended to let off steam boiled over. When trading punches with one of the young enlisted men, who must have been about twenty years old, I wanted to tear his head off, and from the look in his eyes he felt the same toward me. After a few incidents like that, the boxing gloves were taken away. Our captors seemed upset by physical violence.

Christmas came for the third time since my capture. When the Chinese asked the B-29 crew what holidays they celebrated, they mentioned every one they could think of, from St. Patrick's Day to Halloween. The Chinese ignored the list, but they did recognize Christmas as special. In our corridor, we made a Christmas feast from extra food the prison provided and from food packages from home, which the guards had held back in anticipation of the holiday. Fecteau and I had no package, but the crew members shared theirs with us, just as they shared their mail. I devoured Spam, that fatty canned ham, as if it were the finest roast beef. After the meal, we sang Christmas carols and then bawdy songs with lyrics that must have baffled the interpreter monitoring our performance.

These were the only happy days I had in Chinese prison. We talked, joked, and argued incessantly. Our emotions were close to the surface, and a letter occasionally would evoke tears from one of the crew. Spirits were high. The Air Force group were certain that the good treatment signaled imminent release and tried to convince me that Fecteau and I were going home with them. Desperate surges of hope struggled with my sense of reality. The sentences of the fliers ranged from four to ten years, but I was a civilian with a life sentence. My captors were not going to let me off that lightly.

A few days after Christmas, a pair of interpreters came to the corridor and explained they had decided our cells were overcrowded and that two of us would have to be moved. The bombardier and the flight engineer, both older career men, volunteered. They were tired of living in close quarters, especially with the younger crew members, who were quite boisterous. The suggestion took the interpreters aback. They thought the crew would want to stick together. Fecteau and I should go, they said. We didn't argue. As we collected our belongings, the kids of the crew succeeded in extracting a guarantee from the interpreters that Fecteau and I would be brought back each day to visit. One of them tried to cheer me up by shaking my hand and offering congratulations. I was being released, he said. I knew he was wrong. I knew it was the B-29 crew that was going home.

Fecteau and I followed the interpreters to another corridor and into the same cell. But before Fecteau could put his things down, he was told to carry them across the way to a different cell. We both pleaded to be cellmates. The answer was no. Exactly three weeks after we had joined the B-29 crew, we were back in solitary, and I was nearly as flattened as I had been after the sentencing. The future seemed bleak. The next day, the interpreters admitted, with some embarrassment, that they had lied when they promised that Fecteau and I could share recreation periods with the B-29 crew. Perhaps it was from guilt that they brought me a pile of books to read. But the books were small comforts that highlighted the paucity of my situation. Even anticipation of letters and food packages from home did not boost my spirits.

I had been told I could write my family soon after I joined the fliers. I was overjoyed, but the letter proved very difficult to write. I knew the letter would be censored, so I could not unburden myself of the anger and the pain we felt, even if I thought my family should hear about it. Besides, I didn't know how much my family knew about my situation. Did they even know I was alive? There was so much to tell, and so little I could say. My first letter home contained only the predictable vows of love and reassurance that I was doing fine.

Before I got any letter from home, I was surprised to find myself reunited with the B-29 crew again. This time the message was delivered by an interpreter, one we later referred to as "the Kid." He told me that the government wanted to take photographs to send to my family so they could see how well I was being treated. My black prison uniform was exchanged for a new blue quilted suit of good quality fabric. Then I was taken from my cell to what appeared to be a mess hall several corridors away. Fecteau was already there, also in new clothes, as was the B-29 crew. We had an exuberant reunion. I met Colonel Arnold, who had been returned to his crew for this occasion. He appeared in good health, but crew members whispered to me that he had been tortured the week before and forced to sign a false confession. The method of coercion had been arm twisting, literally. His arms had popped out of their sockets. The brutality seemed not atypical and it was years later that I learned UN Secretary-General Dag Hammarskjöld was visiting Peking at the time, to check on the Communists' American prisoners. That was why the confession was urgently needed and why our photographs were taken.[3]

We were photographed outside playing volleyball, even though the day was bitterly cold. We hopped stiffly about, with our necks pulled in and our fists clenched, pretending to enjoy ourselves. In the mess hall, the crew members got new food packages, which were followed by a prison meal of extra generous portions. The interpreters warned us not to gorge ourselves on the provisions from home so we would have room for the second meal. They were worried that we would not clean our plates of prison food, indicating to anyone who saw the photographs of our meal that the prison food was deficient. The interpreters need not have worried. We ate both meals with relish.

After the meal, we were photographed reading mail from home. Neither Fecteau nor I had yet gotten any mail, so we gazed at snapshots sent by one of the crewman's family. I tilted mine toward the photographer, hoping that when his shots were printed someone examining them with a magnifying glass would recognize that the loved ones I so wistfully gazed at were strangers to me. I was also doing the same with reading others' mail, when I got no mail from home. Before we left the crew, I circulated among them, giving each a word or phrase to repeat at the debriefing I knew they would undergo once they were released. The CIA could piece these together; they would give the agency information I had included in my confession. I successfully smuggled out this information to the CIA, the only spy work I had done.[4]

Back in my cell, I found it furnished with a desk and a chair. The nine-inch-high plank bed had been replaced with one that was two feet high. It would be a luxury not to feel I was sleeping on the floor. After I was photographed with my new furniture, the interpreters assured me that they were not just for show and that they would be mine permanently. My purgatory had ended. My real prison life was about to begin. These improvements gave me little pleasure; it indicated that my prison stay would be long rather than short. It left me wondering how long would it be . . .

13

THE CHINA I SAW, WITH
AMERICA IN MY MIND

AFTER THE B-29 crew left, we were back to solitary confinement again. Even with improved furnishings, books to read, permission to write home, and also the expectations of letters from home, nothing could lift me out of my low mood. It seemed there was no end in sight. After a while, I told myself repeatedly, "Have faith in your own government; it will negotiate for your release. It just takes time. You need patience."

As I accumulated packages from home, my cell began to take on the aspect of a hermit's one-room cabin. I threw away nothing of any conceivable use. I stored my possessions beyond my growing library of books and magazines in boxes under my bed. Eventually the boxes crept out from beneath the bed and began to line the walls. Instead of carrying everything in one arm as I did whenever I switched cells in the early years, I now needed several guards to help me. My interpreter tried to persuade me to leave things behind, but I insisted on taking all of it, to the last copy of *Sporting News*.

I changed prisons three times but changed cells many times. The reasons for moving were never explained to me. Fecteau made the moves with me. Though we were usually on the same corridor and for many years shared exercise periods, we were never cellmates.

In August 1955, a time when I was particularly anxious, I was visited by a pompous, strutting young party official who introduced himself as "Mister Chou."* Flourishing a paper document, he said he had something to read to me. The language was formal and convoluted, and by the time he had finished, I realized it was the text of an agreement between China and the United States on the exchange of civilian prisoners.

"Do you have any questions?" Mister Chou asked me grandly.

"Just one," I said. "Does it apply to me?"

The question may have been obvious, but it instantly burst Mister Chou's bubble of officious pride. He blushed, turned, and left the cell without saying a word, leaving me to wonder in ignorance if my release could be arranged. The agreement declared that any American who felt he was improperly detained by the Chinese should inform the British chargé d'affaires. I hesitated before writing for an audience. Petitioning for release was an implicit denial of my guilt, and I was convinced it would offend the Chinese, perhaps leading to a new round of interrogation to remind me of my crimes or making my chances for release even more remote.

Mister Chou finally reappeared a week later, his spirit restored. He made some general inquiries about how I was getting on but did not mention the exchange agreement. When I reminded him of it, he feigned forgetfulness, as though he had never heard of any exchange agreement. I got angry.

"Does it apply or doesn't it?" I asked. "Yes or no?"

Once more Mister Chou's aplomb deserted him. He mumbled, "I'll press on your request to the authorities" and scampered out of the cell. I was exasperated, my sense of justice offended; my outrage made me reckless. I dashed off a note, asking "in accordance with the

---

* Downey reports that a man named Mr. Chou reads a statement presenting him with an opportunity to appeal his detention to the UK chargé d'affaires in Beijing in August 1955. That agreement was negotiated in August 1955 but not reached until September 10, 1955, as will be discussed in chapter 14. It is possible but improbable that the Chinese government was testing out a working draft by presenting it to Downey, but it seems more likely that Downey's account is off by a few weeks—fully understandable given the length and conditions of his incarceration. This would mean that it was later that September 1955 when he moved to the new prison where he met Miss and the Warden.

Sino-U.S. Agreement" to see the British chargé d'affaires. I had the letter taken to the prison warden and then sat back to await the fireworks. It was all I could do.

Two weeks later, an interpreter arrived in my cell and told me to collect my possessions. I was being moved. I beat back the surge of hope that I was being released. Two guards helped me carry my boxes to a small truck. The truck, however, did not take me toward home. It drove me through the gates of a weather-blackened prison in the heart of Peking. I was greeted by a Chinese man with a bushy black mustache and bulging eyes. He was simultaneously arrogant and nervous. He told me I was there to begin officially serving my life sentence. Now I was certain my letter to the British chargé d'affaires had stiffened the Communists' resolve to punish me.

The pronouncement of the mustached man, who apparently was the prison's political commissar, was translated by a tiny young woman. She was chubby and just under five feet tall. Her bright black eyes, obscured by glasses, and her smooth complexion were the only traces of softness in an otherwise severe demeanor. Each word she spoke bore the tone of condemnation or correction. Her English accent was close to flawless and was far better than her command of the vocabulary. I eventually called her Miss, just as I eventually called her boss the Warden. They were to be part of my life for the following ten years.

Initially I wrote home every week, but soon I ran out of things to say to my family. There was nothing hopeful to report. I noticed that the female interpreter, whom we had nicknamed "Miss" and who was always combative and scornful toward us, had been unusually withdrawn. Did she feel sorry for us for not being included with the B-29 crew who went home? I could only guess.

One day in January 1956,* Miss came to my cell and announced that we were to be taken out for a trip the next morning and advised me to get ready when I got up. In the past, we went out of the prison walls

---

* Downey wrote that it was January 1955 when he was invited by Miss and her boss, the Warden, to travel outside the prison and see Beijing. This was almost certainly a typo, as his trips most likely occurred in January 1956, not January 1955. By his own account, Downey does not meet Miss or the Warden until his transfer to the new prison in late summer 1955. Downey

for trials or moved to a different prison. All the activities were done after dark; I had never been out in the daylight, and up to this point I never did get a good look at Peking. The next morning I got up early and sat on the edge of my bed waiting. I knew Fecteau would be on this trip as well. I had not seen him for a month since we were separated and put in solitary cells. Breakfast time came, and instead of the usual gruel and steamed bread, I was served bean curd milk and a long piece of fried dough, a welcome change, to say the least. When the Warden unbolted my cell door, it was full morning.

The small group included Fecteau, me, the Warden, Miss, and a soldier guard who also served as our driver. We boarded a van and were driven through Peking's broad boulevards and their motley traffic; we saw a mixture of vintage cars, bicycles, motor scooters, and carts drawn by animals and people. The sights and sounds were curious and heartwarming.

I should have enjoyed this outing, but there had been no warning until the night before; I didn't know what behavior was expected of me, and I tried futilely to stop myself from wondering whether this excursion was a preliminary to release. How should I conduct myself in order not to jeopardize my chances of going home? I was tense. As it turned out, this trip included a three-hour train ride to a newly completed dam north of Peking, which we dutifully marveled at when allowed to give our opinion. Then it was a three-hour haul back to the city to our cell. On a subsequent trip, we visited a Buddhist temple, a short drive from the prison. We saw older people making their pilgrimages, kowtowing and saying prayers and lighting incense sticks. Some young people stood in clusters, mocking the piety of their elders, and laughing to each other. Miss disapproved of this behavior.

---

also discusses a long period of time after the B-29 crew left the previous prison and before he meets Miss and the Warden. During this time he was kept in solitary confinement. This was also the first time he was allowed to write home, which he did for many weeks until he ran out of things to say. His first reference to trips outside the prison occur in letters he wrote home in February 1956. Since the B-29 crew left the previous prison sometime in January 1955, their departure and the initial trips to tour China could not have occurred in the same month, by Downey's own account.

She said that religion was destructive but the young people should still be respectful.

Our van had gone through Tiananmen Square many times. It was on the National Day of the Revolution, on the first of October, 1956, that I got to see the immensity of the Square. It was well over one hundred acres and was covered with soldiers and a crowd of onlookers. By midmorning on this clear day, we were taken to an observation point. At a distance of a half mile, without warning, the howitzers arranged below us exploded in a twenty-one gun salute, startling us more than the loudest Fourth of July cherry bombs. Chinese prison had accustomed us to silence. In this New China, workers, peasants, soldiers, and artists paraded in formation before a great wall hung with portraits of Marx, Lenin, Stalin, and Mao. Mao, the man himself, was there, dwarfed by his own likeness. As the ceremony came to a close, the throng broke and surged toward him as waves rushing toward the shore. Later, when the crowd dispersed, we went back to the prison, where we waited. Evening came, and we were returned to the Square to see real fireworks, and a more exuberant celebration of the Revolution. This time we sat in bleachers on the Square itself. Our driver parked near cars from many of the foreign embassies in Peking. Though there was no U.S. delegation, there were plenty of American-made automobiles, many new models, the first that Fecteau and I had seen in five years. We grew increasingly excited as we spotted first one sleek model and then another. Mystified by our animated response to the cars, Miss insisted on an explanation. And when we offered one, she reminded us that it was an injustice that such wealth should be expended on vehicles for the rich when the workers needed so much. We couldn't answer her, and luckily the debate ended by the time we reached the bleachers. There we found a crowd as diverse as the parade units we had seen that morning. Nearby sat a contingent of Buddhist monks in saffron robes, who seemed mesmerized by the pageant before them. They seemed to be as detached from the celebration as we were. Watching the magnificent fireworks, I was overwhelmed with nostalgia for the Fourth of July at home in America, and I told Fecteau, "I will go home, go to law school, and run for political office!" Fecteau pulled my sleeve and whispered in my ear, "Don't forget you are serving a life sentence!" He brought me back to earth.

After the crowd moved out of the Square, again we were driven back to prison, the door bolted behind me. Although our outings continued, the following January, in 1956, we were given a four-day tour of Peking and surrounding areas, which was both educational and enjoyable. We were also treated at local restaurants. Our taste buds awakened, and the food tasted heavenly. Even with all these intriguing activities and special treatment, my dream of going home remained strong.

By now I had connected with my family and friends. I received dozens of letters and cards, some from people I never knew. I could not write back to everyone, although I would have liked to. These letters gave me a sense that I was still alive, that I was somebody people cared about, and it connected me with my world. The letters and the packages that I received monthly were my lifeline.

In early spring of 1956, Miss came to my cell and announced we should prepare ourselves for an extended trip that would take four weeks. This proposed trip awoke a hope that I would soon be released. I was ready to see as much of China as my captors would provide. The train would take us to five cities, all in the eastern third of the country. The stops would include Tianjin, Nanking, Shanghai, Wuhan, and Hangzhou. These cities and Peking represented the cultural center of China. Curiously, Canton, which could be too dangerously close to China's southern border, was not included.

Tianjin, once the imperial port of eight foreign countries after the Opium War, was now a bustling city of light industries. Among our stops was a factory that made textile machinery. We heard a monotonous series of lectures on the superiority of Communist technology that was designed, we were told, for efficiency, not for profit like shoddy Western machines. Nevertheless, after the tour, the plant manager offered us tea and candy and asked what we thought of his operation. He seemed disappointed when I gave a vague and desultory response. Outside the plant, Miss scolded me for my rudeness. I defended myself, saying that I didn't think the manager cared to have an archcriminal passing judgment on his factory. That was when I learned that no one except party officials who met us knew who we were.

That made it all the more surprising when the director of a sports complex we visited admitted the Revolution had done little to involve

more women in athletics. Before we left Tianjin, we were treated to its
famous specialty, baozi, a kind of steamed dumpling that Tianjin was
known for. Each city had its own recipe. But to my taste it could not
compare with the sweet, fruit-and-nut-filled variety we got at our next
stop, Nanking.

Nanking was the capital city when the founding father Sun Yat-Sen
established the Republic of China. Now Nanking was noted more for
its culture than its industry. We saw the anthropological museum
where the artifacts of Peking Man were displayed. There was Dr.
Sun's mausoleum. We climbed hundreds of granite steps to reach his
secluded tomb, which revealed itself to be one of the most peaceful
and magnificent memorials I had ever seen. Part of its serenity may
have resulted from the fact that it did not seem to attract many visitors. A faint, faded quality permeated the grounds and the tomb.

There was one other relic I saw in Nanking, this one more personal. I found it when we visited Nanking University with its Western-
style campus. Though she didn't understand why I wanted to, Miss
allowed me to go into the library and down into the book stacks. Just
being among those close shelves of bound volumes reminded me of
Yale and the library job I had held as a scholarship student. My visit
became almost a homecoming when, on one of the Nanking shelves,
I found a volume by Samuel Flagg Bemis, a diplomatic historian who
had been one of my professors at Yale.

I had another reminder of my former life during the time we spent
in Nanking. At a gymnastics meet, we saw teenage girls performing in leotards. After years in prison in which the opposite sex was
represented solely by the interpreter Miss, I was now reminded that
women could be more than just political pedants. The stirrings I felt
were disquieting, less because of any frustrated desire than because
they made me realize how much of myself I had shut away. Repeatedly on the trip I was surprised by eruptions of forgotten emotions.
At the gymnastic match, I was touched to see one of the girls weep-
ing after a poor performance and being consoled by her teammates.
Kindness was not something I saw in prison.

In a Shanghai theater, at a variety show that must have been the
Chinese equivalent of vaudeville, I fought back tears that welled up
unexpectedly at a love duet whose lyrics I could not understand. I

tried to hide my emotion from the ubiquitous Miss, but she saw my flushed face and smiled at my Western sentimentality. The show also included what I at first thought was a wrestling match between two midgets. In fact, it was a single acrobat dressed in a suit painted to look like two people. Later we met the theater director, who evidently felt no compulsion to make any concessions in his lifestyle to the ascetic Communists. He wore an ascot and a flowing smoking jacket and ordered us drinks that were served by an enticingly made-up woman.

Shanghai brought me closer in many ways to the world I had left behind that was lost when I was captured. From high up in one of the city's major hotels, I looked down on streets filled with fast-flowing traffic. We ourselves sped along the Bund, the famous commercial boulevard edging the city's waterfront. When we stopped to walk about, people in Western dress were everywhere. Once we encountered a middle-aged Englishman who nodded to me in a friendly way, though my costume must have puzzled him. I resisted the impulse to blurt out my plight: "I'm an illegally detained American intelligence officer. Help me!" Even if he had understood me and then believed me, what could he do? I also rejected the idea of simply bolting into the crowd. I had nowhere to run to. I was a head taller than most Chinese, so I could not even run without sticking out in a crowd.

To reach Wuhan, we had to swing far south to connect with the rail line that would carry us north. At one station stop, we shared the platform with a very glamorous Chinese woman who was wearing a seductive slit skirt. Fecteau and I simultaneously began elbowing each other in the ribs like school boys at the sight of her. We drew a glowering frown from the stern Miss.

At such station stops, either Miss or the Warden would buy food for the long haul ahead. Among the more extravagant purchases was a glazed chicken that was dismembered and handed out in pieces to us. I grabbed what I thought was a leg and was happily gnawing away when Fecteau began laughing and pointing at what I was eating. I was too eager for meat to pay attention, but what I had taken wasn't a leg. I was holding the neck of a Chicken head, and applying myself to an area dangerously close to the beak. I nearly gagged. This time Miss looked at me, puzzled. She, like most Chinese, regarded the neck and head of chicken as worthy of consumption as any other part of the chicken.

The last leg of the journey to Wuhan was by a ferry crossing the Yangtze River. The river, notorious for its floods, often did its worst at Wuhan. There the Yangtze was a big, powerful, muddy river, like the Mississippi. It was at Wuhan that Mao was to make his famous swim to disprove rumors of his ill health. For several years afterward, thousands of Chinese, pilgrims of Maoism, came to the Yangtze at Wuhan to duplicate his feat.

In Wuhan we visited several factories, including one that made fertilizer. All of them, no doubt, did their part to make the Yangtze browner. Well away from the river's banks, we saw a plaque marking the height reached by a devastating flood in the 1930s. We were looking at the plaque when citizens of Wuhan began to look at us. Within minutes we had attracted a good-sized crowd. Our guard barked at them to leave, but they only fell back a few steps, laughed, and edged forward again. They seemed friendly enough. Wuhan was an inland city, not much visited by foreigners, and perhaps we were the first Westerners some of them had ever seen. It was heartening, too, to see that they regarded our guard, a soldier, with no more fear than they would a local policeman. Once at a soccer match, an enthusiastic fan rushed up to ask us what we thought of the game. He was warned away with two words, "security police," that made him literally jerk backward and retreat hurriedly into the crowd.

It was in Hangchow that Miss decided that Fecteau and I might be enjoying ourselves too much. Hangchow was famous for its resorts on West Lake, a shallow, algae-filled pond that happened to be situated prettily among some very steep hills. It was a Chinese tourist attraction covered with water lilies, arched bridges, excursion boats, food pavilions, guest houses, and tacky billboards. It was also famous for its statue of a kneeling traitor, Chiang Kwei, erected so people could vent their anger at him by slapping it with a stick or kicking it at will. The lake was also known for its carp.

What got us in trouble with Miss was the good humor of our host at West Lake. He was a full-fledged party member whose reserve must have been undermined by the paper moon atmosphere of his assigned post. He was full of energy and he liked to see people happy. When we were served lotus root pudding with whipped cream on top at one of the food pavilions, he offered us seconds. Fecteau and I eagerly accepted. When he took us to the carp pool, he said he needed help calling the carp to the surface. The carp signal was to jump up and down on a stone wall edging the pool. We linked arms and jumped in unison. Thanks to our weight, we proved very success-ful carp callers. As appreciative as we were of our host's kindness, we could not bring ourselves to taste the carp when it was served whole at the banquet. While our Chinese tablemates dove for the carp dish, Fecteau and I asked for scrambled eggs instead. We received looks reserved for idiots.

Miss was already annoyed at our host's indulgences and grew further irritated during a boat ride when we were passed by another excursion boat with students who spotted Western faces they mistook for Russians and waved energetic greetings. Willing to accept even unintended goodwill, Fecteau and I waved back with enthusiastic cheers, while Miss hissed at us that they thought we were "Soviet friends."

In our ongoing political debate, Miss almost always got the last word. And while I never came close to being convinced that Commu-nism was a better form of government than Democracy, there were a couple of times that I had no rebuttal for their arguments. The guard was a tall buck-toothed peasant who was probably seeing more of his country than he had ever expected during our five-city excursion. Though he had fought in the Revolution, he trembled with fright when he had to ride his first elevator in Shanghai. But he was more clever than he looked. He repeatedly beat Miss in the Chinese version of chess. Once, when I was holding forth on the virtues of the two-party system, he described the deaths of his four children. They had lived in a village, like 80 percent of the Chinese population, and they had all died of diseases that could have easily been cured by proper medicine, had it been available. Under the Nationalists, it wasn't. Under the Communists, it was. Many times on the trip, I noticed the deformed feet of women who walk in a certain way due to the custom of binding feet in the old China. The younger women were freed from that custom by the Revolution.

On our train returning to Peking, we saw young women, part of a troupe of dancers, who did their stretching exercises in the corridor outside the passenger compartments. Their lightness and youth only deepened the depression that grew inside me. I couldn't face returning to the prison. Miss asked about my glum looks, and I told her, "The holiday is over." She said nothing, intending to leave me guessing. Fecteau saved me from a blacker depression by suggesting his theory of unscheduled haircuts: he believed that if one gets an unscheduled haircut and face shave, he is to be released. A decade later, his theory was proven true on his own release.

Thoughts of escape occurred idly to me many times during our four-week trip, but only once was the temptation strong and wild. It was at a train station stop leading back to Peking. Our guard, Fecteau, and I had all gone into a restroom together. I finished first and stepped outside onto the nearly deserted station platform and found myself staring at a southbound train. It would have been easy to slip aboard then perhaps find a place to hide for the several-hundred-mile trip to Canton, close to the border. If I could make it that far, surely I could find a way to slip across the border to Hong Kong. But before I could move, the guard emerged from the restroom, and the train began to pull away from the station. As fantastic as my chances would have been, I wondered for years afterward what might have been had I boarded that train going south.

The return to prison did not mean an end to our excursions. We made shorter trips once or twice a year to locations not far from Peking. We went to a model commune, where farmers lived a seemly Utopian life, even though it was just for show. We were given a sample of each of the performing arts: ballet, theater, and, of course, the Peking Opera. My favorite trips were to international sports competitions, the only time I could almost forget where I was for the few hours I was at the stadium.

Fecteau and I were the stars of our own productions. One was at a Peking outing, a visit to a replica of West Lake at the famous Summer Palace, where an empress had a boat built of marble. We had been there several times, partly because we spoke of it so favorably to the Chinese, who were anxious to prove their good treatment of their American prisoners, and partly because they liked to go there themselves. Souvenirs and snacks were sold under a pavilion of highly polished and intricately carved wood that ran for many yards along the shore of the lake. On rowing boats on the lake, Fecteau's passengers were Miss and the Warden, while mine were a guard and a photographer who came along to record our good times for anyone who might inquire after our prison conditions.

It took Fecteau and me only a few strokes to get our steam up. I had done plenty of rowing in my youth, and Fecteau had been in the Merchant Marine. We both began demonstrating fancy strokes and propelling the small boats with a speed that alarmed our passengers. They didn't expect the bourgeois Americans to possess the physical skills needed to row a boat, and they didn't like the threat to their own bodies. I was told to relinquish my oars to the guard, and Fecteau to give his to the Warden. But the Warden soon lost one of his oars, and the guard got stuck on a mudflat. Fecteau and I had our last laugh. Another time, we were on a train trip. The Warden uncharacteristically got into a conversation with us and made the mistake of asking what he thought was an insightful question about American football. A demonstration seemed the best explanation, so Fecteau and I took our positions as center and quarterback in the train aisle, crouching and grunting out down cadences. Then I ran down the aisle to catch the football. Before we could complete our first pass pattern, the alarmed Warden eyed the two monsters he had created and urged us back to our seats.

Our trips outside prison from 1956 to 1964 all added up to less than two months of the twenty years we spent in China. The excursions to the five cities counted for about half of our time outside the prison. I often thought of the significance of that trip, four weeks in five cities, in the spring of 1956. It was the closest prelude to a release. Something happened on the American side that I eventually learned in a 1958 almanac.

Once the Cultural Revolution began to spread, our trips to the outside world stopped. My family had visited me in 1958, 1959, 1960, 1962, and 1964. The Cultural Revolution also stopped my family's visits. By the fall of 1971, my mother was seventy-five years old, and she had just recovered from a minor stroke; she wanted to see me one last time before it was too late. She came with Bill and his wife, Jean.

These trips outside of prison left me with clear and lasting impressions of the Chinese people; they were diligent, good-natured, and friendly toward foreigners. I remembered the constant juxtaposition of new and old, the lorries sharing streets with donkey carts, the bound-feet women and the women in soldier uniforms, the hardworking farmers, and laborers in the factories, all with dignity and good humor. If the purpose of the trips was to educate the American prisoners, I did learn something about China and the Chinese, and I kept an open mind. But it did not diminish my desire to go home. Actually, I missed my country even more.

14

"YOUR GOVERNMENT DOES NOT WANT YOU BACK"

The Failure of U.S.-PRC Negotiations at Geneva

Thomas J. Christensen

ATE SUMMER 1955 was a critically important time in Jack Downey's long drama in China. He and Richard Fecteau were moved to a new prison, where they would first meet their interpreter, Miss. She would be their handler from the Chinese Communist Party and, as it would turn out, also their tour guide of the "New China." By all appearances, these years in the mid-1950s were their best chance at release.

There was likely a political purpose to those tours, one wrapped up tightly in the international politics of the time and Premier Zhou Enlai's diplomatic strategy toward the Eisenhower administration.

* * *

On July 31, 1955, Downey's friends from the B-29 crew finally crossed over from mainland China to freedom in Hong Kong.[1] Downey could not have known that after the crew left his prison in January 1955, their release was still several months away. But he knew something was changing in the relationship between the United States and the People's Republic of China. He reports that, in August 1955, weeks before his move to the new prison, he was approached by a Chinese official named Chou, who read him the contents of an agreement between the U.S. government and the PRC. The agreement was actually finalized on September 10, 1955, during meetings between U.S. and PRC diplomats in Geneva after five weeks of negotiation. It would be the last formal agreement between the United States and the PRC until the Shanghai Communiqué of February 1972 during President Nixon's historic trip.[2]

The Geneva agreement (simply "The September 10th Announcement" in U.S. government parlance) offered all imprisoned American citizens in China the opportunity to write a letter to the British chargé d'affaires in Beijing if the prisoner believed he or she was being unjustly held. Unlike the Truman and Eisenhower administrations, who refused any diplomatic recognition of Beijing, the United Kingdom had formally recognized the People's Republic of China in January 1950, just three months after the founding of the nation, and therefore had a diplomatic mission in Beijing. For their part, the agreement also stated that Chinese citizens in America who wanted to return to mainland China could contact the Indian mission to the United States, since the PRC lacked diplomatic representation in Washington.[3]

Downey recalls being confused by the opaquely worded agreement that Chou read to him. This is understandable. Documents created by negotiating diplomats from hostile countries are often unclear, especially in translation. A degree of ambiguity is usually necessary just to secure the agreement. Downey asked Chou whether the agreement applied to him or not, but he received no answer.

The initial agreement almost certainly did not apply to him. While Downey was indeed a civilian prisoner, he had confessed to espionage and subversion. Chou himself almost certainly did not know the answer to Downey's simple question; he was definitely not in a position of sufficient authority to make such a decision.

Downey did not know the back story of the agreement pounded out in Geneva by the two governments. He only knew that Chou's presentation placed him in a dilemma. From 1953 to 1954, he had written a very long confession about his role as a CIA agent plotting to destabilize or overthrow the Chinese Communist Party with the help of former members of the KMT, the CCP's enemies in the civil war. That confession was used in his conviction and his sentencing to life in prison in November 1954. If he now claimed that he was being held unjustly, he wondered, would this simply upset his captors and leave him with even harsher treatment and even less chance of release? And was he even considered a normal citizen by the CCP? On the other hand, how could a man with a life sentence in a hostile country, almost entirely isolated from the outside world, not seize the opportunity to appeal to the top diplomat from his own country's closest friend and ally? Downey reports that he became frustrated enough with Chou's silence that he fired off a letter to the British mission in Beijing asking for a meeting with a British official.

The document that Chou read to Downey was an agreement negotiated by the U.S. ambassador U. Alexis Johnson and the PRC ambassador Wang Bingnan in Geneva, Switzerland. These two ambassadors had first met in 1954 on the sidelines of the Geneva Conference on Korea and Indochina, which produced a fragile peace in the first Indo-China War between France and the Vietnamese communists. In August 1955, the two diplomats began a series of historic bilateral meetings, again in Geneva, that had been arranged by India and the United Kingdom. Unlike the 1954 discussions, when the two diplomats happened to be in the same place for other reasons, these talks had no such political cover. What was extraordinary about these meetings was that the two nations still had no formal diplomatic relations. The upgrade of bilateral talks to the symbolically higher ambassadorial talks was particularly striking because Secretary of State John Foster Dulles had gone to great lengths to isolate the PRC diplomatically from the United States and its allies.[4] The only other direct bilateral diplomatic contacts had been six brief meetings between U.S. and PRC diplomats at the consul general level in Geneva in November 1954 following the prosecution and sentencing of Fecteau and Downey and the eleven surviving members of the B-29 crew in Beijing. Those talks had produced little but to lay out the U.S. position that the continued detention of the B-29 crew and the four fighter pilots still being held in China (but not the detention of Downey and Fecteau) was in violation of the Korean Armistice Agreement's position on mutual exchange of POWs.

Beijing clearly put great stock in the August 1955 ambassadorial negotiations, which would be carried on for years, first in Geneva and later in Warsaw. Beijing had not yet been recognized diplomatically by several U.S. allies and had to watch as Chiang Kai-shek's Republic of China in Taiwan filled China's UN Security Council seat. In June 1954, Johnson and Wang had begun discussing the disposition and repatriation of their citizens: the Americans still in mainland China after the revolution and the Korean War, and the Chinese still in America following the founding of the People's Republic of China in October 1949. The initial negotiations between Johnson and Wang in the spring of 1954 did not go far. The atmosphere for bilateral cooperation was further damaged by Beijing's conviction of the B-29 crew on charges of espionage in November 1954, along with the separate convictions of Downey and Fecteau that month on similar charges. Unlike Downey and Fecteau, however, the B-29 crew were considered prisoners of war by the United States and many other member nations of the United Nations.

Those convictions occurred during an already tense period in U.S.-China relations. From late summer 1954 through early 1955, the PRC and the United States were engaged in the first of two Cold War nuclear crises. The United States had been moving closer strategically to Chiang's Taiwan after the outbreak of the Korean War, and Mao wanted to prevent Taiwan from allying formally with the United States, as had Japan and South Korea. It was publicly known that Chiang was lobbying hard for such an alliance and, at the time, the United States was creating the multilateral Southeast Asia Treaty Organization (SEATO) to fight communism in Asia. In early September 1954, Mao decided to send a signal to Washington and Taipei—a warning not to get too friendly. He shelled the tiny offshore islands of Quemoy and Matsu, which were controlled by Chiang's Republic of China (ROC) forces, but which lie much closer to the mainland's Fujian province than to the main island of Taiwan. A crisis ensued between the PRC and the United States. Washington sent its military to the region to aid Chiang in supplying and bolstering KMT military garrisons on the tiny islands and to signal American resolve to Beijing. The Eisenhower administration—which placed nuclear deterrence at the heart of their strategy to contain communism—also made nuclear threats against China.[5]

The shelling backfired. The Eisenhower administration helped defend and resupply the KMT garrisons on the offshore islands, and even dropped its long-running reluctance to publicly ally with the ROC on Taiwan. In December 1954, they signed the U.S-ROC Mutual Defense Treaty, which was ratified by Congress in January 1955. From the PRC's perspective, this was a terrible outcome. But there was one upside for Beijing. In a secret clause within the alliance treaty, the United States insisted that the its obligations to Taiwan *did not include* backing the island if it attacked the mainland without Washington's approval. Like Truman before him, Eisenhower worried that Chiang could entrap America in a major war. Even so, the crisis revealed Washington's commitment to protect Taiwan from mainland China. Both the Korean War and the 1954–1955 Taiwan Straits crisis exposed the PRC's near-total dependence on the Soviet Union for nuclear deterrence against a nuclear-capable superpower like the United States. Mao realized this and launched China's indigenous nuclear program in early 1955 (albeit with significant Soviet help at the onset). By 1964, Mao's China had a nuclear bomb.[6]

Despite such daunting international political obstacles, Dag Hammarskjöld's early January 1955 mission to Beijing still took place. There the secretary general successfully planted the seeds for the eventual release in May 1955 of the four fighter pilots who strayed into Chinese airspace during the war and the eleven surviving members of the B-29 crew, who had been convicted of breaching China's air space for the purpose of espionage. The fighter pilots would be released in May with little fanfare. The eleven B-29 crew members were released on July 31 on the eve of the first round of ambassadorial talks between Johnson and Wang. This was several months after the Hammarskjöld mission but still long before the completion of the sentences that they had received in November 1954, which ranged from four to ten years. Ambassador Wang states in his memoir that this concession was an ice-breaking gesture on the part of the Chinese communists, who wanted to use the U.S.-PRC Geneva talks to break China out of its diplomatic isolation in the West and elbow Taiwan out of the China seat at the United Nations.[7]

Contemporaneous documentary evidence from the PRC foreign ministry archives confirms Wang's recollection. Zhou Enlai timed the release of the crew to seize the initiative in the coming negotiations. He believed there was more international and domestic pressure on the Eisenhower administration to adopt a flexible posture toward the PRC. In the talks, Beijing wanted Eisenhower to consider direct ministerial talks between Zhou and Dulles on issues of war and peace related to Taiwan. Beijing believed the United States was paying an increasingly heavy diplomatic price for its position that Chiang's KMT government in Taiwan, not Mao's CCP government in Beijing, was the sole legitimate government of China.[8]

Between the January 1955 Hammarskjöld mission and the August bilateral talks, tensions between the two nations eased. As the Taiwan Straits crisis wound down in the early months of 1955, China and the Soviet Union launched a diplomatic peace offensive that was designed to win over the hearts and minds of neutral countries in the Cold War who might otherwise ally with the United States and its anticommunist allies. For China, this took the form of Zhou's general formulation for China's foreign policy: "The Five Principles of Peaceful Coexistence." In these principles, Beijing expressed its willingness for peaceful—even cooperative—relations with any country, regardless of its domestic regime. The only condition was that the country must respect the legitimacy of the CCP and recognize the People's Republic of China as the sole legitimate government of all of China. In other words, Beijing signaled that it would not support communist revolution in noncommunist states so long as those states had good relations with Beijing. In the same spirit, at the conference of nonaligned developing countries in Bandung, Indonesia, in April 1955, Zhou tried to reassure the diverse set of developing countries that Beijing had no ideological litmus test for friendly relations with fellow Third World regimes.[9]

In Bandung, Zhou said that the PRC would be willing to open diplomatic talks with the United States.[10] The Eisenhower administration took notice, wanting to avoid future military crises with Beijing. Still, Eisenhower and Dulles had no intention of switching diplomatic recognition from Taipei to Beijing.[11] So the bilateral ambassadorial talks in a neutral location, Geneva, became the fallback position. The Geneva talks were designed to address the handling of the citizens still living within the territory of the other country. Lower-level conversations on that topic had been held between the two consul generals in Geneva in late 1954 after the public announcement of the prosecution of the B-29 crew, Downey, and Fecteau. The Chinese delegation took note that Downey and Fecteau had not been included in the initial list of Americans whom Ambassador Johnson sought to free in June 1954. (Only the Chinese delegation could notice this, since the Americans did not yet know Downey and Fecteau were still alive.) As Zhou signaled to Hammarskjöld in Beijing in January 1955, their absence from the American list fed Beijing's suspicions about the real mission of the downed B-29 crew.[12]

There were several reasons for the CCP to connect the missions of Downey and Fecteau to the mission of the B-29 crew. We know from Downey's memoir that the B-29 crew described their mission to their Chinese captors in the exact same way that Downey described his initial cover story: they were distributing political leaflets over North Korea and accidentally entered Chinese airspace. In the case of the B-29 crew, the story was apparently true, although the Chinese could not have known that for sure. In Downey's case, the story was not true, and CCP officials knew this even before his plane was shot down because they had turned at least one of the former KMT soldiers in Downey's operation. This was why soldiers from the People's Liberation Army were lying in wait for the flight's arrival in Manchuria in the first place. It is not surprising that the CCP officials were deeply suspicious of the B-29 crew as well.

Downey's cover story also held that he was a civilian working for the U.S. Army as part of a Defense Department program, and this was the position that the U.S. government continued to adopt even after his trial and conviction was made public. It was one of the many reasons that the Chinese government did not treat Downey and Fecteau as prisoners of the Korean War. Neither did the U.S. government, once it discovered they were still alive in November 1954. Their supposed civilian status also helped explain why it was Zhou, not Hammarskjöld, who raised their names in the January 1955 meeting in Beijing. Hammarskjöld's mission was mainly about the B-29 airmen and the fighter pilots, and he argued that they were POWs who had been fighting under the UN flag in Korea.[13] Including two convicted civilian spies would have compromised Hammarskjöld's argument that the B-29 crew and the fighter pilots still being held by the PRC were true prisoners of war—uniformed military personnel who should be released in accordance with the July 1953 Panmunjom armistice.

The bilateral ambassadorial talks in Geneva that began on August 1, 1955, were designed to go beyond Panmunjom and the Hammarskjöld negotiations and discuss the citizens still living in the other nation. Some of these citizens, like Downey and Fecteau, were in prison; others were not. In the case of Chinese citizens in the United States, many were Chinese students who were studying in the United States before the Chinese communists declared victory in the civil war on the mainland. The United States brought a list of about sixty Americans, including Downey and Fecteau. Washington suspected that at least some of the Americans in Chinese prisons were really political prisoners being held on trumped-up criminal charges to force Washington to negotiate with Beijing. Dulles preferred a China policy of total diplomatic isolation, ignoring mainland China in favor of Taiwan.[14] China suspected that many mainland Chinese in the United States were being discouraged or prevented from returning home by the Americans, perhaps at the behest of the KMT.[15] Beijing had good reason to think so, since they had seen how Chinese prisoners in the Korean War camps were persuaded and coerced to "repatriate" to Taiwan over mainland China.

In the Chinese language, the Geneva talks were about the disposition of "civilians" (*pingmin*), which might also be translated as "regular folks," a category that generally distinguishes ordinary citizens from military personnel or government officials.[16] Downey and Fecteau were not considered prisoners of war by either government. From the perspective of an American English speaker, they were civilians as opposed to military personnel, but they still did not fit the Chinese definition of *pingmin*. In his memoir, Wang distinguishes between journalists and *pingmin* when complaining that Dulles wanted to restrict either kind of contact between the two countries. If the *pingmin* category did not include journalists, it certainly did not include spies.[17]

Washington intentionally left Downey and Fecteau off the lists presented to the UN General Assembly and to Hammarskjöld to increase the chances that China would release uniformed military personnel on the basis that they were prisoners of war. So Johnson must have been surprised in Geneva when Wang initially offered a four-part categorization of the five dozen or so Americans remaining in China. His fourth category was "military personnel." Wang claimed that after the earlier release of the four fighter pilots (May 1954) and the eleven B-29 crew members (July 1954), only two Americans, Downey and Fecteau, were left in his fourth category. Johnson tried to correct Wang. Those men, he said, were not members of the U.S. military. They were civilians working for the U.S. Army. But Wang responded that their "crimes" in China were "military" in nature.[18] Archival materials from the PRC foreign ministry reveal that Wang's instructions clearly separated Downey and Fecteau from *pingmin*. In the eyes of the Chinese, they were spies and military personnel.[19] Since the preparations for the Hammarskjöld visit in early 1955, in both internal discussions and in communications with the UN Secretary General, Zhou had consistently categorized the eleven members of the B-29 crew themselves as "spies" (*jiandie*) despite their military uniforms.

The Chinese may have lumped Downey and Fecteau in the same category as the B-29 crew because of Colonel Arnold's confession. Arnold had said that his crew was part of a larger Air Force unit in the Philippines that coordinated with the CIA to promote subversion in the PRC.[20] This confession dovetailed with Downey's own confession about his "third force" operations on military bases in Saipan and Japan. In Wang's memoirs, he says the conversations between Hammarskjöld and Zhou focused on "thirteen spies"—the eleven crew members of the B-29, Downey, and Fecteau. In describing the release of the B-29 crew at the end of July, Wang also refers to them as "eleven spies."[21] In so doing he was following his internal instructions from the foreign ministry that were sent the day before the crew's release.[22] All of this was a roundabout way for Beijing to insist that Downey and Fecteau were not really *pingmin* and the United States should not assume that they would be readily released following an initial agreement on ordinary civilians. Wang clearly distinguished between the more run-of-the-mill cases of American civilians in China and those guilty of "espionage" (*jiandie*) and "sabotage" (*pohuai huodong*), both calling cards of the OPC.[23] An unpublished Chinese historical retrospective upon the occasion of Downey's death and a published CCP history on the case take umbrage at the way that U.S. diplomats in

Geneva had tried to deny the two CIA officers' espionage by lumping them with *pingmin* in the negotiations on repatriation.[24] Despite Beijing's refusal to categorize them as such, Wang did reassure Johnson that all criminal cases, including those of Downey and Fecteau, were being "reviewed" in August 1955.[25]

The agreements that Wang and Johnson reached in September— and the many more they could not reach—revealed much about the goals of the two countries. Beijing wanted to break out of its diplomatic isolation from the West and its economic and diplomatic isolation from the United States.[26] Beijing's purpose in seeking bilateral ambassadorial negotiations on the disposition of citizens was to plant the seeds for even higher level ministerial talks between Dulles and his Chinese counterparts. Beijing believed that pressure was building on the Eisenhower administration from its allies and from domestic opposition, mostly from Democrats on Capitol Hill, to end its rigid diplomatic isolation of Beijing.[27] Washington had refused such high-level diplomatic contact at every turn, and ever since China entered the Korean War in force in late 1950, reversing MacArthur's offensive toward the Yalu, the United States leveled a trade embargo on mainland China that was even stricter than the one against the Soviet Union and the Warsaw Pact countries. This "China Differential" made little strategic sense, since the PRC instead turned to trade with the Soviet Union and its allies, strengthening China's ties with the Soviet bloc. From the Truman administration's perspective, the Differential was necessary to satisfy the domestic political outrage against China for attacking UN forces in Korea. Once in place, the embargo could not be lifted without raising resistance at home, where McCarthyism was in full swing. And in 1955 that domestic resistance would be bolstered by opposition from the new U.S. ally in Taipei, which had a powerful lobby in Washington.[28]

Dulles had an entirely different objective for the Geneva talks. Washington wanted to avoid granting Beijing even tacit diplomatic recognition that would compromise their strategy. The Eisenhower administration aimed to isolate the PRC and instead recognize Chiang's government in Taipei as the sole legitimate government of all of China. But aside from repatriation of its citizens, the United States wanted the PRC to renounce the use of force against Taiwan or

U.S. forces in the region.[29] The Eisenhower administration knew that the PRC still enjoyed a strong alliance with the Soviet Union in the mid-1950s, and they feared such a crisis could escalate to World War III. But Beijing could not agree to this demand. By renouncing the use of force entirely against Taiwan, especially while there were U.S. forces on the island as part a new U.S.-ROC alliance, Beijing could be seen as symbolically ceding its claim to sovereignty over the island. This could lead to a "two China" solution, in the same way that Korea remains divided at the 38th parallel to this day and the way Vietnam was divided at the 17th parallel in 1954. Perhaps worse still from Beijing's perspective was that this could eventually allow for a fully independent Taiwan with no remaining connection to the Chinese nation.[30]

The United States demanded a full accounting of all American citizens in China and access to them by the UK mission in Beijing. The Chinese communists, predictably, wanted a full list of all Chinese citizens who were in the United States since the founding of the PRC and wanted to secure access to all of them by Beijing's chosen intermediary, the Indian mission to the United States. The trouble, as Johnson reported to Wang, was that the United States did not even recognize Beijing as the legitimate government of China. By the Eisenhower administration's logic, if any Chinese government should have access to all Chinese citizens in the United States, it should be the Republic of China, the American ally in Taiwan, which still claimed jurisdiction over all of China. Washington also feared that disclosing all the names of the Chinese nationals in the United States to the Chinese communists would endanger the families of those people who did not return to China.[31]

In international diplomacy, a core principle for practical deal-making is reciprocity. This principle is arguably even more important in dealings between real or potential adversaries. But reciprocity often means major compromises. This did not bode well for Downey and Fecteau, whose case was the most sensitive and controversial of all the Americans detained in China. And U.S. reciprocity was sparse in the Geneva talks. The Americans would not offer a list of the Chinese living there, nor would Washington agree to allow the UK and India to be formal "representatives" for the purpose of vetting citizens and their desire for repatriation. The PRC initially proposed language that Beijing would "authorize" (*shouquan*) India to vet Chinese citizens in the United States to see if they wanted to return home. To accept such language, Dulles and Eisenhower feared, would be to lend legitimacy to the claim that the PRC was a sovereign nation. So the United States insisted that the UK and India could only be "invited" (*yaoqing*) to play this role, not "authorized" to do so.[32]

Judging from declassified cables, this issue of "representation" by impartial third countries created tension between Johnson in Geneva and Dulles in Washington. Early in the negotiations, Johnson recommended that Washington be flexible on this issue. He sensed, probably correctly, that this would provide Wang a chance to convince his own government to repatriate American prisoners. But Dulles refused Johnson's overtures, convinced he must isolate the PRC regime and instead support Chiang's Republic of China in Taiwan, which was pressuring the United States hard, fearing that it might tacitly recognize the PRC government in the process of negotiating the release of Americans.[33] Dulles's rigidity in August 1955 portended his position much later in the Geneva negotiations, when he refused another overture by Beijing that might have won the release of Downey and Fecteau in early 1957 rather than in the early 1970s.

Johnson and Wang reached a workaround. Their agreement allowed American citizens in China to approach the UK mission there to appeal for repatriation, and the UK government would fund the Americans' travel back home if they could not afford it. Under the same agreement, Chinese citizens could contact the Indian mission to the United States to seek repatriation to "mainland China" (the U.S. government avoided using the name PRC whenever possible). The Indian government would provide travel resources as needed in the same way that the UK government would in the United States. But they agreed that neither the UK nor India would proactively contact the expatriates. In this formula, rather than deputies of the PRC and the United States, respectively, India and the UK were more passive intermediaries, a status that even the Eisenhower administration could accept. Both countries announced their side of the agreement unilaterally, and the United States referred to the agreement as simply "the September 10th Announcement."[34]

Surprisingly, both governments seemed to implement the agreement sincerely. The U.S. government ran tens of thousands of public announcements to inform any Chinese citizens in the country that they had an opportunity to return to mainland China if they so desired. One report found more than two hundred chose to repatriate between 1955 and 1957, and the Indian authorities registered no complaints of the United States obstructing that process.[35] The Chinese government, through officials like Chou, reached out to Americans in China and let them know that they could contact the UK mission in China regarding their repatriation and, in the case of prisoners, any perceived injustice in their detention. As a spy convicted of trying to overthrow the Chinese government and in solitary detention at the time, Downey was a hard test case for CCP sincerity. Who would have known if the CCP never told him of the Geneva agreement?

Despite accusations from Beijing that Washington was not implementing the agreement and was preventing repatriation by mainland Chinese, especially those with useful technical skills, there were only a handful of such cases. Consider the case of Dr. Qian Xuesen, a Chinese rocket scientist and mathematician at Cal Tech who had served on classified U.S. military projects in the 1930s and 1940s involving jet propulsion, rockets, and nuclear weapons. Qian returned to China for a visit briefly following the founding of the PRC and, upon his return to the United States, received extremely harsh treatment there during the McCarthy era. Stripped of his security clearance in 1950, he was then placed under a soft form of house arrest in Los Angeles for the next several years. Like a small number of other scientists with technical information that the United States did not want shared with Beijing, Qian was forbidden by U.S. law from traveling to the PRC.[36]

Ambassador Wang raised Dr. Qian's case.[37] Qian had managed to get a letter to his family members on the mainland in June 1955, in which he wrote that he wanted to return to China but Washington would not let him. Wang carried that letter in his pocket during the Geneva talks.[38] But after the September 10 announcement, the U.S. government relented and allowed Qian to return to China. He departed that same month, just weeks after the liberation of the B-29 crew. The U.S. government claimed he was being "deported" punitively, though this was likely political cover from criticism of the lifting of his house arrest. He received a hero's welcome in China and became the father of the PRC's extremely successful ballistic missile program. That program produced the nuclear deterrent against both the United States and the Soviet Union and planted the seeds for the current conventionally tipped ballistic force that threatens forward-deployed U.S. forces long after the Cold War. When Qian passed away in late October 2009, television coverage in mainland China treated him as a true national hero of the PRC.[39]

Civilian repatriation, as it turned out, was the *only* issue on which Beijing and Washington could agree. For example, the United States proposed a simple bilateral public commitment to "renounce the use of military assets" (*fangqi shiyong wuqi*) to resolve political differences. But the CCP could not make a sweeping commitment to the nonuse of force across the Taiwan Strait. Cross-strait relations were considered a purely domestic issue. But for a high diplomatic price, Beijing was willing to discuss tensions in U.S.-PRC bilateral relations regarding Taiwan. Wang made a counteroffer: Beijing would be willing to issue a statement that "both sides agree that peaceful measures should be used to resolve conflicts and there should be no appeal to arms (*suzhu wuli*); therefore, the two countries will hold ministerial-level talks (*waizhang huitan*) to resolve, relax, and remove the problem of the tense situation in the Taiwan area."[40] It was these high-level talks that were the main prize in the negotiations for Wang's superiors in Beijing.[41]

From the Eisenhower administration's perspective, to accept such a proposal would have de facto recognized the PRC as a nation and reduced Taiwan to an "area" within China as opposed to a sovereign state. Dulles was rigid: the United States would not even suggest that it recognized the PRC as a sovereign state. He famously avoided meeting Zhou during the 1954 Geneva conference, even though they both attended at the same time. He was certainly not going to agree to meet with him now, especially at the expense of the new alliance with Taiwan forged in January 1955. The Americans held the renunciation of the use of force as a prerequisite for any discussions of easing the trade embargo, so the bilateral talks reached a deadlock once the somewhat vague and noncommittal agreement on repatriation of civilians was reached. A joint statement of peaceful intent, ministerial-level talks, or an easing of the trade embargo were all unachievable goals despite multiple meetings between Wang and Johnson from 1955 to 1957.

Undeterred by this deadlock in Geneva, Zhou pushed forward with his peace offensive in ways that apparently had direct implications for Downey and Fecteau. As part of their hostile relationship, the United States and the PRC had blocked each other's journalists from working inside their countries. The Eisenhower administration even forbade American journalists from traveling to mainland China. It was not until 1957 that the families of American prisoners would be permitted to visit.

In August 1956, Zhou announced a unilateral lifting of the PRC embargo on U.S. journalists visiting the PRC. As with the release of the four fighter pilots and the B-29 crew, Zhou was taking the initiative. He proactively reached out to fifteen U.S. news organizations with cables inviting them to send journalists to learn about the PRC.[42]

The American response was telling. In 1956 and through the first half of 1957, Dulles, with Eisenhower's backing, refused to lift the ban on U.S. journalists traveling to the PRC. Journalists lobbied hard to lift the ban. They complained that it violated their constitutional rights. Some went anyway, via third countries, risking Treasury Department sanctions at home for "trading with the enemy."[43] The Chinese side noticed the turmoil that the rejection of Zhou's offer created in America.[44]

Zhou and Wang then proposed to the Americans a negotiated deal. They suggested that the two countries break their mutual isolation by allowing journalists from both countries to travel to the other. But Dulles rejected this deal entirely, calling it coercion and extortion. The idea of Chinese communist reporters traveling around the United States with free rein was anathema to his strategy of isolating the Chinese communists internationally. He thought the deal would make the United States look weak and undercut morale among U.S. allies in Asia. Dulles also expressed concern that any deal on journalists before the unconditional release of the American detainees would encourage U.S. adversaries around the world to take Americans hostage for negotiating leverage.[45]

Dulles's hard line went well beyond journalists. When Hammarsjköld visited Beijing in January 1955, he secured only one immediate concession from the PRC, and that was an offer by Beijing to allow the families of all those detained in China to visit their relatives in prison. This included the families of Downey and Fecteau. But from 1955 to 1957, the State Department denied Downey's family permission to visit him despite Zhou's invitation. Dulles personally wrote to Downey's mother in early 1955 to explain why.[46] (See the letter on pages 251–252 in this volume.)

It was only in late 1957 that Dulles relented and allowed a few reporters to travel to the PRC for a limited amount of time. He still refused to cut a deal with the CCP to exchange journalists, and no PRC journalists would be allowed to visit the United States.[47] But once Dulles allowed journalists to travel to China, he could no longer justify blocking visits to China by the families of Downey and Fecteau. So in late 1957, Downey's mother and brother traveled to visit him for the first time.

Eisenhower and Dulles's diplomatic strategy toward the PRC was markedly different than the one that would later be adopted by Eisenhower's vice president, Richard Nixon, once he assumed the presidency in 1969. Nixon allowed his top foreign policy adviser, Henry Kissinger, to negotiate directly with Zhou in July 1971. Kissinger was to arrange a summit between Nixon and Mao in early 1972. And to prepare the proper "people to people" atmosphere for Kissinger's July visit to Beijing, the United States accepted an invitation for a U.S. ping-pong team to travel to the PRC in April 1971. This icebreaker, which scholars have come to call "ping-pong diplomacy." It was this outreach that expedited the release of Fecteau in late 1971 and reduced Downey's life sentence to five more years before eventual commuting that sentence on humanitarian grounds in early 1973.

Downey looks back on February 1957 as a time in which a similarly dramatic breakthrough in his case seemed possible if only John Foster Dulles had not been so rigid on the issue of exchange of journalists. He reports that in the following year Fecteau received a care package with a 1958 almanac that informed the two prisoners that Zhou had proposed a deal to exchange journalists. If Washington had accepted, this might have freed American prisoners in China. But the deal had been quashed by Dulles as "blackmail." Downey judged this as a missed opportunity for his government to secure his freedom, and he called it a "nail in his coffin." Downey and his wife, whom he met and married after his release from the PRC in 1973, believed that Dulles was to blame for failing to cut such a deal to gain Downey and Fecteau's freedom. The relevant PRC officials seem to agree. In February 1957, one of Downey's interpreters reportedly scoffed at him and said, "Your government do [sic] not want you back."[48] A decade after his release, Downey would return to China, where he was greeted by none other than Wang Bingnan. Wang said that Downey's name had been on his lips frequently between 1955 and 1964 but that to his personal frustration, Washington and Dulles in particular did not want to make a deal to win his release through an exchange of journalists. He told Downey that the CCP leaders had decided that his serving five years in prison would have been sufficient for their purposes if the diplomatic conditions had been better and allowed for a commutation of his life sentence.[49]

Of course, Wang had his reasons to lay blame for Downey's suffering at the feet of the U.S. government. But there is much circumstantial evidence that such an early release was theoretically possible if the U.S. government had not been so rigid. First, we know that in his meetings with Hammarskjöld regarding the B-29 crew and the four fighter pilots, Zhou also raised the even more difficult cases of Downey and Fecteau, who lacked any pretense of being POWs who had served under UN Command. Despite this and despite Downey's life sentence from November 1954, Zhou told Hammarskjöld that he expected that both Downey and Fecteau would eventually find their way home. While Zhou viewed their imprisonment as justified and legitimate, even pointing out that they really deserved the death penalty for what they did, the Chinese premier also clearly viewed them as pawns in his diplomatic game. He would use them, if he could, in opening some form of relationship between his PRC and Dulles's United States.[50] And we know he pursued that strategy in 1955, releasing the four fighter pilots in May and the B-29 crew in late July as an appetizer to the Geneva talks.[51] In his memoir, Wang praises his boss for "taking the initiative" (zhudong) to open a relationship between the two countries. While the efforts failed to produce new ties, Wang argues that it was still successful because it turned world opinion and, to a degree, domestic public and media opinion in the United States against Eisenhower's hardline stance against the PRC.[52]

In December 1956, during a trip to Nepal, Zhou said that a deal to release American prisoners was possible if the United States adopted a less hostile policy toward the PRC. Wang had raised this same idea in Geneva.[53] When they met on Valentine's Day in 1957, Johnson raised with Wang Zhou's earlier negotiating position, but then he insisted that all prisoners needed to be released before discussions about issues like exchanging journalists could even begin.[54] It is clear that Johnson was simply echoing Dulles's view that any deal over journalists without prior release of the Americans amounted to blackmail and the use of Americans as hostages. Dulles had said as much publicly, and we can find the same views in classified documents from the time.[55] Johnson reported back to Washington that Wang claimed China had offered goodwill measures in 1955 by unilaterally releasing the fighter pilots and the B-29 crew, but the United States had not reciprocated. Such reciprocity to the PRC's "friendly gestures," Wang suggested, would be necessary to make progress on other things, like the U.S. demand that Beijing release all American citizens detained in China. But the Americans had simply rejected Zhou's proposal to exchange journalists.[56]

PRC diplomats often speak in these abstract terms about the need for a "proper atmosphere" to proceed with productive negotiations. It seems that Wang was signaling that further releases of prisoners like Downey and Fecteau would be possible, if only the United States would first make some reciprocal goodwill gestures, such as the exchange of journalists. In an interview with a reporter in 1983, Johnson denied that Wang had made any explicit offer to release Downey and Fecteau in February 1957.[57] And the declassified record of the meeting does not specifically mention their names nor any explicit quid pro quo offer by Wang to release the ten Americans still imprisoned in China. But reading between the lines of this discussion, I can fully understand why Wang recalled later to Downey that a deal for their release was indeed on the table.[58] From my analysis it appears that Downey and his family had reason to be bitter that Dulles and Eisenhower did not pursue such a deal at this critical juncture in this saga.

Perhaps the best evidence that the PRC was prepared to release Downey and Fecteau under the right conditions after August 1955 is found in Downey's memoirs. Although he could not have known it at the time, it was almost certainly no coincidence that he was introduced to Miss at his new prison just after the United States and the PRC reached an agreement on civilian repatriation. Starting in early 1956 and through the rest of that year, Downey and Fecteau were taken on goodwill tours of Beijing and elsewhere in mainland China, intended to teach them about the alleged upside of the communist revolution in China. They saw a dam outside of Beijing, a model commune, several tourist destinations, and attended cultural and sporting events like gymnastics. Miss tried to convince them why Chinese citizens held righteous anger at the government of the United States for its hostile policies toward "New China."

We can see the real purpose of their tours in 1956. Downey and Fecteau were being prepared for an early negotiated release if the bilateral Geneva talks progressed in the direction Zhou desired. Downey looked back on those trips as propaganda efforts by the CCP. Even then, he believed the trips were a prelude to his release. He was right to be optimistic, at least as it applied to the Chinese. Downey was serving a life sentence. So why would the CCP care to influence his views of the PRC if there were no prospect he would ever go home?

It appears that it may have been Dulles's rigid approach to diplomacy that kept Downey in prison until the Nixon-Kissinger breakthrough in the early 1970s. The cables between Dulles in Washington and Johnson in Geneva were sometimes tense, as Dulles again and again rejected Johnson's suggestion that he could dangle some diplomatic carrots to Wang on issues like third-country "representation" if it freed more American detainees in China. Johnson's own memoir has a full chapter on the U.S.-PRC talks. He praises Wang's intelligence and diplomatic professionalism. Johnson saves his scorn for Wang's CCP bosses. In general, he spares Dulles any direct criticism. But in one particular passage regarding Dulles, Johnson seems to drop his guard and suggest that Dulles's rigidity had serious consequences for international cooperation: "More than most people Dulles was able to subordinate the innate human desire to reduce conflict with others to a long-term strategy that required writing off normal contact with half of humanity. That sustained toughness [was] completely principled, but somewhat chilling."[59]

Dulles's strategy was very different than that of Zhou, Kissinger, and Nixon. There were real human costs to Dulles's approach beyond abstract concepts like the reduction of international conflict to which Johnson alludes. In the case of Fecteau and Downey, the cost was quite likely more than a decade longer in a Chinese prison cell.

Dulles's concerns—about signaling weakness, undermining the morale of allies in Asia, or encouraging future hostage situations— were overblown at best. As Wang explained to Johnson in February 1957, from Beijing's perspective, the PRC had offered several concessions to break the ice, including the release of the B-29 crew and the four fighter pilots shot down over China. Why would Beijing or anyone else then see the exchange of journalists as a sign of American weakness? Other than Chiang's Republic of China on Taiwan, there is little evidence that other Asian allies would become dispirited in the fight against communism if the United States had allowed PRC journalists to visit America. And Chiang had nowhere else to turn but the United States in any case. The argument that Downey and Fecteau were simply political hostages of the PRC and that bargaining for their release would endanger the safety of Americans traveling around the world can only be sustained if one entirely ignores the two men's original mission in 1952. They were to enter a hostile country without permission, during wartime, to facilitate the overthrow of that country's government. It is hardly the case that they were snatched unwittingly off the street and held for ransom. The high human cost of their incarceration was not justified by the diplomatic benefits, slight at best, of preventing an exchange of journalists between the two countries.

15

PRISON LIFE

N A Chinese prison, a man's five senses do not atrophy because they are deprived of stimulus. Instead, they are always hungry and therefore always acute. Their relative importance, though, may be reordered. The ears begin to tell more than the eyes; smell becomes more sensuous than touch.

In the months of enforced stasis before my trial, I gazed for long periods at the patch of sky visible through my cell window. Since the sky over Peking is hardly a kaleidoscope, my greatest entertainment most days was the sunset. The more carefully I watched the progression from pale blue to indigo on clear days, or pink to deep rust on cloudy days, the more shades of coloring I discovered. Like a new student in painting class, I became aware of colors' subtleties for the first time. One day, at the moment when the sun had fully set, the sky turned a pale green. It was the green of a new apple and it reminded me of a phrase used several times by one of my favorite authors, Erich Maria Remarque. He described sunsets as apple green, and I remembered thinking at the time that he had taken liberties with nature, and disapproving. But that evening in Peking, as an iron grate cut my view, I was oddly pleased to discover my own apple green sunset. In prison, the basic rhythms of nature, the rising and setting of the sun, the shift of the seasons, comforted me against the uncertainty that was my own lot, vulnerable as I was to the caprice of my captors.

I was ordered to wake and to sleep by bells or whistles. I knew breakfast was being served by the creaking of wooden vats and the knocking and sloshing of ladles wielded by guards far down the corridor. Hours on my auditory clock were the quick-step marches of formations of inmates from another prison wing who crossed my corridor twice a day carrying their chamber pails to an outdoor latrine. Their slippers slapped the concrete floor and the lids on their pails clanged, a deep sound on the outward bound trip when the pails were full and a lighter clatter on the empty, inward bound trip.

Even in my own corridor, I never saw my neighbor inmates. Each one of us was fed, exercised, and taken to the toilet in his turn. I kept track of the others' comings and goings by the sliding of bolts and the snapping of padlocks. A door that opened at an odd hour told me that change had come to the corridor. Then I listened hard to see if footsteps or a voice familiar to me had been replaced by one that was strange.

When he was on my corridor, I maintained my companionship with Fecteau in this way, listening for his distinctive cough or his steps. He tended to shuffle and his cough was a deliberately loud double clearing of the throat. In the months after we left the B-29 crew, he was kept in another part of the prison and I could not hear him at all. But I knew he was close and in trouble because during that time an interpreter visited me repeatedly to ask the meaning of some utterly vile curse that only an American could have inflicted. It was funny and embarrassing to define *bastard* and *motherfucker* for a fastidious Chinese, but it was not funny to realize Fecteau was dangerously upset. Who knew what was done with prisoners who repeatedly misbehaved? Months later, when Fecteau and I had a rare chance to talk face to face, he told me that he had been convinced his mail was being withheld. We both had been allowed to write home, and my letters had been answered. But his to his wife had not. He could not know that she had died in a fire not long after returning home from Japan the weekend of our mission. The new husband she had flown halfway around the world to meet had been given up for dead in a plane crash.

Fecteau's anguish was not the only trouble I learned of by listening. Whether they signaled temporary hysteria or a more total snapping of the will, I did not know, but the screams and moans of distressed souls occasionally drifted through the prison corridors. When these arias of bedlam were sung by a woman, I became filled with a helpless protective anger. If they came from a man, my pity would be mixed with scorn. Wailing that lasted only a matter of minutes was painful enough to hear, but it sometimes went on much longer. One man howled for hours, repeating the same lament over and over: "*Mei banfa, mei banfa.* There's no hope, there is no hope." Finally, he exhausted himself, or was silenced by guards. In general, the women were bolder than the men in expressing their despair and anger. A woman who was more flamboyantly insane than broken in spirit taunted the guards by setting up a plaintive chant of "Help me, help me. They are torturing me" in a voice too high-pitched and whining to be ignored. Most guards soon learned, however, to hide their displeasure at her grating cries. But one guard, a former guerrilla who was a fair-minded but quick-tempered fellow, always succumbed. He would shout at her to shut up, pointing out rightly enough that she was not being tortured. At that she would burst into laughter as wild as a witch's cackle that was more disturbing than her moans. I never saw the woman or knew what happened to her. One day I simply realized that I had not heard her in some time. She was just gone.

Not all the sounds I heard were mournful, though. From the alleyway where an insane woman cursed her husband came the simple, lovely sounds of everyday life. Peking seemed to be a city of itinerant workmen, and each day the alley was visited by food peddlers, tinkers, and menders. The knife sharpeners had a particularly musical chant that, when heeded, would be followed by the grinding of blades against their small stone wheels. In summer, purveyors of red bean custard frozen on a stick walked slowly through the alley calling, "Bing Guar, Bing Guar." They were Good Humor men with only one flavor and without trucks. Indeed, I rarely heard the sound of an engine in the alley. All movement was declared by the sound of footsteps or the clatter of cart wheels.

On one Christmas night, my fifth in captivity, the alley was very still, its stillness reinforced by the coldness and clarity of the weather.

Then, at the furthest edge of my hearing, arose voices singing. They came nearer. They were girls' voices, as clear and bright as the night, and they were singing Christmas carols. The tunes were so familiar; I heard the words in English even though the girls sang in Chinese. As they passed in the alley below me, their voices sweetly smashed the brittle defenses I had built around my emotions. I was flooded with homesickness and nostalgia, and the half-triumphant, half-empathetic feeling that China still retained its humanity. I guessed the girls were coming from the Catholic cathedral I knew to be nearby. The Chinese Communist Party was officially atheistic, but in its early years it was more tolerant toward religion than its Soviet counterpart. For years I heard the cathedral bells ring each Sunday. They were silenced finally during the Cultural Revolution.

The Party's paradoxical denial and acceptance of religion was applied directly to me when I asked for a Bible and a missal. I could have the books if I chose, my captors told me, but they would not provide them. As right-thinking Communists, they would not abet my spiritual ruination. It took months, but I got the Bible and the missal from home and I made them part of my daily routine. Each morning I read the appropriate passage from the missal, and each evening I read a chapter from the Bible. Eventually, I read it through several times, and my favorite books, Ecclesiastes, Paul's Epistles, Isaiah, and Psalms, I read dozens of times. In the silence of evening, in the dim light of my cell, I read the preacher's weary summation: "One generation passes and another comes, but the earth endures forever" . . . and I was comforted.

Though the terrifying circumstance of my capture and early imprisonment had quickly restored the active faith I had let slide in my adolescence, the long solitary hours I spent in prison gave me a new and deeper belief. My faith changed from a talisman against fear to the stoic serenity that ultimately my fate was in God's hands, not my captors'. But if faith gave me the strength to endure prison, it also sustained me in the certainty that I would not spend the rest of my life there, that somehow my release would be arranged through diplomatic channels, and that somehow I would survive until it was. It was blind faith and it worked. I learned, too, to accept the passage of time. In the first years of imprisonment, I fretted over each day that was taken from me. I was a young man watching his future recede, and I constantly recalculated my purely speculative law career—which was what I planned to do when I got out—to accommodate my advancing age. Finally, I stopped counting and simply assumed I would go to law school and enter politics, just as my father had done, regardless of my age at release.

And as my career worries diminished, so did my romantic worries. Like most young men, I considered romance an essential component of happiness, and once I got letter-writing privileges, I began to carry on affairs through the mail. At one point I was writing to two women at once, and when we began to voice our hopes for the future, my interpreters, who read all my correspondence, cautioned me that I was failing to take my life sentence seriously. They need not have worried. Even as I wrote, I knew the intensity of my passion was in large part a measure of my despair. Besides, I did "the honorable thing" and broke off the correspondence with one woman I knew I did not love. Then, not long after, I was jilted by the other. Her "Dear John" letter eventually proved a relief. I was learning that there is more to a man's life than profession and passion and that a year, or two or three, taken from that life does not diminish one's expectation of the future.

I was discovering, too, that there were some offsetting virtues to the deprivation of prison. As my hearing and other physical senses became sharper, so did my interior senses. Soon after my stay with the B-29 crew and my return to solitary, I began to receive books from my Chinese captors and in packages sent by my family. *The Pickwick Papers* brought tears of laughter and *A Tale of Two Cities* brought tears of sadness. I was chilled by Dr. Manette's compulsive tapping with his cobbler's hammer, and I worried something similar would become of me. But mostly the books I read were inspirational. I plumbed most of the volumes in Balzac's *The Human Comedy* and marveled at the breadth of his achievement. I read the works of most of the nineteenth-century social realists, who fortunately were considered acceptable by the Communists because they were critical of capitalism and established religions. Of course, I was permitted the great Russian novelists Dostoyevsky, Turgenev, and Tolstoy. I knew the jokes about attempts to plow through *War and Peace*, but I read it seven times, each with more pleasure than the times before.

My standard for what was a great book became that which improved with each rereading. Thus, I came to have high regard for Thomas Mann's *Buddenbrooks*, a book that I decided was a neglected classic. I amused myself by establishing a list of the ten books one ought to have on a desert island. I cheated a little, including Balzac's comedy as one book and an anthology of poetry as another. In fact, I memorized many poems in prison—one of them was:

INVICTUS

Out of the night that covers me,
Black as the Pit from pole to pole
I thank whatever gods may be
For my unconquerable soul.

In the fell clutch of circumstances
I have not winced nor cried aloud.
Under the bludgeonings of chance
My head is bloody, but unbowed.

Beyond this place of wrath and tears
Looms but the Horror of the shade,
And yet the menace of the years
Finds, and shall find, me unafraid.

It matters not how strait the gate,
How charged with punishments the scroll.
I am the master of my fate:
I am the captain of my soul.
William Ernest Henley

—reciting them to myself and taking the deepest pleasure in knowing that if my captors suddenly decided to confiscate my growing library, they could never take away the poems I knew by heart. Also on my list were the Bible and a thesaurus. I rated *Drums Along the*

Mohawk by Walter D. Edmonds as the most free roaming of the outdoor books I read, and *The Reason Why*, Cecil Woodham-Smith's story of the charge of the Light Brigade, as the most skillfully crafted.

But the work that affected me most powerfully was Carl Sandburg's *Abraham Lincoln: The War Years.* Surely, at a pure literary level, it did not surpass all the other classics. Its fascination derived from the quintessentially American character of both author and subject. Sandburg had chronicled the agony and chaos, the pettiness and grandeur of the Civil War that tested the nation as it had tested the tall, homely president who helped the nation survive it. I had been fascinated with Lincoln since my father had taken me to his memorial as a child. And when I revisited the memorial in my final days in Washington before leaving for Japan, I was overcome with what later I could only describe as a palpable religious sensation. In a communist prison in China, Sandburg's *Lincoln* brought me home again. I read the whole four volumes over and over.

In those first years, I read when I could during the day and always in the evening, when I read with permission from the end of supper at six thirty to lights out at nine thirty. But the dim bulb inset high in my cell wall never did go out, and it provided enough light to read by. On many nights, I turned my back to the guards' window and hunched over a book hidden in my quilt. Without my glasses, the book was inches from my eyes and reading like that may have weakened my already poor vision. My nose was stuck, literally, against the pages.

Though I read for hours with the most intense kind of involvement, books could not absorb all the extra psychic energy that prison life gave me. For a few months I kept a sort of diary and fancied myself a cell-bound writer. But when the interpreters confiscated it, I resolved never to write seriously again in prison. My thoughts were the one thing my captors could not control, and I vowed that I would never jeopardize their sanctity by committing them to paper. The letters I wrote didn't matter. I knew they would be censored, so I filled them with banalities and small talk.

I was more successful as my own Russian instructor than I was as a writer. In college I had been talked out of taking Russian by an adviser. Then, as a CIA officer, I had wished I knew the language of our chief adversary. In prison, I was taken with the idea of reading the great Russian writers in their own language. So after some years, I acquired a basic Russian grammar and began teaching myself. I studied for several hours each day, memorizing words by rote. It was an unsophisticated method, but within a year I was reading some of the simpler Russian novels, albeit with frequent side trips to a dictionary and a rather free interpretation of some phrases. I read parts of *War and Peace* in Russian.

Not all the uses of prison solitude were intellectual. I read sports magazines sent to me from home as avidly as I read the classics. The amount of mail I could receive was strictly controlled, and all of it was censored. When Maxim Gorky spoke of the censor as wandering through a book like a pig through a garden, I knew what he meant. *National Geographic* was about the most hard-hitting example of Western journalism I was allowed. Once I discovered that a photo accompanying an article about an athlete had been ripped out of a magazine because a barroom nude could be seen in the background of the photo. I noticed the picture lying in a waste bin. No matter, it was the sports that I was interested in.

My college buddy Bill Fisher gave me a subscription to the *Sporting News*, the weekly sports newspaper, and I was addicted immediately to its columns of stories and statistics. I followed all sports through all seasons, becoming devoted to teams and players I had never seen. When my family sent the first issue of a new magazine called *Sports Illustrated*, I was overjoyed. They came four or six or eight editions at a time, and their arrival was a bonanza. Often I could reconstruct whole segments of a season in a single evening's reading. But sometimes the latest issue stopped just before the resolution of an important match or championship series. It was like listening to a ball game on the radio and having the power go out with the score tied and men on bases in the bottom of the ninth inning. Except instead of waiting a few hours for the power to return, or until delivery of the morning paper to learn the outcome, I had to wait a month or more for the next package from home. The sheer normalcy of the seasonal cycle of sports comforted me as much as the grand passages I read in books.

The packages from home consumed much of my attention. They were the main element in the "improved conditions" promised after the Secretary-General Dag Hammarskjöld of the United Nations made his inspection visit in January 1955. When the first package arrived a couple of months later, I opened it as reverently and eagerly as a child would a Christmas gift that had beckoned for weeks from under the tree. But the appetite with which I might have received the edible contents had been tempered by my stay with the B-29 crew. I had shaken like a leaf when I opened a can of Spam, and in our one-day reunion for photographs, they smuggled me a supply of food and cigarettes. Still, the contents of the packages were vitally important to me, and since their weight could not exceed eleven pounds, a standard set by the Red Cross, their contents had to be carefully considered.

My early letters home read in part like shopping lists. I wanted canned meats like corned beef or Spam but not chicken. If I asked for a jar of peanut butter, it meant I could not receive a jar of jam or a tin of coffee. And when the jars established their propensity to break in transit, no matter how carefully packed, the package contents shifted toward canned and boxed goods. Apparently my family presented the jar breakage problem to the Cross & Blackwell Company, so I began receiving specially canned jams and jellies. I appreciated them greatly because of a sweet tooth that refused to die during two years of eating the blandest of food. One glass container that was worth the risk of breakage was the one holding the peanut butter; its weight also meant that I had to give up other items.

Getting the contents of the package changed required fine timing. Since I was allowed to write only once a month to my family, and since it took six to eight weeks for the packages to be delivered, I had to guess what I would need three or four months in the future. If I thought I had laid in an ample supply of canned meat, I might ask for a more frivolous substitute in the next package. More than once I miscalculated my rate of consumption and the delivery of the packages. Then I was left without the supplement to prison food I had come to depend on. Not having peanut butter to spread on the steamed bread I got each morning was not just an annoyance; it could also be a painful disruption of a fragile routine I had created to shield myself from the harshness of prison life.

I also received food packages from the Red Cross, and I tried to coordinate their contents. The Red Cross package was standard and tended toward the incidental. There was a roll of toilet paper, which I thought a waste of space, and a box of Rye Crisp crackers, which I considered about as unappetizing as prison food. But there was also instant coffee, sugar, and cigarettes.[1] I acquired a great stockpile of things like plastic spoons, which came in every package and for which I had little use.

In the weeks before the packages started to arrive from America, a Chinese Red Cross representative visited my cell once a week always bearing the same gifts: two slices of white bread spread with margarine. I ate them, but I wondered if his visits had a greater purpose than the delivery of a bad sandwich. His silence offered no explanation. The prison had some mysterious routines of its own. Every day guards brought me three chunks of hard candy and a piece of fruit with a precision and faithfulness suggesting that that exact combination was specified in the Geneva Treaty. The fruit was either an apple or a tangerine. Once on an apple day, I happened to ask if any tangerines were available. The request caused the guards to retreat outside the cell, where they deliberated for some minutes. Finally, they substituted a tangerine. Once the food packages began to arrive, the Red Cross gentleman disappeared, as did my ration of candy and fruit.

Before they passed the packages on to me, guards would inspect them, opening all cans and jars, and thus increasing the rate of spoilage. They persisted in this practice, my interpreters informed me, because they feared my government would try to poison me. They seemed offended when I laughed at this nonsense, but they kept on. The preferred method of inspection was to probe my food with silver chopsticks, on the theory that the presence of cyanide or common poison would cause the silver to turn black, an antiquated technique the Chinese had used for centuries.

Personally, I was more concerned with prison sanitation, or the lack of it. When I discovered my jailers simply tossed my empty food tins in an unused cell, I began to wash each tin meticulously before discarding it. I didn't want my garbage to nourish any more bacteria or vermin than already were loose in the prison. I was appalled the first time I stepped away from the toilet and looked down to discover I had intestinal worms. I had been feeling more tired than usual, but that was no warning for the slimy white creature that rose from my feces like a cobra. I captured one about a foot long and took it in a jar to one of the guards, who received it with chagrin. Worms were so common that they kept a powerful purgative handy. By the next day, my system was flushed out, but it took some time before I felt wholly clean again.

My only serious illness in prison was also centered in my gut, though doctors never found the cause. It occurred in a spring following three years of bad harvests. Everyone was on short rations and for two months my prison diet had consisted of gruel for breakfast and boiled cabbage for lunch and dinner. There was absolutely no variation in the menu. One day without warning, I became nauseous. Later I added diarrhea to my symptoms. The Chinese always suspected that any prisoner's illness was psychosomatic. But when my distress persisted, they sent me to the infirmary. The first night there, I sweated profusely and I was fed intravenously. The doctors appeared quite concerned, while I fanned the faint hope that my sickness would be severe enough to scare them into sending me home.

The infirmary was on an upper floor of the prison, and it afforded a pretty view of Peking. Trees planted after the Revolution were coming into full foliage and their leaves glistened in the post-dawn mist. In the distance shimmered Coal Hill, where the last emperor of the Ming Dynasty hanged himself in 1644, and which now was as lovely and green as the new trees.

The landscape may have been tranquil, but what finally settled my stomach was a diet of arrowroot cookies, a cure apparently as well known to the Chinese as it was to American mothers. The cookies were succeeded by an egg custard laced with soy sauce. It had a freshness and delicacy that nothing in my prison meals or in my food packages could approach. To my starved taste buds, that hospital custard was ambrosia. After I was returned to my cell, fifteen pounds lighter, food on the corridor improved noticeably, and we even got some custard now and then. The guards resumed testing my food from home with the silver chopsticks, but after months of negative results, they relaxed their vigil against the possibility of my being poisoned. Since their doctors could not explain my illness, and since they could not admit their prison regimen may have been the cause, the Communists preferred to believe my disease had been shipped from the West.

I almost wished I had gotten sick more often in prison. The kindness of the doctors and nurses was a welcome relief from the stern and indifferent treatment I got from guards on the cell corridor. The tension that established itself between the guards and me in the very first months diminished only slightly over the years. I resented their control over me, and they resented the demands I made on them, as small as they might be.

Among the guards' daily chores was boiling water for the prisoners to wash with or to drink. Often by the time the water was brought to the cell, it had cooled to a temperature fine for washing but not good for instant coffee. Each morning, I waited to see how hot my water ration would be. Water that was too cool meant the start of a bad day. Both Fecteau and I complained to the interpreters and stressed the importance of piping hot water, though we hated to ask for special treatment. Eventually the guards were persuaded to pour us coffee from the kettle they kept boiling on their own stove in the corridor. It was a privilege given only to us American prisoners.

Hot water was not a problem in winter, for then small pot-bellied stoves were installed in each cell, and we could boil our own. But the anxiety about receiving not-hot water was replaced by the fear that the coal fire would burn out during the night. Worse than the cold and the tedium of rebuilding the fire was the loss of face to the guards, who would scold our carelessness and then grumble about having to fetch more firewood.

Tending the stove fire, like everything else associated with the harsh Peking winter, demanded much of my energy. When the dust storms came from the Gobi Desert, the stove fires had to be carefully banked against the wind that blew so hard it leaped down the stove pipes and threatened to extinguish the flame. The smaller fire meant colder cells, and everyone, guards and prisoners, would wrap themselves in as many clothes and blankets as possible. Prison routine was reduced to the minimum while we rode out the storm. When it was over, I would pour coal on the fire and try to regain some of the lost heat.

The coal came in various forms. The preferred version was what was called coal balls, a mixture of coal dust and sand, compacted with a small amount of water. Though they were inspired by the need to conserve fuel, the coal balls actually burned better in the small prison stove than pure coal nuggets. They ignited more easily and they burned more cleanly. When consumed, the coal balls left a residue of coal kernels. A handful of these thrown on a banked fire provided a quick burst of heat that was just right for boiling a pot of water or for warming hands on particularly frigid mornings. The coal balls normally were piled in the cell corridor, but when they were not available, prisoners were given the ingredients to make their own, or ordinary coal nuggets were provided. The nuggets had to be pulverized. Either process was a dirty one, and it was only with painstaking care that cells were kept from becoming as black as the inside of a coal mine.

Just preparing for bed in winter was an elaborate process. I took off the top layers of clothing, which after a time included sweaters and wool shirts sent by my family. Quickly, I replaced my outer clothes by wrapping myself in two quilts. Using my belt, I secured the quilts below my ankles so that they would not come loose during the night, exposing my ski-stockinged feet. Finally, I wrapped the bundle I had made of myself in an old overcoat, tying its sleeves to secure it. At last, I thought as I listened to the wind howl through the cracks in the cell wall that could never quite be sealed, I was warm.

Much of prison life was composed of such trivial ritual. If it was not dictated to me, I imposed it on myself. In its observance, I could forget the larger facts of my existence, that I was serving a life sentence in a hostile land. So I arose each morning and did my calisthenics, toe touches, squats, stretches, and push-ups; I rolled my bedding into a back rest and washed my face in silt-filled water; brushed my teeth and spit into my chamber pot; read my missal and ate my gruel, all the while trying not to think too hard about myself. My horizons shrank, and I was immersed in getting through that day and the next one, and then I'd look up and notice another month, another year, had rolled by.

16

CELLMATES

ONE TIME, when I changed prisons, officials led me through the prison corridors, and guards, trailing behind us like porters on a trek, carried my books and clothing. We stopped at a cell. The door was unbolted and we all trooped in. I ducked my head as had become a habit from the low doors of my previous cells. There was a milling about as my boxes were deposited along the wall. The cell gradually emptied and I was alone, except for one shadowy figure I had barely noticed. He did not move to follow the other Chinese out the door. When the door was closed and the bolt was slid home, he was locked in with me. I had a new acquaintance; this was my first cellmate.

His last name was Wu. He was very slight; his black prison clothes hung on him like a shroud, and he behaved in such a perpetually nervous and frightened manner that he seemed to have shivered away his bodily substance. The cell was very much like the one I had left, except the floor space was diminished by the addition of a second plank bed and my stuff. We shared a desk and, involuntarily, each other's miseries.

Wu was in his early forties and had been a professor of French before his arrest. He came from a well-to-do family; his father had been a diplomat. During World War II, Wu worked as an intelligence officer for the Nationalists. After the war, while the Nationalists were still in control of Peking, Wu returned to teaching at QingHua [Tsinghua] University. Later, Wu was accused of contributing to the death of a pro-Communist student. He was sentenced to death, but the sentence was suspended for two years. If he showed proper contrition, the death sentence could be commuted. By the time I met Wu, his sentence had been reduced to fifteen years. His fate was entirely in the hands of his captors, and he was scared to do anything that might displease them.

Nevertheless, he could not hide his affection for things French, a symptom of bourgeois leanings certain to irritate the Communists. When he was in the grip of self-pity, which was often, he would pace the cell muttering to himself, "C'est fini; c'est fini."

Wu taught me to sing "La Marseillaise" in French and I sneaked him American cigarettes when he ran out of the Chinese brand. We also shared food, mine from my food packages and his brought to him by his wife or his father. They came faithfully once a month. One time he brought back a great delicacy his wife had made; pigeon eggs suspended in aspic. The meat of the eggs was a true blue and the yolks a bright yellow. They tasted delicious, and I ate more than I had intended.

It was after one of his father's visits that Wu told me he had engaged a lawyer to reopen his case. His father had told him the Party was making one of its great reform efforts, this one focusing on courts and prisons. If Wu was scared when I first met him, now he was in a permanent dither. As weeks went by, he continuously paced, smoked, and mumbled to himself. Finally a party official visited Wu. He asked why Wu had not previously declared his distance from the student's death. Wu said he had been afraid his protest would anger his captors. A short time later, Wu was released.

As he prepared to leave the cell, we both kept silent, each of us afraid that any display of friendship would arouse suspicions against Wu. At the last moment before he stepped through the door, Wu turned and looked at me. I said to him, "Bon chance, mon ami." He held my gaze another second then turned away and disappeared into the corridor. That was the way prison acquaintanceship ended, as abruptly and finally as the bang of a cell door.

Wu had been released in the fall of 1957. A few weeks after his departure, I got another nerve-jangling command to collect my belongings. This time the trip was short, down the corridor three doors to Uncle's cell. He was tall for a Chinese man, about five foot nine. He had a long, square face and a large nose. The Chinese tended to look askance at the large nose of Westerners. The epithet "Big Nose" in particular was reserved for the Russians. When Uncle and I got to know each other, we would playfully ridicule each other's nose. Once we even measured noses to see whose was longer. The dubious prize went to Uncle, and I never let him forget it.

Uncle was in prison because he was a captain in Peking assigned to the anti-Red squad of the Nationalist government. He was educated in an American missionary school, and he bragged to me about having a love affair with an American teacher. He had a wife and a concubine, who lived in the same compound. Uncle's worldly attitude toward women was a refreshing change from the normal Chinese fastidiousness about sex. He had many other decadent Western proclivities to go along with lust. In fact, he was enamored of everything Western, and that accounted for much of his trouble with the Communists. Uncle was able to carry on a long conversation with me in English but much less in written form. Uncle's addiction to the West extended to coffee. He must have been delighted to have an American for a cellmate, if only because I got coffee in my bimonthly food packages. On those mornings that I failed to offer him coffee, Uncle became withdrawn and sullen. I always had the notion that his taste for coffee was more Western affectation than a true liking for the brew, and I occasionally resented having to share my limited supply.

Similarly, feelings on both sides became tender when I had to share food with Uncle or subsequent cellmates in times of bad harvests. It was impossible to eat spam, or even peanut butter, while the fellow sitting across from me had only boiled cabbage. My weight went down to 165 pounds, the lowest since I became an adult. Since prison policy discouraged sharing, I had to sneak food to Uncle. We ate our meals with one eye on the cell door peephole.

Uncle liked to tell stories of his concubine, who was a Peking opera actress; she had become a minor star and had even performed in Paris. For a time after his arrest, she visited him in the prison. But she was pressured by the Communists to end their relationship. She moved out of his compound and then out of his life. Uncle's wife, who was a peasant girl, remained loyal to him throughout his imprisonment. She was the mother of his several children.

If any time in prison could be said to have been pleasant, then such a time occurred for me at the start of the new decade, the 60s. Uncle and I, and Fecteau and his cellmate, were transferred back to the star-shaped prison on the outskirts of Peking. For several seasons in a row, harvests had been poor, and odd plots of land everywhere in the city were being turned into vegetable gardens. Our cellmates read about the civic agricultural effort in the newspapers they received, and we asked if we could participate by cultivating the small, irregularly shaped courtyard we used for outdoor exercise. With picks, shovels, and our bare hands, we excavated a three-foot layer of packed earth and rubble. Each day, all day, we shoveled and sifted, using sticks and string to construct an even grade. The work was productive, if tedious, but blessedly absorbing.

We planted carrots and tomatoes in a rectangular plot and green peppers, cucumbers, and corn in narrow beds running along the base of the courtyard walls. Our Chinese cellmates were particularly adept at building the gentlest of grades into the garden, so that by pouring water in at the upper end, the entire length of the garden, almost sixty feet, irrigated itself. I alone abstained from the long debates about best planting methods. When it came to gardening, it seemed everyone considered himself an expert. Fecteau had a way with tomatoes, but he had less success with carrots. He insisted the sprouts had to be transplanted after they reached a certain maturity, while others argued that they only needed to be thinned. A compromise was struck in which a portion of the carrot crop was thinned and another transplanted. All the carrots continued to grow, but those that were moved developed into twisted grotesque carrots. It seemed we had neglected to loosen the soil to a depth that could accommodate the carrots' growth. They burrowed down a few inches, and when they hit hard-packed dirt turned sideways and then back on themselves.

None of us ever solved the pepper problem; they had a tendency to fall from the vine when only half-formed. Our corn grew well enough, but we couldn't convince Uncle and the other Chinese that they were good to eat. They considered corn fit only for pigs. We persuaded the guards to boil it for us, and Fecteau and I enjoyed a reminder of American summers. Our cellmates nibbled at the corn with a skeptical curiosity.

Corn was not the only bit of American culture for which our Chinese cellmates had no taste. Athletic competition was another. In the same courtyard where we had our garden, there was an exercise bar and a quoits set. In the previous prison in downtown, I had rarely seen Fecteau, since we had separate exercise periods. But back in the star-shaped prison, Uncle and I, Fecteau and his cellmates, of whom he had a succession, all went out together. Each session started out peacefully enough; we loosened up with calisthenics and jogging. Then we hit the exercise bar where Fecteau and I began to match pull-ups. Our cellmates liked neither the exertion nor the competition. Dick stopped straining himself after he reached twenty at a time. I kept practicing until I broke forty, though there was some grumbling from Fecteau and the cellmates that my form was suspect. They were sour grapes as far as I was concerned. From the daily pull-ups my hands became covered with thick callouses. Once, after we had missed outdoor exercise due to our four-week, five-cities travel, I threw myself back at the bar eagerly to determine how far off I had fallen during the days of little physical activity. I had barely started when I felt myself slipping; the tighter I gripped the bar the more I slipped. Then I realized it was my hands. Without daily toughening, my callouses had softened and now they were peeling away from my hand like a glove. I went to the infirmary, where my hands were bandaged. As soon as I could, I resumed my pull-ups and built back up to over forty.

I was obsessed by records and victories. Fecteau and I learned to hoist ourselves astride on an exercise bar and do rotary spins like gymnasts. We counted these, too. And we had jump rope marathons, each of us trying to make as many revolutions as possible while the other did his best to break the jumper's concentration by any means guile could suggest. By my count, I got up to three thousand revolutions. Then I read in *Sports Illustrated* that a young girl had done fewer than that and had still made *The Guinness Book of Records*.

Our jump rope competition was child's play compared to the intensity of quoits and badminton. The quoits were made of horsehair. Fecteau and I played alone when we couldn't convince our cellmates to join in. Without normal outlets for proving our self-worth, the games took on an exaggerated importance. When we won, we were exultant, and when we lost we were downcast and ill-tempered. The contests often became heated, embarrassing Uncle and the other cellmates, who disapproved of such blatant aggression and bad behavior. Fecteau had the much finer touch at quoits, and I plotted and practiced for hours in hopes of beating him. Finally, in one tingling game in which ringer topped ringer, I won. My feeling of triumph was so overwhelming, I wondered at my lost sense of priorities even as I celebrated.

If quoits was Fecteau's game, mine was badminton. We had no net, only the rackets and a supply of shuttlecocks. Our court was defined by the jutting walls and overhanging roofs of the courtyard, and we created imaginary out-of-bounds lines running through the air. In a way, our game resembled medieval court tennis. We would smack the bird as high as we could, hoping it would come down in some cranny where a return would be difficult. Too often, though, the bird landed on a roof and we had to plead with a guard to fetch it and throw it down. They grew tired of the exercise, and as the shuttlecocks wore out, they were not replaced, ending our badminton careers.

When there were no games to play, I jogged. My route naturally always followed the outline of the particular courtyard I was put in. None of the courtyards were ever large, and so I always ran my route in tight circles. In the end I was jogging ten miles a day at fifty-eight laps to a mile. I ran alone and lived alone by then.

Uncle and I had been cellmates for six years when he developed a chronic intestinal disorder. He had diarrhea and then nausea. As was usual, the guard suspected the illness was psychosomatic and Uncle suffered for days while they waited for him to grow tired of his charade. I was obliged to become a nurse, a role I resented and felt guilty for resenting. I also resented having to do all the cell-keeping chores and felt guilty about that, too. But the greatest strain was watching Uncle suffer, seeing him retching repeatedly into his urine bucket as his misery continued. The best I could do was to give him condensed milk when I got some in my food packages; it stayed down only some of the time.

Finally, Uncle was moved to a cell where he would be alone. When we could, on our way to exercise or to the toilet, Fecteau and I popped cigarettes or food packets through the open peephole of Uncle's cell door. He was emaciated, and he had a luminous look in his eyes. Some days later my prison antenna told me Uncle's cell was empty; he had been released with about four years left to serve on his fifteen-year sentence. We never had a chance to say good-bye, and I never knew what happened to him afterward.

In the early years in prison, I had longed for companionship. Fecteau and I had begged to share a cell. But in my last years, I cherished my isolation. I knew I could outwait my captors, and I didn't need the depressions and fears of some strangers. The tedious burdens and daily indignities of prison life were better borne alone.

17

KEEPERS AND COMRADES

AFTER MY CELLMATES, Miss was the person I saw the most in prison. Several times a week, sometimes every day, she visited our corridor to check on the Americans or to give us instructions. Whatever was the case, she never passed up a chance to correct our wayward thinking. When I was in the infirmary with my intestinal ailment, Miss was there, watching passively while I disrobed for an examination, including a rectal probe. She stayed with me around the clock when I was first admitted to the infirmary. She translated my description of my symptoms to the doctors and the doctors' questions and comments back to me. We rarely talked, but in one conversation, in which I tried to explain Yale's position in American society, I cited examples of graduates of Yale who had distinguished themselves with good deeds.

"Yes," she replied dryly, "and you have done just the opposite." That was pure Miss. Born in south central China, Miss was a Han, as the majority of Chinese were. She came from an upper middle class family and had attended college where she studied English. Her social activities included western dances. During the time we knew her, she was married and had a son. She took only a few weeks for maternity leave. When the child was older, she would occasionally bring him with her to prison. She was often brusque with us, but with the child, she was unfailingly patient and gentle.

Miss's downfall was that she deluded herself about having exorcised her elitist inclinations. She was condescendingly gracious toward the guards, most of whom were from peasant stock, and the more she gushed about how much intellectuals like her had to learn from the peasants like them, the more irritating, I suspected, she became. She was a bourgeois young woman working overtime to become part of the proletariat.

It was just such people who became victims of the Cultural Revolution. When she was "overthrown," she lost her interpreter's job and the position she had had not long before as party secretary at the prison. For her rehabilitation, Miss was assigned to do menial chores so that she might acquire a true egalitarian spirit. I saw her once from my cell window; she was being denounced in the basketball court just below. Later I saw her carrying buckets of manure hanging from a shoulder yoke, and she was dressed in tattered clothing. It seemed to me she was making a very dramatic showing of her penance.

Despite her posturing and her constant willingness to criticize us, Miss was bright, and when she chose, she could converse engagingly. Certainly I preferred her to her successor, a young zealot we had nicknamed Woo Woo. He was skinny and with such large eyeglasses he reminded me of a grasshopper. But he was not one to fiddle away his time. He arrived on our corridor with the energy of a missionary fresh from divinity school. He immediately set about raising our political consciousness, and for a time we were reimmersed in propaganda. With the addition of an intellectual prisoner named Ma Hua, who was both egotistical and arrogant, our political study turned into high gear. The study group began as a crash course, six hours a day, six days a week. We each described our personal backgrounds, and then we proceeded to read party literature. My fear of brainwashing had subsided. I quickly learned to ignore the assurance that we could honestly broach disagreements with Communist theory and practice. Everyone in the group was trying to protect himself, and the surest way to do that was to criticize whoever was foolish enough to raise a genuine argument. We became adept at disagreeing just strongly enough and just often enough to make a convincing show of willingness to study. When Fecteau and his cellmates merged with our group, the group study became more bearable. I faithfully read all my assignments for the next day's class so that I could be certain I was protecting my right to read *Sports Illustrated* in the evening. This was the time Fecteau and I quickly fell to sharing news from home, exchanging reading materials, and talking about sports. It was impossible to police us, and soon the interpreter or guards stopped trying. More people in the study group meant the burden of criticism could be borne by more shoulders. Besides, there were more people to socialize with, and it was just more pleasant.

As for Woo Woo, who chose to live on the corridor near his charges, his fervor soon waned. We settled into a functional relationship. He brought us our mail and our food packages, and criticized us and gave us cause to gripe, just as Miss had done. But we rarely got into a spontaneous exchange of words with him. Only a few of the interpreters or guards stayed with us for any length of time. The practice was to rotate them frequently to prevent them from becoming familiar with any prisoner. So our interactions with them were characterized more by detachment and correctness than anything else. Rarely was there any overt hostility. My angriest incident occurred in the mid-1950s, when I was in extreme uncertainty about my situation.

I had been feeding a pair of long-haired rabbits for some weeks without interference, when one day a young guard in a watchtower overlooking the courtyard shouted to me and waved me away from the rabbits' cage with his machine gun. His voice was arrogant and the command without reason. I snapped. I turned toward him, screaming and swearing at the top of my lungs. I alternately pounded my chest in a challenge for him to shoot and thrust my arm up in an obscene gesture. Uncle was with me, and he placed a hand on my shoulder, trying to calm me. I shook it off and kept yelling at the guard, who by now had leveled his gun at me. The row continued in a standoff until one of the interpreters came rushing out to see what was going on. I angrily told the interpreter I didn't see any damn reason why I couldn't feed the damn rabbits when I had been doing it for weeks. By then I had blown off enough steam to allow myself to be led back inside the prison. After much deliberation, the Chinese informed me I would be permitted to continue feeding the rabbits.

It gave me some comfort to know that they could be reasonable, and I had won the argument. But I was disturbed by the blackness of my own anger. As for the guard, he must have been transferred, for I never saw him again.

On the other hand, a guard who became too friendly was just as likely to be transferred. Even if a guard was not removed for smiling, or struck up a conversation, he would be counseled to keep his distance from the Americans, and then there would be a mutual awkwardness for some days until we regained our cool. I came to discourage any overtures that were made, for my own sake as well as theirs. When the small comfort of their friendliness withdrew, the absence only reminded me of the emotional barrenness of prison. So the guards came and went over the years, only a few making any lasting impression.

Among those who did make an impression was a rotund middle-aged fellow we called Mister Fat. Even other guards called him that, though he was not grossly overweight by Western standards. He was an old soldier being rewarded for his service with a lowly prison sinecure, and nothing could shake his loyalty to the Mao regime. His skin was the color of earth. Mister Fat had little patience for the intellectuals who were in his charge. They were truly effete; some had never had to do the simplest physical task. Usually he treated their ineptness with indulgence or good-natured scorn. But he had a temper, too. Once, his angry shout startled the whole corridor when whining came from a toilet that someone had defecated on the floor. Listening for a few moments, he roared, "Well, clean it up."

I was not immune to Mister Fat's vocational instructions. It was he who ordered me to do my own laundry and tailoring. He told me there were no such services in the prison. All clothing and bedding was washed by hand in the cell. The lighter stuff could be managed reasonably enough, though in my first attempts I flooded the cell with my laundry water. Our quilted winter jackets and blankets were too heavy to be washed in one piece. They had to be disassembled and washed piece by piece then reassembled; it was like a jigsaw puzzle. When I finally stitched them together after several tries, my jacket had shrunk by half a size. I figured out to sew scraps of cloth across the portion that rubbed against my neck; it was easier to remove the ragged doily and clean that instead of the whole jacket. Mister Fat approved of my resourcefulness.

We once had an enthusiastic young guard we called Fat Kid. He grew up in the years after the Revolution and thus benefited from the improved lot it won for peasants. He was better educated than the old soldier and the guerrillas who were peasants. He was also more naive. He would bang into my cell at unpredictable hours to deliver what he must have regarded as inspirational lectures in Marxism, dragging Ma Hua out of Fecteau's cell to act as translator.

"I have observed your conduct," he would begin, pacing solemnly with his hands clasped behind his back, as though he was on the quarterdeck of the Emperor's barge. "You have been conserving the People's coal. Very good. And I hope you will also conserve the People's water, and the People's food, and the People's toilet paper."

He paused dramatically then asked, "What do you think of my words?"

"I think your words are full of, ah, good," I'd answer, and his severe expression would disintegrate into a huge smile.

He was husky, big by Asian standards, just under six feet tall, and built like a barrel. In winter, if I stepped outside to fetch a bucket of coal, he would scold me for not dressing warmly and jam a hat on my head, or run after me outside to deliver the cap with his own collar open. Oddly, for someone so beefy and cumbersome, he was a very good basketball shooter. Outside my window, I saw Fat Kid sink shot after shot.

There was only one guard in whom I felt any abiding trust, however. I called him Gary Cooper because he was tall and wiry and almost never smiled. He was another peasant who had been through the wars, literally. No situation—a madwoman's rantings, an intellectual's whining, an American's tantrums—could fluster him. He was the warden—the man in charge. He sat at a desk at one end of the corridor, a short-brimmed Mao cap habitually on his head. When he was on duty, I relaxed as much as I ever did in prison, for he was there when I began serving my sentence officially in the fall of 1955 and had followed us from prison to prison. He knew the Americans and their idiosyncrasies, and he was the one who broke in new guards when they arrived on the corridor. He was also there to see us released. The laconic and rugged Chinese peasant alone was my constant companion in prison. He was like a rock, when I went from fear to despair to resolve, from youth to middle age.

Cooper and I never carried on any extended conversations; indeed, we rarely communicated in any fashion beyond grunts and gestures. But I sensed he liked me or at least felt sympathy toward me. His most demonstrative moment came late in our acquaintanceship, about the time of President Nixon's visit to China. All the guards were called off the corridor to a meeting, and Cooper returned unusually excited. He rushed into my cell and gestured toward Mao's book, required reading for study groups.

"Read book! Read book!" Cooper said over and over with great earnestness, picking it up and banging it to make his point. I understood he wanted to guarantee I would be able to pass any final political exam that might bar my release; he cared about what was happening to me.

So there were Miss, Cooper, Woo Woo, Mister Fat, and Fat Kid; I knew them best and I knew them not at all. Their lives were as locked away from me, by our mutual reserve, as mine was locked away from a normal life. Most of my prison encounters made no more impression than a scene glanced from the window of a moving train. Most were indeed stolen glances through a crack in a door or over a window transom.

From the day Fecteau and I boarded the fateful C-47 aircraft, we were never far from each other as we moved from city to city, from prison to prison. Especially in the early days, not a day went by that I did not count on him to be near. I knew instinctively that he was going through the same ordeal as I was. We lived on the same corridor for many years, and the desire to get in touch was always strong. But we were always separated by heavy doors, and walls made of cement and stone. In the late 60s, I did have limited custodian status, though I was not permitted to roam the prison grounds, nor was my cell left unlocked. My privilege was to be let out for a few hours in the evening to sweep the corridor, clean the toilet and empty the garbage, chores I did in rotation with Fecteau and other prisoners. The Chinese may have thought that my willingness to do menial chores proved I had taken their political lectures to heart and overcome my bourgeois intellectual pretensions. In fact, my passivity was a defense against their intrusions, and the chores were a great relief from the tedium of my cell.

Brooms and mops and other cleaning apparatus were stored in an uninhabited cell at one end of the corridor. The storage room was divided in half by a makeshift wall of bed planks. Over the top of the planks I could see bulging burlap bags. On my first several visits, I ignored the bags. One day, when I was certain the guard on duty was occupied at the opposite end of the corridor, I stretched out my arm and plunged my hand into the top of one of the bags. I came out with a handful of envelopes and quickly tore one open. It was a Christmas card to Fecteau. I tore open another. It was another card to Fecteau, and every one of the envelopes in my hand bore a postmark several years old.

I stuffed a couple of envelopes inside my winter quilted jacket and returned the rest to the bag. I casually moved toward Fecteau's cell, pretending I was cleaning. At Fecteau's door, I stopped and bent down as if to pick up some trash and instead tried to slip one of the cards under the sill. The guards were still engrossed at the other end of the corridor. The card passed halfway under the door then buckled. I hissed, hoping to attract Fecteau's attention, but to no avail. A guard turned in my direction just as I managed to slip the card all the way through. I stood up and tried to act nonchalant. The guard said nothing and turned away again. His lack of suspicion was no evidence that the Chinese were extraordinarily trusting or lenient. Rather, I thought, it derived from their utter confidence that their prisoners were so cowed that none would dare attempt any subterfuge and, therefore, they didn't look for any violation.

As my years in prison piled up, I knew of only one escape attempt. It was in the late 50s, in the prison in the center of Peking, when a loud crack made me jump up from my desk. What I immediately recognized as a gunshot was followed by an eruption of sirens and bells and great commotion. I could see nothing from my window. Soon I learned one prisoner had boosted another over a wall while in the exercise courtyard. I never knew what happened to the prisoner who sacrificed himself or if the other prisoner made good his escape. I doubt he did. As for me, I knew there could be no escape; there was nowhere for me to hide or to blend in; I was a foot taller than an average Chinese, and my skin was so light I would stand out without even trying, although this did not stop me from dreaming from time to time. In the corridor, I was able to exploit my captors' complacency. They couldn't know that any American given a few liberties would soon take more.

On subsequent visits to the storage room, I grabbed more letters from the second bag. I hid them under my bulky jacket until I could return to my cell to read them. Then on my next outing, I would exchange them for another batch. Nearly all were Christmas cards to either Fecteau or me from people we did not know. There were hundreds of them, all dating from 1961. In one I found a newspaper clipping that showed photos of Fecteau and me; it said we would be spending our tenth Christmas in prison. I guessed the article had elicited an avalanche of mail that the authorities decided not to deliver. Perhaps they wanted to deprive us of the comfort of knowing that so many people cared about us. It was, in fact, deeply comforting to discover the cards, even several years late, and it gave me additional pleasure to have uncovered the Chinese secret. But counting backward, I realized that it was shortly after the Christmas of the waylaid cards that our mail was ordered restricted to letters from family only.

My janitorial duties also allowed me to perfect an old intelligence skill, the reading of trash. It told me much about the comings and goings on my corridor. I detected the arrival of a new prisoner when I emptied trash cans and noticed food wrappers printed in German. When the wrappers stopped showing up, I knew he had been moved from the corridor. I kept track of the corridor's population, which never exceeded more than seven or eight. Our isolation was so strictly enforced that I never saw some prisoners who stopped on the corridor for only a few months. There were other prisoners I glimpsed rarely as they passed my door peephole. Occasionally I stole a look through theirs. The isolation stopped when I had my first cellmate in 1959. Later, we had a political study group. My last four years in prison, I went back to solitary.

Among the more enigmatic inmates was an Englishman who had made the mistake of displaying a camera at a construction project he was working on in China. He may have had clandestine motives, but it was likely just an innocent indiscretion, and it earned his three-year sentence. He was too frightened to respond when I peeked in at him or when I whistled "Yankee Doodle" as I passed his cell. I did not begrudge him his silence. However, I was exasperated years later when I learned that after his release, he testified before a U.S. Senate subcommittee investigating relations with China. The Englishman had conveyed an image of Fecteau and me as having been reduced to "zombies." It was a grossly ill-considered statement that caused our families great pain and worry, since they had no way of checking our condition during the Chinese Cultural Revolution. I had more success communicating in the later years of the '60s with Philip Smith, Hugh Redmond, and Bob Flynn. All were Americans from the war with North Vietnam, another Communist regime.*

When Philip Smith arrived on the corridor sometime in late 1965, I whistled the theme song of the U.S. Air Force while I was mopping the corridor. I let him know that there was an American here, and I knew who he was. But he was going through a hard time adjusting his expectations to his treatments. He fought tooth and nail against their orders and got into trouble.

By the time Smith arrived on the corridor, the political study group started in early 1959 was still going strong but with varying frequency and participants. The Communists took the political education just as seriously as they took the Cultural Revolution. The same political education classes were conducted in every city neighborhood and in every country village. They wanted to make sure that everyone saw the light of Communism. I became certain that the Communists would not let me go until they felt they had made some progress in teaching me the evils of imperialism. After a few years of classes, we reached an accommodation of wills. They knew they weren't going to convert me to Communism, and I would listen patiently to what they had to say.

One Fourth of July, Smith made an American flag and taped it to his cell wall. When he refused orders to take it down, there were some real fireworks that ended up with Smith being overpowered

---

* Redmond was actually captured in Shanghai in 1951 as he attempted to board a ship for San Francisco. Redmond is discussed further in chapter 18.

and handcuffed. No doubt Smith would have had us digging an escape tunnel if such a scheme had been remotely possible. Instead, he devoted much of his energy to our elaborate message-drop system, not that we had much urgency to communicate until Bob Flynn arrived.

Bob Flynn, an American Naval pilot, was on a mission over North Vietnam when he was shot down on August 21, 1967. Flynn was on the prison corridor for several years, but I saw him only a handful of times in all those years. He was a tall, gangling young man with sloping shoulders, and he was from a small Minnesota town near the Mississippi River. Flynn was easygoing most of the time, but now and then I could hear him shouting angrily at some affront by the guards. Our message-dropping system finally had a purpose.

We met the mother of Hugh Redmond first in January 1958 when he was still imprisoned in Shanghai. He was transferred to Peking in the late 60s for a reason that was never explained to me. By then, he was a middle-aged man, but still full of energy and charged with fire. We were passing through an exercise courtyard doorway while he was carrying some wet laundry. We both knew that meeting was unintended, so we did not speak. He was pale with darting eyes of such intense blue they approached turquoise in hue. The glances that I managed through his peephole showed a curly-haired man in a corduroy jacket. I scratched him a note asking if he wanted to risk communicating secretly. A few days later a large wad of toilet paper popped through my peephole and landed on the floor with a thump. How he managed to sneak such a bulky message past the guards, I could not imagine. The toilet paper contained a detailed account of his arrest and trial, a history he expanded in subsequent notes. When he learned I was studying Russian, he sent me long lists of Russian obscenities.

Redmond had been an Airborne Infantry Major during World War II and was decorated as a hero. His hometown of Yonkers, N.Y. raised a million dollars to buy his release. The Communists rejected the ransom, however. After the war, Redmond had gone to work for an import-export house and married a White Russian. It was his wife who had caused him to stay in China after the Revolution. His wife and his fluent Russian helped him to survive for a while, but in 1951, he was accused of some transgression against the Revolution and was put under arrest. He got in more trouble in 1957 when he complained to an American youth delegation that his trial had been a farce. I had been visited by the same delegation, which consisted mostly of adults with pacifist or socialist sympathies. They had traveled to China in defiance of the State Department. I remembered that I spent a tense half hour with them trying to answer their questions in a way that would neither make me appear craven nor offend the Chinese, who stood with us, smiling or scowling at every response. When Redmond's remarks were reported by the delegation on their return to the United States, the press release found its way back to China. The Communists reacted by putting Redmond in solitary confinement and stopping his mail and food packages for two years. Redmond had been brought to Peking at the height of the Cultural Revolution. The Chinese accused him of contacting a United States general just after the Revolution. He claimed that accusation was nonsense. In one of his notes to me, he wrote, "They've told me my sentence will be increased. I already have a life sentence."

By then, the harsh prison treatment had already taken its toll on Redmond. He was physically thin and weak, with high blood pressure. I felt an impotent anger when I saw him shivering in his cell with only his corduroy coat to protect him from the chill. But his spirit was still fiery. I often heard him angrily lecturing the Chinese in their own language. Once the Russian language fell out of favor after the Sino-Soviet split, in the mid-sixties, it took him about a year to become fluent in the enormously complex Chinese language. Fecteau and I did what we could to help him. We dropped packets of tea and coffee and sugar through his peephole. At Christmas, we took a greater risk, hiding packages of food in loose cinder blocks in the exercise courtyard where we knew Redmond would find them. We could not give him much because Redmond had to consume everything immediately; in his bare cell there were no hiding places to cache any surplus.

In the spring of 1971, I was happy to learn that Redmond was again receiving Red Cross packages. A few months afterward, through a crack in the courtyard door, I saw him climb into a jeep and watched him driven out of the prison. I assumed he was being returned to Shanghai. Later that year, I read in my *Yale Alumni Magazine* class of

'51 class notes that "Richard Fecteau, the man who had been captured with Jack Downey, had died." I knew for certain that Fecteau
was alive down the corridor; I heard his cough several times a day.
I immediately guessed that the class secretary had mistaken Richard
Fecteau for Hugh Redmond, who had died. In the next issue of the
magazine, there was a correction.

The Chinese press had reported that Redmond had committed
suicide, though I didn't believe that for a minute. He had defied the
Chinese so vehemently that they never even attempted to subject him
to the innocuous political education classes. He was indomitable. He
defied the Communists but talked optimistically of our chances for
release. I assumed Redmond had died of a heart attack and that the
Communists were embarrassed to admit that a prisoner in their care
had died of illness. Somehow, it did not occur to them that suicide
was an even more damning indictment of their custody, yet another
cultural difference between East and West.

18

A PINHOLE VIEW ON A MASSIVE TRAGEDY

1958–1970

Thomas J. Christensen

MBASSADOR WANG respected Ambassador Johnson, but he believed Johnson was under such strict control by his superiors that he could not function as a diplomat. He could not even negotiate deals. (Johnson similarly expressed respectful views of Wang as a professional but recognized that he was under tight constraints from his superiors.) Wang claims that, after Johnson could not accept Zhou Enlai's overtures, the U.S. ambassador became "dispirited" (*jusang*) and began smoking constantly.[1]

Declassified documents seem consistent with Wang's account. Johnson clearly wanted to end the talks altogether in early 1957 but was ordered by Washington to sustain them. Secretary Dulles thought that American willingness to talk to the Chinese communists, even if those talks produced no concrete results, made Washington appear more reasonable to allies and neutral parties. Many of those allies and neutral parties were critical of the main elements of Washington's China policy: economic embargo, diplomatic isolation, military hostility toward the People's Republic of China, and a formal alliance with Chiang Kai-shek's Republic of China on Taiwan. Dulles also believed that if the PRC were to use force against Taiwan while the United States was still conducting talks, the international reaction toward the PRC would be harsher than if the United States had broken off talks before the conflict erupted.[2]

Diplomatic talks between the United States and the People's Republic of China continued in fits and starts until 1970. The talks in Geneva ended in December 1957 when Johnson was appointed the ambassador to Thailand. Diplomatic contacts broke down entirely in the first half of 1958 when the Eisenhower administration offered to continue talks but below the ambassadorial level.[3] Affronted, Beijing cut off contact. This may seem petty, but recall that one of Zhou's goals in agreeing to ambassadorial talks in the first place was to eventually upgrade them to ministerial talks between Dulles and Zhou himself. Refusing Zhou's offers of cooperation and then downgrading the U.S. representation added insult to injury. Eventually, in July 1958, Washington offered to reopen ambassadorial talks in Warsaw, another country in which both countries had embassies.

The talks began again in Warsaw that September but in a much more hostile international context than Wang and Johnson had enjoyed in 1955. They were in the midst of a second U.S.-PRC crisis over the KMT-held offshore islands of Quemoy and Matsu, which Mao began shelling with heavy artillery the month before. Wang again represented the PRC, and Jacob Beam represented the United States. But the topic of conversation was the Taiwan Strait and how to avoid war between the United States and the PRC, which was, after all, an ally of the nuclear-armed Soviet Union.[4] Detained citizens like Downey and Fecteau were not discussed.

The domestic environment in China in September 1958 was hardly conducive to an offer of leniency regarding the two spies. That summer, Mao had launched the utopian and ultimately disastrous set of radical economic policies that fell under his Great Leap Forward. Among other things, he ordered the communization of farmland, forcing farmers into militarized work brigades under the slogan "Everyone a Soldier," and attempted fast-paced industrialization in part by creating backyard steel furnaces in rural areas. These amateurish mini-factories did little more than provide an occasion for farmers to melt down previously useful metal implements in the hope of transforming them into industrial-grade steel. Production quotas

were set ridiculously high, only to be raised higher still by local officials in competition with each other to impress party leaders.[5]

Mao hoped that China would surpass England and then the United
States in national production and, in the process, reduce its reliance
on Soviet assistance for economic development. The call for "self-reli-
ance" was particularly important because Mao distrusted and disre-
spected Stalin's successor, Nikita Khrushchev, whom he considered
more of a bureaucrat than a revolutionary or a statesman. China had
become highly reliant on the Soviet Union for economic and tech-
nological development during the CCP's rather successful First Five
Year Plan from 1953 to 1957. Thousands of Soviet experts assisted in all
aspects of China's industrialization. Beijing also remained reliant on
Moscow to deter the United States, a nuclear superpower allied with
Mao's old civil war enemy in Taiwan, and to develop its own military
capabilities at home, including a nuclear weapons program launched
in January 1955.[6]

Whatever its ambitions, Mao's central plan was one of the great
disasters of the twentieth century. Between thirty and forty million
Chinese would die of famine and famine-related disease during the
years of strict communization from 1958 to 1961.[7] Especially when
one adds the millions killed in the initial land reform program following the founding of the PRC and in the later Cultural Revolution,
it is fair to estimate that Mao's policies killed many more Chinese
than the Japanese invaders ever managed to during the 1930s and
1940s. China's rural economy would not recover until the early 1960s,
when the CCP retreated from the Great Leap. Production targets
were lowered, small parcels of land were returned to farmers, and
industrial workers were given some individual incentives to work
more productively.[8]

The second nuclear crisis between the United States and China
in the Taiwan Strait was a by-product of Mao's domestic plans. Just
as the CCP began implementing the most radical aspects of the Great
Leap Forward, on August 23, 1958, Mao ordered the People's Liberation Army once again to shell the tiny offshore islands of Quemoy and
Matsu with heavy artillery. He aimed to create an international crisis
just short of war, an event around which he could mobilize his population to sacrifice for the Great Leap Forward.

Quemoy and Matsu lie only a few kilometers from the mainland coast in the province of Fujian, one hundred nautical miles from the main island of Taiwan. In 1958 they were home to large forward-deployed garrisons of Chiang's KMT military. The status of the islands was left ambiguous in the 1954 U.S.–ROC Mutual Defense Treaty, and the Americans were never comfortable with Chiang placing so many troops there. Washington wished that Chiang would abandon the islands, albeit not under duress. For Chiang, the islands were important symbolically because everyone on the mainland and in Taiwan saw them as part of the mainland's Fujian province, and so occupying them served his argument that his government, not Mao's, was the sole legitimate government of all of China. Such an argument was essential to Chiang's political legitimacy on Taiwan itself. There, Chiang was an outsider from the mainland. His only claim to authority on the island was that Taiwan was part of the larger Chinese nation of which he was the legitimate ruler.[9]

As Mao predicted and actually wanted, the United States chose to support Chiang and intervened in the crisis to escort the KMT ships resupplying the offshore islands. The United States also supplied cutting-edge military equipment to Taiwan, including the Sidewinder air-to-air missile, which devastated Mao's young air force in dogfights. The PRC did not take the islands, but Mao did not necessarily intend to. What he really desired was a crisis just short of a full-scale Sino-American war. He could mobilize his citizens around such a crisis, fomenting nationalist fervor that he could direct into supporting his restructuring of Chinese society. Mao's propaganda machine linked agricultural and industrial targets to the patriotic mission of standing against the U.S. imperialists and "liberating" Taiwan.[10]

If Dulles's rigid approach to diplomacy had not fully sealed Downey and Fecteau's fate as long-term prisoners in China, the second crisis in the Taiwan Strait certainly did. The crisis itself ran the risk of escalating to nuclear war. Within China it intensified widespread anti-Americanism during Mao's mobilization drive for the Great Leap Forward. Such an atmosphere was not the place for anyone to suggest releasing the two American prisoners.

Downey himself saw the results of the Great Leap. He noticed his food rations became smaller and less diverse in these years, though he attributed this to bad weather and poor harvests. That is likely what they told him; it is the standard explanation for famines in communist regimes from the Soviet Union to China to North Korea.

The People's Republic of China has been a great scientific experiment pitting the power of markets and capitalism against communist ideology. Even though the form of government has held constant from 1949 to the present, China's years of highest growth were when the Chinese Communist Party gave individuals selfish incentives to produce more and invest in their futures (1953–1957, 1962–1965, and especially since Deng Xiaoping's reforms were launched in 1978). The economy has been much weaker, sometimes disastrously so, in highly ideological periods like the Great Leap Forward and the Cultural Revolution from 1966 to 1976).

From his prison cell, Downey could not have known that while his own rations were declining, he was still much better off than millions of Chinese who were sometimes left to scour the countryside for leaves and tree bark to eat. Local leaders in many areas had tried to impress their superiors with their high productivity by passing off the strategic stores of grain as recent harvests. So when disaster struck, those stores were depleted, and the safety net was gone.

Mao did not warn Khrushchev about the Great Leap Forward or the shelling that yielded the Taiwan Straits crisis, and tensions between Moscow and Beijing were high. Relations had begun to sour two years earlier when Khrushchev launched a de-Stalinization campaign without conferring in advance with Mao, who believed he himself was the most experienced international revolutionary and a natural leader of international communism following Stalin's death in 1953.

Khrushchev's ideology rankled Mao. Khrushchev believed there could be a "peaceful transition" to socialism through parliamentary processes in capitalist countries and that the Soviet Union and the United States could establish a "peaceful coexistence." These views ran directly against Mao's revolutionary exhortation that "power grows out of the barrel of a gun." Khrushchev also believed the Great Leap Forward was utopian and ill-advised. He visited Beijing in late July and early August 1958 to improve relations with Mao, but the meetings were contentious. Mao failed to warn him that he was about to spark a major confrontation with the United States that could have escalated to World War III. In 1959, Khrushchev and Mao held another contentious summit, and Khrushchev decided not to honor an earlier agreement to transfer a sample nuclear weapon to the PRC. In 1960, Moscow abruptly withdrew the thousands of Soviet technical and administrative experts that had helped China in its industrialization in the 1950s. These Soviet advisers took their blueprints with them. The Sino-Soviet rift was now clear and deep.[11]

Such a split between the two communist giants was something Washington had hoped for since the creation of the PRC in 1949. The Truman administration thought that if they could find a way to create diplomatic contact with Beijing, they might exploit such a split whenever it occurred. But the domestic environment at the end of the 1940s, Truman's need to mobilize the United States for the Cold War around a clear and simple message of anticommunism, and the outbreak of the Korean War in June 1950 and its escalation to a Sino-American conflict later that year all made that impossible. When Eisenhower took office, he hoped to catalyze a Sino-Soviet split through a very tough policy of diplomatic and economic isolation of the PRC. He believed such pressure on the PRC would make it more dependent on the USSR, a condition that would eventually drive a wedge between the two communist allies. Unfortunately for Downey and Fecteau, that pressure campaign overlapped with the Geneva talks from 1955 to 1957.

While the Americans hoped for a Sino-Soviet split in the 1950s, they did not anticipate that the split would make the communist bloc *harder* to contain. Mao's rejection of Khrushchev's more moderate stance toward the capitalist world and his belief that he, Mao, should lead the international communist movement only encouraged him to support communist revolutions abroad, particularly in Vietnam.

In 1956, with support from the Americans, South Vietnam backed out of the scheduled nationwide elections that would almost certainly have unified North and South Vietnam under communist rule. Mao began supporting efforts of the North Vietnamese communists and their leader, Ho Chi Minh, to foster communist insurgency in South Vietnam. Ho had a long history with the Chinese communists and had fought with the PLA in China against the Japanese during World War II. Perhaps more important, his was a rural communist revolution, just like Mao's. The Vietnamese revolution and Chinese support for it would become Mao's flagship example of why new communist revolutions in the developing world should lean toward China, not the Soviet Union. The Sino-Soviet ideological rivalry was growing.

Chinese advisers and Chinese supplies supported Ho in his struggle against the French in the First Indochina War, which ended with the 1954 French defeat at Dien Bien Phu and the negotiations in Geneva that followed it. In Ho's later war against South Vietnam and the United States from 1964 to 1975, Chinese material and personnel assistance to the Vietnamese communists was essential. In just the first four years, some 260,000 Chinese troops would rotate through Vietnam. Chinese histories claim that a large percentage of downed U.S. aircraft flying over North Vietnam were hit by gun positions manned by Chinese forces. At its peak, the Chinese presence in Vietnam was 170,000 troops in 1967. They were mostly involved in air defense and reconstructing infrastructure damaged in U.S. bombing runs. Beijing also provided a defensive guarantee that China would repel a ground invasion of North Vietnam if the United chose to cross the 17th parallel, just like they had repelled MacArthur in Korea after he had crossed the 38th. The geographically more distant Soviets could not match China on that score and the Vietnamese communists knew that.[12]

Khrushchev was much less interested in supporting revolutions in far-flung lands. Instead, he sought some sort of modus vivendi with the United States. While Vietnam bordered China, it was very far from the Soviet Union. Still, Khrushchev had to worry about the Soviets' reputation within the international communist movement in competition with Mao's China. So, before he fell from power in 1964, he began to increase Soviet support for revolutions in the developing world. Experts on Soviet foreign policy argue that Khrushchev's decision to transfer nuclear weapons to Castro's Cuba, which sparked the extremely dangerous Cuban Missile Crisis of 1962, was made in large part as a way to compete with Mao for the hearts and minds of the Cuban communists. Khrushchev became interested in North Vietnam in the early 1960s, and the Soviet Union under his successor, Leonid Brezhnev, supported Ho's cause much more robustly once the United States intervened directly in 1964. Until the Soviets and Chinese actually started firing on each other in 1969, the great beneficiaries of this competition for ideological leadership between Beijing and Moscow were leaders like Ho Chi Minh, who skillfully played the two communist allies against each other to maximize support for his revolution. The biggest losers in this struggle were arguably the United States and its anticommunist allies, who faced a better supplied and less compromising communist enemy in places like Vietnam.[13]

Downey would see some of the results of these geopolitical machinations when two American airmen shot down by Chinese antiaircraft gunners during the Vietnam War entered his prison. Downey says they had been shot down over North Vietnam. One of them, Philip Smith, had actually unintentionally strayed into Chinese airspace over Hainan Island when piloting a mission over the Gulf of Tonkin in 1965.[14] The Chinese claim that the second downed airman, Robert Flynn, was also shot down over Chinese airspace, but Flynn insists he was some twenty miles on the North Vietnamese side of the border with China in the summer of 1967. He was surprised to be taken into custody by what appeared to him to be Chinese troops. He claims that he was transferred to China for propaganda purposes so China could more effectively criticize the ramped-up U.S. bombing campaign at the time. Once under the control of Chinese troops, Flynn may also have been transferred to China to mask the large Chinese military presence in Vietnam at the time, of which Flynn claimed he was previously unaware. Like Downey, both Smith and Flynn would cross over into Hong Kong in early 1973 following the Nixon administration's rapprochement with China. The official U.S. position on Flynn's flight was that he was shot down within China, consistent with the official Chinese position. This was a source of great frustration for Flynn. He was the navigator on his doomed flight and prided himself on his skills.[15] It is unclear whether the American position was sincere or was simply adopted to avoid contradicting Beijing and thereby securing Flynn's release.

By supporting revolution in Vietnam and increasing tensions with the Soviet Union, Mao had adopted a very risky approach to the Cold War. He was confronting both global superpowers at the same time.

The year that Flynn was taken prisoner, 1967, was near the peak of Mao's radical foreign policy agenda. Not only was Chinese troop presence in Vietnam at its peak, but Beijing was busy scuttling proposed peace negotiations between the United States and the Vietnamese communists, even though both Washington and Moscow supported such peace talks. Mao warned the Vietnamese that they were a trap laid by the United States with the help of the Soviet Union, which had left the path of true communist revolution. Soviet material aid to the Vietnamese communists had grown sharply after the massive U.S. intervention that began in 1965, and it now outstripped Chinese material assistance. But Mao accused the Soviets of providing the aid as another trap: Moscow was trying to convince the Vietnamese communists to adopt a less aggressive stance toward revolution in South Vietnam. And Mao and his advisers reminded his Vietnamese comrades that only China could defend North Vietnam against an American ground invasion across the 17th parallel.[16]

What complicated Sino-Soviet relations further was Mao's next domestic political movement launched in 1966, the Great Proletarian Cultural Revolution (or Cultural Revolution, for short). This highly ideological campaign was an effort by Mao to destroy what he argued were conservative, Soviet-style bureaucratic attitudes within the Chinese Communist Party. Mao invited citizens, especially Chinese youth, to lash out at authority all around them for being insufficiently revolutionary and insufficiently loyal to Mao. Many youths, too young to remember the earlier revolution, seized the opportunity to rebel against their elders, brandishing the "Little Red Book" of Mao's quotations as an ideological bludgeon. Many citizens were already angry at their local party cadres for the suffering wrought by the Great Leap Forward, so Mao was lighting a match in a tinder box. In Beijing, Mao used the Cultural Revolution to purge his most powerful deputies, even Liu Shaoqi and Deng Xiaoping, two of the top five leaders at the time. Liu would die in prison of untreated medical conditions. Deng would bide his time in exile in the countryside until he returned to power in fits and starts in the 1970s before securing his position as China's supreme leader following Mao's death in 1976.[17]

Other Chinese elites suffered terribly. Peng Dehuai, the hero commander of the Chinese People's Volunteers in the Korean War, was publicly humiliated and beaten by Red Guards. He would eventually die in detention.[18] Many mid-level Chinese elites, particularly in the cities, were "sent down" to the countryside to learn from the rural poor how to be better revolutionary citizens. The technical and administrative brain drain from government, industry, and academia was enormous. People with bad family backgrounds—meaning their parents or grandparents were rich or middle class—were attacked and suppressed with the greatest vigor.

During this Cultural Revolution, the Chinese ideologues began to level scathing criticisms against the Soviet Union. Chinese citizens abroad would protest outside Soviet embassies around the world accusing Moscow of having gone "revisionist," selling out the true communist revolution. Chinese diplomats became involved in revolutionary activities in countries that had generally been cooperative with the PRC. Zhou's Five Principles of Peaceful Coexistence were in the rearview mirror now. Chinese in communist countries became brazen in their complaints that those countries were too close to the Soviets and too far from the true Maoist path. Back in Beijing in 1967, the Soviet Embassy was surrounded by angry Red Guards for two weeks, Soviet diplomats and their families suffered humiliating personal attacks, and the street outside the Soviet Embassy was renamed "Anti-Revisionist Boulevard."[19]

If there was anything more damaging than being associated with the Soviet Union in China in the second half of the 1960s, it was to be associated with the United States and its capitalist allies. Besides a "bad class" background, a major black mark on one's record was association with Americans and Westerners of all types. Red Guards set the British diplomatic compound in Beijing on fire.[20]

Downey saw at least this part of the Cultural Revolution from within his jail cell. He reports that his handler, Miss, was treated harshly within the prison. She was demoted from managing and interpreting for two prize prisoners, Downey and Fecteau, to carrying buckets of manure on a shoulder yoke. She also received frequent criticism in struggle sessions in the prison's exercise yard.

Downey reports that Miss came from a family that was well-off before the revolution. She had a supportive but condescending attitude toward poorer Chinese citizens. Such an attitude was the hallmark of an avant-garde Leninist Party led in large part by middle-class and upper-middle-class people like Mao, Zhou, and Lenin himself. Downey writes that Miss's less-educated peers could not have avoided noticing her condescension. The Cultural Revolution provided the ideal cover for these peers to settle that score. It gave the blessing of the "Great Helmsman," Chairman Mao, in meting out punishment to haughty elites.

Miss's fluency in English could hardly have helped her political situation. English was often a target of criticism by radical Red Guards. For Chinese citizens, knowing English was enough to earn one a beating; it was worse still if one had learned the language abroad or had been tutored before the revolution by foreign teachers or in international schools.[21] The professor of history Shen Zhihua reports that he was detained during the Cultural Revolution and accused of studying English.[22] America was still the enemy for China, and there were few actual Americans to bully and reeducate in China. So any Chinese with some connection to the United States would just have to do.

Downey was subject to political education classes himself during those years. From his description, these were not the rough, often violent struggle sessions to which "bad class" or "Western-oriented" Chinese were subjected. Estimates of deaths from political violence in the Cultural Revolution vary and credible statistics are hard to come by, but conservative estimates generally start at a million and range up to 1.6 million.[23]

One American whom Downey met and learned to admire in this period did not fare so well. Hugh Redmond had been detained in Shanghai in 1951 as he prepared to leave China. Downey reports that Redmond, a decorated World War II paratrooper, had moved to China before the Revolution and married a Russian woman he met there. Downey claims that Redmond remained after the Revolution to do business but was arrested as a spy. Downey refers to Redmond with great admiration. According to him, Redmond resisted all sorts of pressure from the CCP. Downey and Fecteau would sneak him small portions of food in the common area when they were outside their cells.

According to published histories, Redmond was indeed a spy who had been turned in to the CCP by his wife.[24] It is unclear whether

Downey knew this and, as a CIA officer himself, decided to keep it secret. Unlike all the other American prisoners, Redmond would not make it home. The CCP reported that he committed suicide in custody in 1970.[25] Downey never believed that story. He believed that Redmond likely died of illness for which he received insufficient medical treatment and the CCP covered this up by declaring that he died by his own hand.

We do not have reliable death statistics from the Cultural Revolution in part because many casualties of political attacks were reported as suicides rather than homicides, as Redmond very well might have been. And since family members were coerced to turn on each other, even children against their own parents, it would not be surprising if the suicide rate in China did skyrocket in those years. In that era in China, a grim term arose: "death by enforced suicide." Many thousands of people met this fate, and in certain periods of the Cultural Revolution they accounted for the vast majority of deaths related to politics in places as varied as Beijing and Yunnan.[26]

Ambassador Wang Bingnan himself would get caught up personally in the political and social turmoil of that time. After returning to the foreign ministry from Warsaw in 1964, Wang was a senior official there until 1967, when he was reportedly dragged into detention in the basement of a hotel by Red Guards. There, they reportedly showed him photographs of the battered and beaten corpse of his second wife, whom his captors said had committed suicide.[27] Wang survived, though he reportedly suffered a heart attack in detention. He mentioned to a visiting Johnson in the early 1980s that his wife, whom Johnson had met, did not survive the Cultural Revolution.

As for Redmond, it is clear that he paid the ultimate price for refusing to confess to espionage or allow himself to be politically indoctrinated. Coerced confession, which the CCP called "self-criticism," was the preferred tool of psychological control during the Cultural Revolution. Downey reports that the CCP did not even try to reeducate Redmond, but that did not prevent them from treating him harshly. Redmond's next-door neighbor in prison, Flynn, communicated with him by Morse code. Flynn said that Redmond expected to die in prison because of untreated health conditions. He died in 1970, the year before Kissinger's secret trip to China, which would eventually secure the prisoners' release. Later, Flynn said that Redmond had been tortured to death.[28]

Though Downey survived, he was hardly unscathed by the Cultural Revolution. One of the few bright spots in his life in prison would come to a cruel and abrupt halt during those years of radical turmoil in China. His mother and brother could no longer visit. Those periodic visits, which began in 1957 and continued through 1964, would stop until 1971, when the Nixon administration initiated diplomatic contact with the People's Republic of China.

19

FAMILY VISITS

AFTER MY life sentence was announced by Communist China to the world and the United States, I was allowed to send letters home and also allowed to receive letters and packages from home. The packages and literature continued reliably month after month to the very end of my twenty-year prison ordeal. All my mail and reading materials were heavily censored at the Chinese end. As for my immediate fate, I knew only what the Chinese chose to tell me; no contact with American diplomatic personnel was permitted. I had to deduce from slanted and stale Chinese government publications about events of the larger world. At one time or another, I was allowed to receive the *New Yorker, Sports News, Sports Illustrated*, the *New York Times* book review, *Yachting, Yale Alumni Magazine*, and *National Geographic.* From all of those sources, I learned to read between the lines, to extrapolate from omission, and to discount for propaganda. I assembled a much better picture of what was going on in the world than the Chinese ever suspected.

I continued to revise my own forecasts of release according to the fragmented information that found its way to my cell. Fecteau got a copy of the *Herald Tribune* almanac in 1958; listed among significant events of 1957 was a Communist Chinese government proposal to release its American prisoners if the United States allowed the exchange of journalists. The then Secretary of State John Foster Dulles had vetoed the overture as "blackmail." I knew then and there that this was the last nail in my coffin. Dulles would not lend legitimacy to the Communist regime by permitting its newsmen to write about it; Fecteau and I were the pawns to be sacrificed in this political struggle. My only chance for release would have to come from another administration.

When the Eisenhower presidency gave way to John F. Kennedy's, I watched for new incentives offered to China. I had watched Kennedy's political progress with high hopes, since he, too, was an Irish Catholic and had gone to Choate School, although he attended Harvard instead of Yale. His success nourished my own dreams of entering politics someday. One morning I heard Fecteau calling down the corridor to me in an unprecedented breach of prison rules: "Kennedy's been shot!" The report was contained in a couple of paragraphs on the fourth page of the *Peking People's Daily*, which Fecteau's cellmate, Ma Hua, had been reading. The report was so brief, it made no sense. I couldn't imagine what really had happened, but even reading the news in a cell nine thousand miles away, the death of a President whom I had never seen hit me like a body blow. Later my mother sent me a copy of the *Warren Commission Hearings*; it reads like a gripping novel.

Just as all the presidential transitions made me reevaluate my chance for release, so did visits by my family. There were six visits: three by my mother and brother Bill together, two by my mother alone, and one by Bill alone. Though my family had negotiated at length with both governments to arrange the visits, I was never informed of them in advance. The Chinese didn't consider it their job to tell me, and my family feared that last-minute complications, of which there were many, made writing ahead imprudent. So their visits were announced with the suddenness of an old school chum telephoning to say he was in town and inviting himself over.

January 10, 1958, was the date for the first visit, arranged again by the International Red Cross. The day before, a guard opened the door to my cell and instructed me to follow him to the Warden's office. There I learned my mother and brother were in Peking and they would visit the prison the next day. The Warden also told me that my family might be anxious about my fate and that I could feel free to discuss my "crimes" with them and "bring them comfort." His suggestion raised one of many worries in my mind associated with their arrival. The Communists, I guessed, expected me to confirm my guilt to my family, and my spontaneous confession would then be used in China's ongoing propaganda war against the United States. Since I was still in a Chinese prison, my government might still be insisting that I was a Defense Department civilian, which had been my cover story. Besides, I did not yet know what was happening in the negotiations conducted by my government on my behalf. Again, I was confronted with a moral crisis. If I spoke, would it be a form of betrayal to my government? If I didn't, would it jeopardize my chances to be released? My other worries about this visit concerned my family. I fretted about the expense of the trip and the physical strain it would be for my mother, who was then sixty years old. In addition, I worried that the Communists might detain them. Under all these specific worries was a growing emotional tension about seeing my mother and brother; it would only emphasize how destitute my prison life was and weaken the shell of defense I had built.

I solved one problem. I decided to tell my family I had been given permission to talk about my "crimes" and then be guided by their reaction. In the morning, I got an extra bath and a shave, things usually allowed once a week. Finally, in the early afternoon, Miss escorted me off the corridor to another prison wing and a sparsely furnished office. A photographer and a woman with a tape recorder soon joined us, confirming my fear the Communists would use the visit for propaganda purposes. I waited with them a few minutes until the door opened. If either my mother or brother looked older than when I last saw them seven years ago, I didn't notice at first—they looked great to me. We all immediately began laughing and hugging and doing our best to ignore the location of our outwardly happy reunion. Then I noticed that Bill had changed from a nineteen-year-old boy to a six-foot-two young man.

My family brought me a bonanza of food and books and told me about their trip. They had traveled with the mothers of Fecteau and Redmond and had been besieged by the press until the moment they boarded the plane for China. Their visit was an historic one. They were the first Americans citizens authorized by the U.S. State Department to visit the People's Republic of China. The drama of mothers enduring hardship for their endangered sons was certain to get a lot of press coverage when they returned home. I dreaded discussing my case with them. We had been talking for some minutes when I decided to mention it.

"Mother," I began, "the Chinese told me I'm allowed to speak to you about my crimes."

At the mention of the word "crimes" the whole room grew tense and my mother began to cry. I looked over her shoulder at my brother, and he shook his head to signify that the subject should be dropped.[1] I inwardly heaved a sigh of relief and changed the subject. And when it became clear there would be no confession, the cameraman and his partner left, visibly disgruntled. In all, my mother and brother stayed about two hours, saying they would come back twice more before they left China.

The next day the Warden called me out of my cell and asked why I had failed to discuss my crimes. I told him that he was mistaken and that she had cried when I brought up the subject of "my crimes." The Warden looked displeased. The next time my mother and brother came back, only the Warden, Miss, and a guard attended, and they never mentioned that particular issue again.

If my refusal to mention my crimes damaged my situation, I never knew about it. The Warden never repeated his suggestion on any subsequent family visits. The incident was typical of the Communist Chinese; they applied as much pressure as they could to elicit the response they wanted without actually demanding that response. Then, if the pressure were resisted, they would either drop the whole matter or impose some kind of punishment. Except for that single confession attempt, they did nothing to exploit my family's visits. In fact, they treated my mother and brother courteously, allowing them to tour Peking and even helping them to shop. My mother brought me new treats every time she came to the prison. Whatever luxuries had been eliminated under the Communists, some survived, and my mother found some excellent French vanilla ice cream, which I devoured with pleasure. She also bought less perishable food like cheeses and nuts, which kept my cell larder stocked for months after she left.

At the end of their first week in Peking, my mother and Bill applied for a week's extension on their visa, which was granted, so they were able to pay me three more two-hour visits before they left the country. The same pattern was followed on their later visits in 1960, 1962, 1964, and 1971. My brother Bill visited me alone in 1959 for one week; he was working in a U.S. bank in Singapore to be near me. Even our conversations followed the same pattern; we avoided some topics. They brought me up to date on friends and relatives back home— who had gotten married, who had got what job, who had died, and who was doing well in school. Since our meetings were monitored, we dared not discuss even rudimentary questions such as how I had been treated during my years in prison or what Washington had told my mother about my chances for release. During all her visits, my mother generally maintained a brave front until the last moment of the last day. Then she cried. Miss and the Warden, unrelenting in their scorn for me, were visibly moved by her tears.

On the final day of their first visit in 1958, the Chinese allowed us to have a kind of party. Fecteau and I were brought in together for a feast prepared by our mothers and Mrs. Redmond, who had returned from visiting her son Hugh Redmond, imprisoned in Shanghai. Some of the food they had prepared themselves, and some they had bought already cooked. It seemed the Chinese invented take-out food first, as well as macaroni and gunpowder. The stores sold neatly engineered, three-piece food pails that were ideal for transporting a three-course hot meal. The food at our prison banquet was delicious and affection abundant. All three mothers treated Fecteau and me as their own sons.

During that first visit, my mother had been able to get an audience with the Chinese Minister of Health, a woman named Li Teh-yuan, who was also the director of the Chinese Red Cross. She was the widow of "The Christian General," a warlord who had converted to Christianity and converted his troops accordingly. She expressed sympathy for my mother but said I could not be released and denied my mother's request to see Zhou Enlai.

Between trips to the prison, my brother and the two mothers were taken to the Summer Palace, the Temple of Heaven, and to a school. When my mother was taken to the Peking Opera, however, she found the music so discordant she asked to leave after the first act. On her 1960 solo visit, she encountered Edgar Snow, an American journalist,[2] who happened to be staying in the same hotel. Snow had known Mao before the Revolution succeeded and was one of the most trusted American friends of the Communist leaders. Snow kindly sent me a practical gift with literary overtones. My mother brought it with her when she came to the prison the next time; it was one of his shirts, complete with ink-stained pocket. I liked the irony of China's greatest American friend giving the shirt off his back to China's greatest American criminal. I wore the shirt until it disintegrated, as did most of my clothes.

The Cultural Revolution interrupted my family's visits. There was a seven-year hiatus before they made their final trip in the fall of 1971. By then, I was watching with restrained hope the diplomatic overtures of President Richard Nixon and Secretary of State Henry Kissinger. The United States ping-pong team toured China in the spring. Then, in the summer I was stunned when interpreter Woo Woo called me to his office and read the announcement that Kissinger had met the Communist leaders. Kissinger had made a secret flight from Pakistan to Peking, and it had been arranged that Nixon would visit China early the following year. I tried not to betray my excitement. When Woo Woo asked me what I thought of the news, I told him it was inevitable that the Chinese people and the American people would be friends. But inwardly I was packing my bags; the visits signified the strongest prospects for our release in nineteen years.

My private hope had soared. When my mother and Bill arrived in November some weeks later, on her fifth visit, Woo Woo advised me that I could tell them that my case was being reviewed by the government and that the prison authorities had given me a good report on my conduct. My dilemma was similar to the one I had faced on her first visit. Now, however, I didn't worry about abetting a propaganda effort if I talked about my crimes; I worried, instead, about encouraging my mother too much. At seventy-five and in frail health, she might be devastated if the release was promised and then postponed. After an agonizing night before she arrived, I decided to inform her of the hopeful news. She was thrilled and seemed to understand that nothing was certain, though she and Bill went home expecting my release any week.

In December, when the Communists announced they would release two Americans, our families and the media, which were following our case closely, assumed that the pair would be Fecteau and me. But what ensued was what I had feared for my mother.

The signs that Fecteau was to be released first grew over the next few days as he began to receive his meals ahead of the rest of the prisoners on the corridor and then got an unscheduled medical examination. Fecteau's old theory about watching the barber for hints of freedom did come true for him. The barber visited him and he was allowed a bath at an unscheduled time. I knew then Fecteau was definitely going home without me.

One evening in early December, the corridor was very quiet, when I heard the telltale footsteps stop at Fecteau's cell. His door was unbolted and a few minutes later I heard the footsteps proceed off the corridor, this time joined by the peculiar shuffling rhythm I knew to be Fecteau's. Then I heard a jeep engine start and I knew that Fecteau was going home. Nineteen years and one month before, we had been shot down together. I still believed my own freedom would be given to me soon, but I could only guess when. The corridor was now deadly quiet, and I had never felt more alone.

I was deflated but not surprised. I had always suspected that the Chinese's meticulous sense of form would require them to keep me longer than Fecteau, since I was considered the greater criminal, and since my sentence had been more severe. Over the years, Fecteau and I had had very few opportunities to converse freely. When we did talk about release, it tended to be about ice cold beers and the steaming hot showers we would have when we got out. Fecteau dreamed of spending weeks on a tropical island then returning to his old neighborhood and finding work as a football coach. My dream was hiking the Cape Hatteras National Seashore, seeing Yale football games, and entering law school and a public service job.

A few days later, Woo Woo finally told me that Dick had gone home and my sentence was being reviewed. I would not be released immediately, but a reduction of my sentence was possible.

Not long afterward, I was led to a one-story building abutting the exercise courtyard. Three unsmiling military officers were waiting for me. They reminded me of my original sentencing, and they asked predictable questions about my conditions and my crimes. I thought that it would be typical of them to reduce my sentence to ten more years and expect me to be grateful. I knew I couldn't endure ten more years. Five years, I could handle, I told myself. And five more years was what they told me. I calculated it would be December 1976. I would be forty-six years old, and I would have spent half of my life in prison. I responded to the tribunal's generosity with a perfunctory "Thank you."

For the first time in nineteen years my future was defined. Knowing how long I had to serve gave me the impulse to start counting the days to my release, but I refused to follow it. I preferred to think that I still could be freed at any time through negotiation, and I could forget the days more easily if I did not scrutinize and log each one as it passed. The fixed sentence also relieved me of the pretense of paying attention to their political preaching. I knew that they had to recognize that they had exacted a severe punishment for my crimes. They could no longer lecture me about their benevolence. So when Woo Woo told me I was to move into another cell, I flared up and told him I preferred to stay where I was. As a prisoner, my cell remained one of my few possessions. The outburst, however, was also evidence of how strained I was. The Chinese themselves had begun to treat me warily, precisely because I so rarely acted up. The longer I maintained an apparently calm demeanor, the more they feared an explosion. In the face of my anger, Woo Woo withdrew his order. I was permitted to take what I wanted from the books, food, and clothing Fecteau had left. But I was not allowed to share the booty with Smith and Flynn.

After Fecteau's release, I submerged myself in daily routines but still kept an eye on the rapidly warming relations between the United States and China. When President Nixon made his historic visit to China in early 1972, my hope for an earlier release again inflamed. I observed my twentieth Christmas in prison with a solitary meal of special prison food and some treats from home. I knew my mother's

Christmas would be another sad one as well. I regretted that I had caused her so much heartache.

In early March 1973, a Friday evening, the announcement came from Woo Woo. He found me in the television room, a place I was permitted to visit about every six weeks. I was watching a ping-pong match with a guard.

"Downey, I have good news for you," said Woo Woo, bursting in the door. He continued, "Our government is going to release you. I do not know when it is going to happen, but when it does, it will be quick. You are being released because of your good conduct, your mother's illness, and because of the changed relationship of our two countries." He waited a minute for my reaction. I kept my composure.

He said with more urgency, "It may happen any time. You had better go back to your cell and get ready."

I looked at Woo Woo and told him what was uppermost on my mind.

"If it is okay with you, I'd rather see the end of the ping-pong match," I said.

Whatever Woo Woo thought my reaction would be, he didn't expect that, and he was utterly nonplussed. But he let me watch the rest of the match. And I did. Back at my cell, I prepared for bed and fell asleep after only a few more tosses and turns than usual. My feeling was simply, "It is about time." My reserved reaction was not to deprive Woo Woo of a melodramatic ecstasy from me. I had locked so much of myself far away to survive imprisonment that it would take some time before I found enough of myself to feel like celebrating anything.

The next day, Saturday, Woo Woo told me I would probably leave on Sunday; he added excitely, "The government has made special arrangements. And today, you may visit shops for souvenirs."

Souvenirs! I looked at Woo Woo with exasperation on my face and said, "No thanks!" Woo Woo was again disturbed by my response. I was his most cheerful prisoner and my refusal to accept his government's supposedly generous offer made him worry that I was more hostile and a lot less "reformed" than he had thought. He said nothing and scurried out of my cell only to return a few minutes later, asking if I would be willing to loan Phil Smith money. Smith, who was also to be released, was Woo Woo's most troublesome charge. Woo

Woo had to have been surprised that Smith had accepted the shopping trip offer as much as I had rejected it. I lent Smith forty dollars from the money my family had left. Later in the day, he returned with some rather exquisite ivory carvings. I wished I had not been so petulant. It was a sure sign we were being released, since such fraternization had never before been allowed.

The sky, when I finally glimpsed it on Sunday morning, was low and glowering, not good weather for flying. Soon after breakfast Woo Woo appeared and told me to collect my things for the trip to Peking Airport where I would board the weekly flight to Canton. From there, I would cross the border to Hong Kong. My things, consisting of the accumulated books, magazines, and clothing of twenty years and whatever food and toiletries I had not used, were to be left behind. I didn't want to take any of it with me. I wanted to leave prison exactly the way I had entered, with just the clothes on my back. I told Woo Woo so, and there was a debate among the prison staff before they gave in. Their problem, I suspected, was that my imperialist possessions could not be given to the people, yet as thrifty Communists they were loath to destroy useful goods.

I finally left the prison carrying one small bundle and accompanied by a guard, a new interpreter, and another party official. The drive by jeep to the airport took forty-five minutes. We arrived midmorning, well before the scheduled noon flight to Canton. Just before twelve, the loud speaker announced in English that the flight would be delayed an hour because of weather conditions. A couple of hours later, the speaker announced another delay, and then "the flight is canceled." I was told to gather up my stuff. We all climbed back into the jeep, drove the forty-five minutes back to the prison, and I returned to the corridor I thought I had left forever. When my cell door slammed shut, I began to laugh and couldn't stop.

It was another in a series of mishaps that were the story of my life. I had been sent to fight for a country I didn't know, to train guerrillas whose language I didn't speak; I had been shot down on a flight I wasn't supposed to be on and sentenced to life in prison for sticking a pole out of an airplane. Now I was being set free, and bad weather had grounded my ride home. With my luck, I figured China and the United States would go to war that evening.

I did not spend another night in prison, however. After supper I was taken back to the airport to meet a military flight, specially arranged for me by the Communist government. It arrived in Canton sometime after midnight. I was taken to a guest house on the outskirts of the city. When the morning came, I noticed the weather was wonderfully lush and warm compared to Peking's usual March bluster. After breakfast we drove by jeep to the train station, and we were soon chugging through the south China countryside. Rice fields stretched off in all directions. I was working harder and harder to keep my excitement under control. I did not sleep, yet I did not feel tired.

The train reached the end of the line at the Shum Chu border station, a low, featureless building of concrete and brick. We disembarked and I was told to wait in an empty room. Whoever came to meet me would find me dressed in the traveling attire of a Mao suit, high-topped sneakers, and a Boston Red Sox cap that Fecteau had left behind. The next person through the door was an American in the uniform of the Red Cross. He was flushed with emotion and inquired with great sincerity after my well-being. I told him I couldn't be better; then he was called out of the room without explanation. I wondered if something had gone wrong, but he reemerged a few minutes later and assured me we would cross the border momentarily.

Free territory itself was visible through the window. All we had to do was step from the border station and traverse a covered bridge that crossed a narrow ravine. It was so close and so simple, but what was delaying us? A diminutive Chinese party official who had traveled with us all the way from Peking stepped forward. Our party of six had included two guards, an interpreter, a purser, and this man, whose role I was unable to decipher. Now he extracted a paper from his tunic pocket and sternly read from it. It was a parting admonition that reminded me I had committed crimes against the people of China and that the people had forgiven me for my crimes. It ended by urging me to work for good relations between our two countries. Then he put the paper away and told me to go.

Go I did, my heart beating faster as I turned my back on China. I crossed the wooden bridge into the British colony of Hong Kong. A small crowd of people were waiting for me on the other side. Among them were British officials and officials from the State Department and the CIA, as well as a photographer. I smiled at them, but the person who attracted my attention was a bear-like British policeman in full uniform. I felt a little diffident striding toward him in my Mao suit and sneakers. But when I reached him, he threw himself back and snapped off a magnificent salute. I felt a lump in my throat, "Boy, this is the first act of dignity shown me in twenty years." I was finally back among friends.

20

U.S.-PRC RAPPROCHEMENT AND JACK DOWNEY'S RELEASE

1968–1973

Thomas J. Christensen

T
HOUGH HE would not be released from prison for five more years, 1968 was a very important year for Downey. It was that year that Americans largely concluded that the war against the Vietnamese communists could not be won at acceptable costs, at least not by them. From Beijing's perspective, this rendered even smaller the prospect of the proxy war in Indochina escalating into a full-scale Sino-American war.

At the same time, from spring 1968 through March 1969, ideological conflict between Beijing and Moscow would morph into direct hostilities along their shared border. Earlier in the decade, the two communist superpowers had been competing more and more to support revolutionary parties in places like Vietnam and Cuba and accusing each other of departing from the true path of Marxism-Leninism. In early 1969, this turned into a direct Sino-Soviet military confrontation. With America's desire to exit the Vietnam War and the escalating tensions between China and the USSR, rapprochement between China and the United States seemed both possible and desirable for Mao and the newly elected American president, Richard Nixon.

Over the next two and a half years, Beijing and Washington moved in fits and starts toward the diplomatic breakthroughs of the early 1970s. In July 1971, Henry Kissinger secretly went to Beijing to meet

Premier Zhou Enlai. In February of the next year, Nixon made his historic trip to the PRC. Sino-American rapprochement would also win the early release first of Richard Fecteau in late 1971 and, eventually, Jack Downey in 1973.

1968 AS A TURNING POINT

The year began with the Vietnamese communists' Tet Offensive, a full-scale assault on military and government positions in South Vietnam. As a military operation, Tet was an utter disaster for the North Vietnamese communist forces and the Viet Cong, their insurgent allies in the south. They lost almost every battle, beaten back by U.S. forces, South Vietnamese forces, and even by diplomats and security details with sidearms at the U.S. Embassy in Saigon. But while the Vietnamese communist military losses were extensive, they had won a political battle. The breadth and intensity of the attack shook the Americans back home. The government and especially the military had been exaggerating successes in the war effort and systematically underestimating and underreporting the remaining strength and resolve of the Vietnamese communists.

Suddenly, after three years of war, the enemy appeared to the American public to be much more powerful and resolute than they had been told, and there was no evident end in sight. Walter Cronkite, the CBS newscaster and among the most trusted men in America, appeared shaken by the breaking news of Tet. He suggested on air that the government had not been truthful about the war. The political fallout was dramatic and immediate. President Johnson would decide not to run for a second full term in 1968. And the antiwar movement in America, previously limited to a relatively small number of vocal activists, became much more mainstream. Public optimism about the war in Vietnam, which was still relatively strong before Tet, turned suddenly into widespread pessimism.[1]

At home, America was in turmoil. Civil rights protests sometimes morphed into violent inner-city riots, especially following the April 4 assassination of Martin Luther King Jr.and later, the assassination of Robert F. Kennedy, a leading Democratic Party candidate for the presidential nomination. These tragic events were followed by a Democratic National Convention in Chicago that was full of protests, riots, and widespread police brutality. America hardly looked like a nation with the capacity or desire to fight a new war in Asia with Mao's PRC.

It was in this environment that Nixon secured the Republican Party's presidential nomination and later the presidency itself. Downey's mother, Mary, could not have been encouraged by this. Little in Nixon's past suggested that he would be willing to make the necessary concessions to open relations with Mao's China. He had cut his teeth in Washington after World War II as a strident supporter of Joseph McCarthy's cynical efforts to weed out alleged communists from American society. He was Dwight D. Eisenhower's vice president when he and his secretary of state, John Foster Dulles, rejected Zhou's proposals to open up contacts between the two nations.

There were two early clues, however, that suggested Nixon might be open to a more pragmatic approach to the PRC than his Republican predecessors if the opportunity presented itself. One was an unusual article that he published in *Foreign Affairs* in 1967, in which he suggested that China needed to be brought in from the cold and that, under the right conditions, the United States should pursue closer contacts between the two nations.[2] A second clue was his campaign rhetoric about his desire to end the Vietnam War, albeit on terms consistent with national security interests.[3] To end such a war would require direct, high-level diplomatic engagement with the Vietnamese communists.

In the previous Republican administration, in which Nixon served as vice president, Dulles had refused to engage the PRC entourage at Geneva in 1954 and had discouraged his diplomats there from any negotiation with their PRC counterparts. The Eisenhower administration also refused to join the United Kingdom and France in signing the Geneva Accords, the negotiated settlement that ended France's war with the Vietnamese communists. The eventual formation of the bilateral Geneva talks in August 1955 was really the exception and not the rule for U.S.-China diplomacy under Eisenhower. But Nixon's article and his campaign rhetoric suggested he might take a less rigid and more pragmatic stance toward Asian communism, if the right opportunities presented themselves.

Those opportunities indeed presented themselves in 1969, when the last eight years of ratcheting Sino-Soviet tensions broke out into direct military conflict. During the Cultural Revolution, the Soviets had begun building up forces along the border they shared with China's northeast and northwest and along the long Chinese border with Mongolia, a Soviet client state at the time. Though these deployments had been building for years, they suddenly looked far more sinister to the Chinese because of what had just happened in Eastern Europe. In 1968, Alexander Dubcek, the leader of the Czechoslovakian Communist Party, responded to public pressure by instituting liberalizing reforms that reduced the state's grip on the economy and allowed more freedom of expression and political competition. Fearing a dangerous precedent for communist authoritarianism, Leonid Brezhnev, leader of the Soviet Union, ordered armored Soviet and Warsaw Pact forces to invade Prague. They put down the protests, removed Dubcek from power, and restored a pro-Soviet government.[4]

Mao himself was no pro-reform liberal, but he had good reason for concern as he watched the Soviet invasion of the Czechoslovakian capital and "the Brezhnev Doctrine" that accompanied it. According to the doctrine, any previously communist government aligned with the USSR that left the true Marxist-Leninist path, as defined by Moscow, must be corrected, which could mean Soviet invasion and the overthrow of its wayward leadership. In the Sino-Soviet ideological struggle within the communist camp in the 1960s, Moscow and Beijing routinely labeled each other's ruling party "revisionist." Suddenly, Soviet troops along the Chinese border began to look ominous indeed.[5]

Just weeks before a major CCP meeting in April 1969, Mao ordered an ambush on Soviet forces on Zhenbao Island in the Ussuri River. Both sides suffered hundreds of casualties, and it would go down as the first major military clash between two nuclear-armed nations in world history.[6] Once again, Mao proved—as he had proven before by ordering the crossing of the Yangtze River in 1949, the crossing of the Yalu in 1950, the shelling of Quemoy and Matsu in 1954 and 1958, and the deployment of many tens of thousands of troops to fight the Americans in Vietnam—that he was hardly shy about the use of force to achieve his political and military objectives.

Why did Mao so boldly attack his much more powerful ally? Experts offer three major explanations. These arguments are not necessarily mutually exclusive, and perhaps a combination of all three was at work. One possible reason was domestic. To exploit a clear external threat would force greater internal party unity after three years of chaos and factionalism in the Cultural Revolution. The second possibility was that Mao wanted to deter the Soviets by demonstrating Chinese resolve. He intended to remove any misconception in Moscow that it could treat China as it had Czechoslovakia. This argument seems highly credible because Mao—as he demonstrated in Korea and in the Taiwan Strait in 1954—had a tendency to use force to counter trends running against his interest. Mao may also have been sending a signal to the new Nixon administration. The Sino-Soviet rift is real, deep, and here to stay, so now is an opportunity for Washington and Beijing to improve their bilateral political relations.[7]

Although Moscow chose not to escalate the conflict, the Soviets seemed as much provoked as deterred by Mao's gambit. The Soviet build-up in Mongolia and along the shared border with China would continue through the 1970s, eventually constituting around fifty infantry divisions, more forces than the Soviets deployed in Eastern Europe to confront NATO.[8] The Soviets never invaded with those forces, but one prominent Chinese historian suggests that Mao himself was surprised and displeased by the intensity of the Soviet reaction.[9]

THE U.S.-PRC BREAKTHROUGH: 1969–1972

If Mao intended to impress Washington with his anti-Soviet credentials by moving against Soviet forces, this signal was fully received and understood by the Nixon administration. Kissinger, a Harvard professor, assumed his role as Nixon's national security adviser in January, two months before the Zhenbao ambush. Kissinger was aware of Nixon's earlier *Foreign Affairs* article regarding a potential opening with China, and it was clear even before the Sino-Soviet clash that this was the direction in which Nixon wanted to move. But in his White House memoir, Kissinger writes that he did not take the idea seriously until he saw the reports of the Sino-Soviet border conflict. At the time, U.S. officials believed, incorrectly, that the Soviets had initiated the attack, which made the PRC seem even more threatened, and therefore even more reliable as a potential diplomatic partner of the United States.[10]

The summer of 1969 saw several clashes along the border with the USSR in China's northwest Xinjiang region, and there were hints that the Soviets might launch a preemptive strike against China's nascent nuclear weapons arsenal.[11] In August, Nixon suggested to his top advisers that the United States shared one core interest with the PRC: opposition to the USSR. Kissinger called this "a revolutionary moment in U.S. foreign policy: an American president declared that we had a strategic interest in the survival of a major Communist country with which we had had no meaningful contact for twenty years and against which we had fought a war and engaged in two military confrontations."[12]

Of course, the Nixon administration also faced the knotty problem of withdrawing from the Vietnam War on acceptable terms. Washington knew that the Vietnamese communists had long relied on Mao's China and that China had actively worked to scuttle peace negotiations between Hanoi and Washington during the Johnson administration. The Soviets had encouraged Ho Chi Minh to enter such negotiations as early as 1965, but Mao had rejected the idea, warning his Vietnamese comrades that this was a trap set at their expense by corrupt Soviet "revisionists" who only wanted to appease the American enemy.[13]

The Americans believed that as the Sino-Soviet rivalry sharpened to an outright conflict, this might soften Mao's attitudes. In 1968, China began removing most of its forces from Vietnam and, late in the year, became much more receptive to the idea of peace talks between Washington and Hanoi, which had begun in that year, the last of the Johnson administration.[14] If Washington could coordinate with Beijing, this could ease the Nixon administration's considerable burden in ending on acceptable terms an increasingly unpopular war that it had inherited from its Democratic Party predecessors, Kennedy and Johnson.

In Nixon's first year as president, American diplomats stationed in nations that also had relations with the PRC began reaching out to their Chinese counterparts. Beijing could not help but notice this, and that was the point. Walter Stoessel, the U.S. ambassador in Warsaw, was ordered to initiate contacts with the Chinese officials in the Polish capital. Through his efforts, the ambassadorial talks in Warsaw were restarted in January 1970.[15]

These breakthroughs were all the more extraordinary because war was still raging in Indochina between the United States and China's communist allies in Vietnam. Events in that war would delay the rapprochement. In April 1970, Nixon ordered the invasion of Cambodia to root out Vietnamese communist bases along what was called the Ho Chi Minh Trail. This led to intense protests in America, especially at universities. At Kent State, the National Guard fired upon a crowd of protesting students, killing four people. Beijing protested as well, breaking off the Warsaw talks in opposition to the escalation. It was only after U.S. forces withdrew in June that diplomatic contacts between the Chinese and Americans were re-started.[16]

On October 1, Mao sent a signal to Washington that he wanted to begin talks at the highest level. October 1 is National Day in the PRC, the celebration of its founding. At the traditional festivities in Tiananmen Square, Mao invited the American journalist Edgar Snow to stand next to him on the rostrum, where he told Snow that he would welcome a visit by Nixon.[17] Later that month, *Time* magazine published an interview with Nixon, who made what Kissinger called a "pregnant" remark. He said, "If there is anything I want to do before I die, it is to go to China. If I don't, I want my children to."[18]

By year's end, leaders from the two governments began communicating through the governments of third countries, especially Pakistan, about the prospects of more formal diplomatic talks, precisely what Zhou Enlai had sought in the mid-1950s. In January 1971, Zhou signaled that there was just one single stumbling block keeping them from a breakthrough in bilateral relations: Taiwan. It seemed to Kissinger that the ongoing confrontation on different sides of the war in Vietnam would no longer prevent contact between Beijing and Washington.[19] The geopolitical stage had been set for U.S.-PRC rapprochement.

In an interview with the author, Kissinger summed up the Nixon administration's reversal of past policies toward Mao's China: "Ours was a different kind of negotiation. We moved from a pattern of confrontation and non-recognition to a pattern of diplomatic contact and gradual sharing of objectives on which we could cooperate, including the containment of the Soviet Union."[20]

Nixon's approach was the polar opposite of Eisenhower's. Eisenhower and Dulles had tried to isolate Beijing diplomatically and humiliate it publicly, even on issues like the detention of two confessed spies. During the Eisenhower years, Washington never even admitted privately to China that Downey and Fecteau were spies. Instead, the U.S. government publicly dismissed those accusations as lies and political propaganda. Dulles also rejected Beijing's requests for people-to-people exchanges, calling them "blackmail." It was as if Downey and Fecteau were common American citizens who had been snatched off the street, whisked away to a Chinese prison, and held for political ransom. The proposal for people-to-people contact between the two countries was just another communist trick that could only benefit Beijing at Washington's expense.

In contrast, the Nixon administration began approaching Beijing through several channels and treating its government with respect. In a government report from February 1971, the first time in such an official document, the United States government referred to China by its formal name, "the People's Republic of China."[21] The next month, the government offered blanket permission for American citizens to visit the PRC, a stark contrast with Dulles's policy in 1955 of refusing permission for travel there by American journalists and, initially, even by Mrs. Downey, whom Zhou invited to visit her son during the January 1955 Hammarskjöld mission to Beijing.[22]

The starkest contrast from the Eisenhower years came at an international ping-pong tournament in Japan. Both American and Chinese teams were in attendance, and some of the players became friends. Mao and Zhou saw in this a fine opportunity to build bridges. They overrode a resistant Chinese foreign ministry, which was almost certainly paralyzed by fears related to the Cultural Revolution, and ordered the PRC national team to invite the American team to visit China for a tournament.[23] American diplomats in Japan accepted the invitation.[24]

When the American team visited China the next month, they offered to host the Chinese team in the United States the following April, a venture supported by a relatively new U.S.-based nonprofit called the National Committee on U.S.-China Relations.[25] Such was born what the press would term "ping-pong diplomacy," a phenomenon popularized in the Hollywood blockbuster *Forrest Gump*.

Kissinger credited Zhou for this brilliant tactic. A friendly sporting event could lower the emotional and political obstacles to the high-level government contact that Zhou had sought with the United States since the 1950s. And if, for some reason, the United States continued to refuse such contacts after this very friendly and very public event, Washington, not Beijing, would appear to be the stubborn party.[26] World opinion was peculiarly important to the PRC at the time because Beijing was lobbying to replace Chiang Kai-shek's Republic of China in the China seat at the United Nations, which it finally did in October 1971. Zhou himself greeted the U.S. ping pong team at a welcoming event at the Great Hall of the People.[27]

In the coming months, Nixon and Kissinger used the Pakistan channel to arrange for a secret visit to China. In July, Kissinger traveled to Beijing to exchange broad-ranging views on issues around the world, explore the aforementioned areas of potential cooperation, and prepare the way for Nixon's summit with Mao early the following year.[28] When Nixon visited in February, Washington and Beijing finessed their differences and jointly issued "the Shanghai Communiqué," which included tracts in which each side individually offered its own quite different viewpoint on Taiwan's status in relation to the mainland. The PRC, of course, said it was the only legitimate government of China and Taiwan belonged to China. The United States only went so far as to "acknowledge" without dispute the view of Chinese on both sides of the Taiwan Strait that there is one China and Taiwan is part of it. But Washington did not affirmatively accept that Chinese view as its own, thus preserving the intentional American ambiguity on Taiwan's sovereignty created by Truman when, at the onset of the Korean War, he ordered troops into Korea and the navy into the Taiwan Strait. The U.S. legal position on Taiwan's undetermined sovereign status remains to this day.[29]

Washington and Beijing's agree-to-disagree statement on Taiwan allowed the United States and China to move on to particularly pressing issues for the Americans: containment of the Soviets and negotiation of a peace agreement in Vietnam. The common interest in opposing the Soviets would take concrete form in late 1971 as U.S. officials began sharing with Beijing sensitive intelligence data regarding Soviet deployments on the Chinese border.[30] And while Mao and Zhou were not going to give up their long-standing support for the Vietnamese communists, soon after the Kissinger visit in 1971, Zhou traveled to Hanoi and urged his comrades to negotiate in good faith with the Americans and limit their demands by focusing on the withdrawal of U.S. forces from the south. Although Zhou was not particularly successful in convincing the Vietnamese communists to moderate their demands, the spirit behind his message demonstrated a shift in Beijing's strategy. China was now actively promoting peace negotiations between Hanoi and Washington instead of obstructing them.[31]

SECRECY AND PAIN

Kissinger's trip in July 1971 was shrouded in secrecy. He embarked from Pakistan after feigning an illness there. Not even Japan, America's closest ally in Asia, was informed in advance. Even William Rogers, Nixon's secretary of state, was kept in the dark until the last minute. This secrecy carried over to the details of the U.S.-PRC conversations as well. It was perhaps necessary to secure the early release of Fecteau in 1971 and Downey in 1973. But for those fifteen months after Fecteau was released and before Downey joined him, that same secrecy left Downey's mother and brother frustrated and suspicious. They worried that his release was not on Nixon's agenda during the outreach to China. When Nixon went to China in February

1972 and returned without her son, Mrs. Downey already had a jaded view regarding persistent promises from U.S. officials that winning his release was a high priority. And learning that Fecteau had been released in December of the previous year could only have frustrated her more.[32]

What Downey's family didn't know was that his release was always on the Nixon administration's diplomatic agenda, but it was kept a closely held secret. As Kissinger said in an interview, "From the first visit, I never failed to raise Downey's case. Since someone extremely close to the President was raising the issue so often, the Chinese had to know it was an issue of high importance to the President."[33] The archival record bears this out: Kissinger consistently requested Downey's release in diplomatic discussions with Chinese officials.[34] Chinese historical coverage of Downey's case similarly notes the fidelity with which Kissinger pursued his release, noting that he was wrestling with Zhou over issues of geostrategic importance yet always appealing for commutation of Downey's sentence.[35]

Though Eisenhower and Dulles had persistently sought the release of the two spies in the Geneva talks, their approach was markedly different from that of Nixon and Kissinger. Because the Eisenhower administration refused to recognize that the two detainees *were* spies, they approached their release as something that was owed to the United States, a correction of a wrongful conviction. When Dulles publicly accused Zhou of blackmail when Zhou offered to ease tensions by an exchange of journalists, it was simply salt in the wound. As Downey realized later in prison when he read about these statements in a 1958 almanac, this approach had devastating results for the two prisoners.

Nixon's approach was different. As Kissinger recalled, "Our whole approach was the opposite of the approach of previous administrations, which was to shame and pressure China to yield; and China then would have to yield to a country that did not recognize them but wanted them to do [that country] a favor."[36] The desire not to shame China publicly was related to the aforementioned secrecy that kept Downey's family in the dark about the importance of his case in the proceedings. According to Kissinger, "From the first day, we presented this not as a public issue but one on which China's behavior

would affect our attitude toward the overall endeavor we were under-
taking with China."[37]

Perhaps most important, the Nixon administration admitted to
the Chinese government that Downey and Fecteau were spies who
entered China illegally to subvert the CCP. Whereas the Eisenhower
approach was to scold, the Nixon approach was to be contrite. They
did not raise the request for release as a legal or human rights issue
but as an opportunity for the PRC to make a voluntary humanitarian
gesture of friendship toward the United States and its people. "No
country can send a spy and then appeal for his release as a question
of rights," said Kissinger.[38] The prisoners' release, Nixon and Kissinger argued, would have a salutary effect, helping to reduce resistance to the controversial process of rapprochement with such a
recent and bitter enemy. There was no quid pro quo implied in the
discussions about their release. As Kissinger put it, "The Chinese
never asked for anything in return for Downey's release. By releasing
Fecteau and Downey they were making concessions indicated by the
international situation."[39]

Kissinger's surprise visit intended to secure some concessions
from the PRC that would smooth the pathway for Nixon's own visit.
In a conversation in the Oval Office, Nixon told Kissinger and General Haig that "prior to a summit certain accomplishments should
be arrived at between the two governments." The first item on the list
is the "the release of all U.S. POWs held in China."[40] This shorthand
expression included Downey and Fecteau even though, technically,
they were not POWs.

After Kissinger's conversations with Zhou, he wrote in a classified memorandum, "At the very end I said that we would be grateful
for a pardon of all or some of the four Americans still held in China
when the PRC thought conditions were ripe. We were not making a
request and recognized it was China's matter to decide, but we would
consider their release a voluntary act of mercy. Chou [Zhou] said that
their law allowed shortened sentences for good behavior and they
would continue to study the matter. (This could well mean they might
make a gesture.)"[41]

Kissinger returned to Beijing in October to make further preparations for Nixon's trip the following February. While there, he made

an even more explicit admission that the two men were indeed spies from the CIA. The exchange between Kissinger and Zhou follows.

> DR. KISSINGER: Those two and then the two pilots. But they are two separate cases. When I was here last time, Mr. Prime Minister, I knew only that you held these prisoners, but I did not know the facts, because I could not inquire for obvious reasons. I have now inquired, and I find that Fecteau and Downey did engage in activities that would be considered illegal by any country.
>
> PM CHOU [PREMIER ZHOU]: That's right.
>
> DR. KISSINGER: Therefore, our plea to you has nothing to do with the justice of the case. In fact, we concede that you have a correct legal case. But if, as an act of clemency, you could consider that they have been punished sufficiently, it would make a very good impression in the United States.
>
> PM CHOU: According to our legal procedures, if a criminal in our prisons behaves himself well, that is, if he confesses to his crime, then we can lessen the sentence.
>
> DR. KISSINGER: I don't know whether they have confessed.
>
> PM CHOU: They have all confessed. And it is possible in about two months' time we may consider lessening the sentences of some of them who have behaved themselves well. As for who that will be we will tell you later. In the early part of this year we already released an old man, Walsh.
>
> DR. KISSINGER: I am aware of that. We would do our best to see to it that anyone you release would not engage in any propaganda against the People's Republic when he returns.

Kissinger wrote a memo to Nixon summarizing his meeting with Zhou:

> Since July, I had checked into the actual circumstances concerning Downey and Fecteau, whom the Chinese had claimed were CIA agents. They indeed were, and the CIA, for its part, would be willing for us to admit their activities if this were required to get the men released.

Chou [Zhou] concluded by suggesting that they could move on
the two agents first, pointing out that they had already served long
sentences and that Fecteau's term was almost completed. I said this
would mean a great deal to the American people and we would treat
any release as an act of clemency.

Thus in the near future we might expect a release of Fecteau and
perhaps the shortening of Downey's life sentence . . . *However, it is
absolutely essential to keep this information secret, for any public disclo-
sure of Chinese intentions would almost certainly wreck our chances for
early releases.*[42]

Kissinger's humanitarian request lies in stark contrast to Eisenhower's pressure campaign. He also clearly believed that public disclo-
sure of the request would endanger the prospect of the prisoners'
release. He very well may have been right about the need for secrecy
because the United States was asking the Chinese government to
commute a sentence delivered by its own courts. To do so after such
a request from a long-time enemy had been made public could cost
the PRC on the international stage, as Beijing might appear to be
caving to U.S. pressure and admitting that it had been in the wrong
all along. On the other hand, Beijing would gain maximum benefit
from the release of the two spies if it were seen as taking the initiative
and making a humanitarian gesture to improve relations with the
United States. Kissinger's prediction at the end of the memo came
to pass by the end of that year. After his July visit to Beijing, the PRC
requested that Paris be their new contact place rather than Pakistan.
On December 10, the U.S. Embassy in Paris was informed that Fecteau
would be released across the border shared by the PRC and British-
controlled Hong Kong in December, and Downey's life sentence
would be reduced to five additional years in prison.[43]

The two Vietnam War POWs, Robert Flynn and Philip Smith,
remained imprisoned. It would have been unusual for the Chinese
communists to release Vietnam War prisoners before their Vietnamese allies had. This was especially true when the terms of exchange
were a sticking point in the peace talks in Paris between Hanoi and
Washington.[44] Perhaps for the first time, Fecteau benefited from *not*
being labeled a prisoner of war.

But why did the Chinese government not release Downey at the same time? At their sentencing in 1954, Downey was convinced that he had received a harsher sentence because the Chinese falsely believed that he was the operation leader and Fecteau was his junior partner. The reality is they were both recently minted and relatively junior CIA officers. Downey wondered whether this misperception was because he had graduated from Yale, a university that was famous in China, and Fecteau had graduated from Boston University.

By 1971, Mary Downey was elderly and in declining health. When the news broke that just Fecteau was to be released without her son, she was heartbroken. She had advocated for her son's release for years and, despite her failing health, had braved her last trip to Beijing with her other son, William, that November. After the release of Fecteau, the relationship between Downey and his mother, of which the Chinese were well aware, became the core of the Nixon strategy. They appealed to Beijing for an even earlier release (before 1977) on humanitarian grounds. Eventually, this approach would pay off.

During his February 1972 trip to China, Nixon raised Downey's case with Zhou:

PRESIDENT NIXON: There is one personal matter which I would like to submit for the Prime Minister's consideration. That is the problem of Downey that Kissinger discussed with him in October.

PRIME MINISTER CHOU [PREMIER ZHOU]: Downey?

PRESIDENT NIXON: The American prisoner. We know that Downey was guilty. We know also the Prime Minister's government has shown compassion in commuting his sentence to five years.

PRIME MINISTER CHOU: Mr. Fecteau has already been returned.

PRESIDENT NIXON: Fecteau's and Harbort's[45] release had a very good impact on our country . . . . What I now present to the Prime Minister for consideration is not a request—there is no legal basis—and he has no obligation to act, but Downey's mother wrote me before I came. She is now seventy-six years old. She is not well. After five years she will be eighty-one and the possibility that she will not be alive when her son returns is quite obvious. I told her I would raise the subject with the Prime Minister. You must make this judgment. It would be a very compassionate act, especially since the mother is old and not well. It would have an enormously good impression in the United States, as you know when you were there (looking at Ch'iao [the foreign minister who had traveled to the UN late the previous year]), the story Harbort and Fecteau did.

. . .

PRIME MINISTER CHOU: Last year we already commuted his sentence to five years. And it seems he has behaved rather well recently. And therefore it is possible for us to take further measures when we have the opportunity. Of course, that will take some time. It is a complicated process for us because there are no relations between our two countries and there exists no legal precedent.[46]

When Nixon returned from China on Air Force One without Jack, Mary Downey was once again bitterly disappointed.[47]

After Fecteau's release became public, Downey's fate drew even more attention. At the same time, the Nixon administration was negotiating the release of American service personnel captured as prisoners in the Vietnam War, so the topic of American prisoners was very much on reporters' minds. Just as in the Korean War, a major sticking point in Kissinger's simultaneous negotiations with the Vietnamese communists in Paris was the disposition of prisoners of war. As with the B-29 crew at the end of the Korean War, the Chinese communists were holding two Americans flyers, Flynn and Smith, in the same prison as Downey and Fecteau. But just as the fate of the B-29 crew was linked to the Korean War armistice, so too the release of Flynn and Smith was tied to the Paris Peace Accords with North Vietnam. But Downey's case could not be so easily tied to either negotiated peace as he was not, technically or legally, a prisoner of war.

In this context, the Nixon administration needed a public relations position on Downey in case reporters asked questions. An early conversation along these lines took place between Kissinger and the PRC foreign minister Qiao Guanhua in Shanghai in February 1972 during Nixon's trip. There was obviously going to be extensive press engagement following the release of the Shanghai Communiqué and no one knew if questions about Downey might arise.

> DR. KISSINGER: They probably will also ask me about Downey. I will say we recognize this is a matter of Chinese domestic jurisdiction, but we are of course concerned about it. But it is not an international matter as such.
>
> VICE MINISTER OF FOREIGN AFFAIRS CH'IAO KUAN-HUA [QIAO GUANHUA]: Yes, and I would hope that when you reply to that question you will reply just in the way you put it now because that will facilitate how we deal with this matter.
>
> DR. KISSINGER: You can be sure.
>
> VM CH'IAO: We don't want to complicate this matter.[48]

Even this brief exchange is rife with political meaning. Kissinger tells Qiao that the American side, if it needs to discuss the case publicly at all, will treat the case as a domestic legal matter for China, not something that Beijing has any international obligation to resolve related to international agreements, treaties, or international law. Qiao replies that, from the CCP's perspective, such handling of the issue is essential to its early resolution.

Nixon and Kissinger's approach clearly had an impact. In June 1972, Zhou told two visiting senators that Downey's case was receiving renewed consideration.[49] Later that month, Kissinger visited Beijing again and had the following exchange with Zhou.

> DR. KISSINGER: Yes, as always when I am here I feel obliged to say a word about Mr. Downey. And I can only say again we don't contest the justice of the sentence, but we would appreciate an act of clemency, particularly in view of the age of his mother.
>
> PRIME MINISTER CHOU [PREMIER ZHOU]: We have taken note of this. Your president mentioned this too.
>
> DR. KISSINGER: Yes, but I will be asked by the family of Downey when I return, and I wanted to be able to say I had raised the issue.
>
> PRIME MINISTER CHOU:: So far as I know Downey is in good health. I just asked Mrs. Ma to check up on it.[50]

The United States and North Vietnam finally reached a peace deal on January 27, 1973. A cornerstone of this deal was the agreement on the exchange of prisoners of war. It was no surprise, then, when Nixon held a press conference a few days later that a journalist asked him about the three prisoners still in China. This was the first time Nixon had made any public statement about Jack Downey:

> Downey is a different case, as you know. Downey involves a CIA agent. His sentence of 30 years [*sic*] has been, I think, commuted to 5 years, and we had also discussed that with Premier Chou Enlai [Zhou Enlai]. I would have to be quite candid: We have no assurance that any change of action, other than the commutation of the sentence, will take place, but we have, of course, informed the People's Republic through our private channels that we feel that would be a very salutary action on his part.
>
> But that is a matter where they must act on their own initiative, and it is not one where any public pressures or bellicose statements from here will be helpful in getting his release.[51]

The family members were disappointed in Nixon's statement because they believed its roundabout language that the case "involves a CIA agent" fell far short of publicly recognizing that Downey himself was indeed a CIA officer. They worried it did not constitute the public apology for his mission that they believed would finally secure Downey's release. They assumed instead that Nixon's mealy-mouthed statement would only further aggravate Zhou.[52]

But according to Kissinger, Nixon was not trying to be evasive about the nature of Downey's background. "This was a deliberate decision by President Nixon. By making this statement granting that he [Downey] was there illegally, President Nixon could move the issue to the compassionate level. It was not being treated as a human rights violation."[53]

In the years leading up to this press conference, a man named Jerome Cohen had been leading a public campaign to win Downey's release by persuading the government to admit he had been a spy and apologize to China for conducting subversive espionage during the Korean War. Cohen was a professor at Harvard Law School and is a leading American China specialist. He had also been a classmate of Downey's at Yale. In 1971, Cohen wrote an opinion piece for the *New York Times* in which he asked whether Downey would attend his twenty-fifth college reunion, after having just missed his twentieth. From his understanding of the Chinese political and legal system and from meetings he had with Chinese officials in the PRC and at their embassy in Ottawa, Cohen believed that only such an admission could persuade the Chinese to release Downey on humanitarian grounds. He had gathered solid evidence that Downey was indeed a spy, and he included this in his piece, which was published just days before Kissinger arrived in Beijing on his secret trip.[54]

Over the next two years, neither the family nor Cohen could have known that this was precisely the approach that Nixon and Kissinger had taken in meetings with the PRC leadership, the minutes of which were classified as top secret. They hoped for some public recognition of these facts by the government if it might free Jack.

Then, in March 1973, Mary Downey suffered a massive stroke. The month before, Kissinger had met again with Zhou in Beijing to discuss the cases of Downey, Flynn, and Smith.

> CHOU EN-LAI [ZHOU ENLAI]: Oh, yes, there is some matter I would like to tell before I forget it. That is about the two American pilots here. [Author's note: Zhou is referring to the navigator Flynn and the pilot Smith]. That is, it has been decided that since the Paris Agreement has been signed we would release those two pilots during the period of the release of prisoners from Vietnam.
>
> DR. KISSINGER: Will that be announced publicly?
>
> CHOU EN-LAI: You can use it when you go back and meet the press.
>
> DR. KISSINGER: Can I say it?
>
> CHOU EN-LAI: And there is still one more—that is Downey. His attitude has been the best among the three because he probably knows he now has a chance to get out. But in accordance with our legal procedures, although his term has been shortened, he will have to wait until the latter part of this year. You can tell his mother he is in excellent health.

DR. KISSINGER: His mother has been quite ill. May I tell this to
his mother, that he may be released in the latter part of
this year?

CHOU EN-LAI: Yes. *If her situation becomes critical, you can tell us through
your liaison officer, Ambassador Huang Hua.* His behavior has
been very good. It seems to be too good.

DR. KISSINGER: We have no means of communicating with him so we
can't tell him to become a little worse.

CHOU EN-LAI: [*Laughs*] But perhaps when he goes back he won't
behave exactly the same as he does. It won't be too much in his
interest to do so.

DR. KISSINGER: But these are gestures that are very important to the
American public and will be very greatly appreciated. As I said
before, Mr. Prime Minister, we recognize that Downey is in
prison for reasons that are part of your legal system, and that
he was correctly charged. *And the President has said so publicly.*
So we consider this an act of compassion. With respect to
the two pilots we have received many questions about them,
and we will appreciate it to be able to say they will be released
during the period of the release of American prisoners in
Vietnam.[55]

Zhou did not challenge Kissinger when he described Nixon's statement at the press conference as a public recognition of Downey's
culpability under Chinese law. He simply encouraged Kissinger
to contact him quickly if Mary Downey's health took a turn for the
worse. A retrospective account of Downey's case published in China
states that, at the January 1973 press conference, Nixon simply publicly admitted Downey's culpability as a spy inserted into China.[56]
However dull his language, Nixon's press conference statement had
performed as intended.

When Mary Downey had a stroke, her younger son, Jack's brother
William, contacted Kissinger. Kissinger in turn contacted Zhou with
the news in exactly the manner that Zhou had requested in advance
during the February meeting.

On March 12, 1973, John T. Downey was released from prison, and
he rushed to his mother's side in a Connecticut hospital.

CONCLUSION

Nixon's approach to the detention of Downey and Fecteau was markedly different and obviously much more effective than Eisenhower's. But we should resist overly simplistic comparisons. The approaches were different, but so were the strategic settings in which they took place. Nixon could only achieve his diplomatic breakthroughs because certain strategic realities had changed. Sino-Soviet ideological tensions had escalated through the 1960s into direct military confrontation by 1969, and American public opinion had turned against the Vietnam War such that the United States sought an exit at acceptable costs.

Still, opportunities must be seized to be realized. The Nixon administration agreed to the sort of high-level direct diplomacy that Dulles had so resoundingly rejected. And there are few better examples than the case of Downey and Fecteau's release to demonstrate the benefits of direct high-level diplomatic contacts, even between hostile powers with opposing ideologies.

Secret, high-level diplomacy was essential to Downey's release, but also important were the actions of individual citizens operating outside of the state. Groups like the United States Table Tennis Association and the National Committee on U.S.-China Relations, and the "ping-pong diplomacy" that they fostered, created an improved environment for diplomacy. And perhaps more is owed to one private citizen—the courageous and steadfast Mary Downey—above all others in this saga. It was her severe illness that gave China the excuse to release Jack on humanitarian grounds, avoiding any appearance that they were bowing to pressure from Washington. Still, one wonders if this would have played out in the same way if she had not herself visited China several times, always comporting herself cordially and respectfully with her handlers from the Chinese Red Cross and with prison officials. Her reflection on her first two visits to China captures her generous spirit and diplomatic demeanor: "If anyone should hate these people, I should, but the individual Chinese I met in Peiping [Beijing] were kind. Without a doubt, I met a selected group, but even on the street, I never saw any hostility toward me. In spite of all the problems our Government is having with Communist China, the people were very understanding. I don't know about their leaders."[57]

21

COMING HOME

GOING HOME, I felt calm. I had waited over twenty years and three months for this moment, and it was finally here. The cluster of officials who greeted me warmly at the border led me a half mile through a railroad yard to a British helicopter. It lifted off as soon as we were strapped in. The day was clear, giving me a good view of the city that stretched out below, looking as intriguing as I had imagined it in a thousand daydreams. The view from the air was all that I was going to see of Hong Kong. It was a short hop. We alighted from the helicopter and walked directly to the hospital plane, and within minutes the plane headed southeast and flew over the Pacific Ocean.

The rescue plane had been diverted from ferrying American prisoners of war from Hanoi. It carried nurses, medics, and a doctor, all of whom were anxious to help me and who seemed a bit crestfallen to find me in such good condition.

I was pleased to find on board a complete change of clothes: plaid sports jacket, slacks, shirt, tie, socks, and shoes, all my size. Later I learned that this had been Fecteau's suggestion; he had traveled from Peking to Pennsylvania in his Mao suit and had walked around on Hong Kong streets and landed on American soil in that outlandish garb. A CIA man on board this plane explained to me the circumstances of my release. My mother, who had a mild stroke before her last prison visit with me in 1971, had had a more massive stroke in early March this year, 1973. She was now hospitalized in New Britain General Hospital. Dr. Henry Kissinger contacted the Chinese Premier Zhou Enlai to plea for leniency. However, it was my mother's deathbed wish to see me home that finally accomplished the task. President Nixon called and gave the good news to my brother Bill that the PRC had agreed to release me immediately. Soon I was racing against the clock to reach her. Just as I always had faith that I would not spend the rest of my life in prison, I now believed that I would see her alive.

In Manila, I was transferred again to an American Air Force plane. I was met by my brother, Bill, who explained that our mother had fallen into a coma, and whether she would emerge was in the hands of God. Within a half hour we were in the air again, and as the plane droned toward a refueling stop in Alaska, members of the crew slept, but I could not. The euphoria of freedom and the anticipation of being back to Connecticut kept me awake. In Alaska, the commanding officer of the air base where we stopped was our host at breakfast. Then we took off again, flying against the sun. Night came quickly. Somewhere over the Midwest, the pilots invited me into the cockpit. I gazed at the stars spread out against the sky; the view was both beautiful and serene. I was surprised to hear radio messages to me. "Welcome home, Mr. Downey." "We're glad you're home, Mr. Downey," they said, and my pilots handed me the radio mouthpiece to let me respond. "Thank you for your good wishes," I said. These pilots were men I admired. They knew who I was and were wishing me well. I was grateful, and it confirmed that I was back in friendly territory.

As we got near Bradley International Airport in Hartford, another surprising message came through; Governor Thomas J. Meskill would be there to greet me. When my family moved to New Britain in 1941, thirty years earlier, Tommy had lived a few houses down the street. We had been friends from the day he came over to meet the new neighbors. I was eleven and Tommy was two years older. He recruited me to deliver newspapers, and later he arranged my first date.

As we descended over the last ridge of low hills to a landing, I saw a crowd of about two to three hundred people bunched along a fence.

As we drew near, the crowd seemed to erupt, throwing hats or whatever in the air, waving arms, and jumping up and down. As the plane finally rolled to a stop, the door opened. I saw the governor standing at the foot of the ramp. I bounced down the steps and engulfed him in a bear hug. We were then swept toward the fence and were surrounded by reporters and photographers. I managed to say how glad I was to be back and thanked people for their welcome, as I was being moved toward a waiting car. In the commotion, I saw a tall, patrician gentleman yelling and struggling toward me but being held back by a policeman. It was Putney Westerfield, my college roommate and a dear friend. I got to see Putney a few days later, and I learned he had been one of several old buddies and roommates in the crowd. (Yale roommates Jim Healey and Rupe Vernon and buddy Robert Longman were there also.)

I was put in a car which became part of a police-escorted motorcade, and we roared south on the interstate. People in the cars we passed waved and shouted greetings. Apparently my arrival had been reported live on radio and television. At the hospital, another crowd was waiting, and as I was pushed and pulled toward the entrance, they surged around me, clapping, cheering, and calling my name. A few of the women even kissed me.

I reached my mother's room to find her propped up in bed, connected by a web of tubes to an assortment of hanging bottles. Her white hair was strewn over her pillow, and she had just emerged from a coma. She must have either watched or listened to the television, for she seemed very much aware of the commotion.

I stood on one side of her bed, surrounded by lights and people, and a doctor leaned toward her from the other side of the bed. "Mrs. Downey, John is back to see you," he told her.

Looking up at me with a smile, she said in a raspy voice, "You're a celebrity now. Don't let it go to your head!"

Everyone in the room—doctors, nurses, relatives, hospital administrators, and I—burst out laughing. My dear mother might have looked close to death, but she had not changed from the indestructible mother I had known all my life.

The reunion lasted only a short time, for my mother tired quickly. I was admitted to the hospital to be near my mother and to have my own series of medical tests performed. I learned a third member of my family was in the hospital, too; my aunt Kathleen had had a heart attack. I arrived on the evening of March 12, and the next day, I had a news conference with representatives from all the major news networks in the country and reporters from Boston, New York City and the Connecticut local papers. The interview lasted almost an hour. I remember one notable question: "Have you told them anything?" My honest answer was, "I suppose I gave them every bit of information I had." I didn't elaborate and left it at that. My instinct told me that I would not lie to my people. If I did, and they hailed me as a hero, I would have my conscience to contend with for the rest of my life. Another reporter asked how I liked the Chinese people. My answer was, "I don't mean to sing their praises, but my impression is they are decent people, very hard-working by our standards. They have had very few worldly goods, but they are pretty active, and in high spirits."

Not long after the press conference, my mother fell back into a coma. A priest was called to administer the last rites. The doctor said my mother must recover consciousness within forty-eight hours to have any chance of survival. Learning that people in a coma can hear what is going on around them, I spent much of the next two days sitting by my mother's side, telling her I was home and thanking her for everything she had done for me. It seemed ironic and unfair that she should die now, after waiting more than two decades for me to return. The last rites proved premature; she did come out of the coma a month later and began a slow recovery that, sadly enough, was never to be complete.

After the news conference, I took a brief walk in a secluded area and was feeling great. I had hardly slept in the last seventy-two hours, so the doctor gave me sleeping pills. I dozed off for only a few hours, a pattern that lasted for a week; I was too keyed up at being free. A few nights later, when I left the hospital for an evening dinner with my brother and his wife, and a college friend and his family, I discovered alcohol had no more effect on me than the sleeping pills did. I recall the intoxication from revelries of college and carousing with my CIA buddies. Now, after years of involuntary abstinence, my capacity for drink seemed to have increased threefold. Neither did I gain weight, despite consuming gallons of ice cream and ginger ale over those first months of unrestricted access to food that I had missed.

In the first week after my mother regained consciousness, I had only brief conversations with her, but I kept my monologue going. My conversations with my brother and sister-in-law, however, were endless. My brother and I said all the things we had been unable to on his visit to China; nor could I share much in the letters I wrote home. Close friends also came to visit, including Dick Fecteau, who drove down from Massachusetts. We took up where we left off, joking about our shared celebrity status, just as we had about our captivity. In the hospital I got the first sackful of letters that had arrived steadily for days. Most of them were welcome home notes from people I didn't know, expressing admiration or sympathy or both.

Among those who wrote were most of my B-29 buddies, who had been released eighteen years earlier. The gist of their notes was "Thank God. Now we don't have to worry about you anymore!" The saddest letters were from those families who had sons, brothers, or husbands missing in action in the Korean War. Some twenty-five wrote and asked if I had seen a young man, followed by a name and a description. I had to answer each one and explain that I had no information about their loved ones.

Whenever I left the hospital for brief excursions in the first week, and after I had moved into my mother's New Britain apartment, I was often stopped by people on the streets expressing tender, heartfelt kindness. People were glad to see me home; they empathized with my prison ordeal and offered help, handshakes, and hugs and kisses. I couldn't believe so many people cared about me. It did not take many such encounters before I realized that a generation of local school children had grown up saying prayers for me or writing letters to Chairman Mao asking for my release. Though strangers to me, they had acquired a personal stake in my fate. I was moved by their overtures. But I was feeling emotionally exhausted, and even talking to relatives drained me quickly. I repeatedly fought an inclination to withdraw into solitude.

I also found my attention span was very short; I seemed barely able to finish even a single response to the hundreds of letters sent to me without becoming distracted. Into my hospital room flowed a constant stream of visitors, medical personnel, relatives, friends, and strangers. Given my keyed-up state, I wonder how I passed the driver's license test in that first week. My brother let me practice driving using his Cadillac, which had power brakes and power steering. Still, I found it tough to maneuver on those cramped New Britain streets. When the inspector from the Department of Motor Vehicles came to the hospital—his visit was one of the many courtesies and concessions given me in those first weeks—I managed to inflict no damage to anything, except perhaps to the inspector's nerves. He passed me, however, and I got my driver's license.

Because of my mother's illness, the CIA debriefing took place in the New Britain area, rather than at Valley Forge Military Hospital. My contact from the Agency instructed me on the details of our rendezvous. On a certain hour of the morning, I was to wait in my mother's car—an aging white ark of a vehicle—in her driveway. A black Ford compact would drive by and I was to follow it. The arrangement seemed preposterously clandestine. But on the appointed morning, the car appeared, driving slowly by the house. I followed it several miles to a motel on the Berlin Turnpike, a highway dotted with an inordinate number of restaurants and motels that had been abandoned. We met in the motel every day for more than a week, and then, to protect our cover, we moved to a Holiday Inn just off the turnpike in Meriden. If anyone recognized me, I was to say that I was at the motel for a job interview. But no one ever did notice me entering or leaving our meeting places. The debriefing itself consisted mostly of my talking into a tape recorder and telling everything I could remember from the previous twenty years.

The debriefing might have been expanded to provide a kind of cathartic transition back to a more normal life, but it was not. I continued to have difficulty concentrating and was irritated by my failures. I repeatedly left things—a raincoat, an umbrella—whenever I went anywhere, or lost them altogether. I was particularly distressed to mislay a fountain pen the same day I had bought it for myself. My car trips became unintended adventures, since my absentmindedness seemed to increase as soon as I got behind the steering wheel. One evening, I got lost trying to cover the short distance between my mother's apartment and a movie theater in Berlin. On another

AFTERWORD

Jack Lee Downey

Dear Slew,

God knows where you are now, fats, but I assume this'll reach you sooner or later. After 4 mos. of nothing I got a good job that lasted 2 mos. [and] gave me some experience, and enable [*sic*] me to lose about 23.4 lbs.—now down to 200—but in the last 2 weeks the job has petered out & the world is slowly but perceptibly turning to shit—I'm feeling qualms of conscience about the service since this job hasn't turned out quite the way I expected—although it may within the foreseeable future—& that's the damned rub—I'd hate to quit & then see the roof cave in the next day . . .[1]

As a child, it never occurred to me that there was anything peculiar about a grown man pacing around the bathroom, carrying on a full outdoor-voice conversation with himself. In the 1980s, Dad spent a considerable amount of time in the only room in the house where he was guaranteed uninterrupted privacy, chatting away with some imaginary interlocutor. I was as nosy as any other kid, but the prospect of eavesdropping felt like a violation. What I did overhear just seemed like conventional banter—about current events, politics, the weather, college football. Dad never seemed self-conscious about this habit. It always felt like this was somehow sacred time, not to be interrupted nor interrogated.

Just the same, it seemed completely normal that he would steal off by himself on weekend afternoons to grab a coffee and pastry and sit alone in his parked car for several hours with a newspaper. Every once in a while, I'd be walking or biking around downtown New Haven and I'd inadvertently roll up to his car parked on a quiet side street, flanked by the esoteric affectations of Yale University's neo-Gothic architecture, and catch him reading the sports section while listening to local news radio.

By the time I was in high school, I had some sense that these habits were a kind of spindly tether to his past. That although he was typically hypersocial and gregarious, his retreats into solitude and confined spaces were an acquired taste cultivated over more than two decades in prison. The picnicking in the parked car habit is actually something I inherited from Dad. But by all external appearances, he was so acclimated to life after prison that it was just these faint traces of his past trauma that endured, occasionally bubbling to the surface in ways that mostly blended into the wallpaper of his everyday life. Dad was always the oldest person I knew. Compared to my peers' parents, he seemed ancient, and I went through cycles of paranoia that he could die at any moment. Most nights he would nod off in front of the television, and I would spend what felt like hours watching the gentle rise and fall of his chest, to make sure he was still breathing. He could be a robust snorer, so sometimes visual confirmation wasn't required.

Very gradually, it dawned on me that some people in my orbit believed my father was a national hero. I was born in 1980, the very tail end of Generation X, so just a bit too young to remember Dad's self-admittedly quixotic attempt to run for U.S. Senate, which inspired him to write—although never publish—a memoir with the help of the *Hartford Courant* journalist Joel Lang. We never had dogs or cats when I was a kid, but we did have an assortment of small reptiles, a box turtle named "Soup," and a revolving door of freshwater fish that I attempted, in vain, to keep alive.

The Hamden Plaza, a strip mall just outside of New Haven, was most well-known as the "Ghost Parking Lot"—an art installation that served as the final resting place for fifteen vintage car corpses, partially sunken into parking spaces and then paved over with asphalt. But to me it was home to an incredible Chinese buffet—the type that Chinese families ate at—and, more importantly, the local pet store. Once, my mother and I went in to get a few new fish. I was on a mini-shark kick (not great, ecologically speaking). At the checkout, the cashier, probably about Mom's age, noticed the surname "Downey" on her bank card, which she clearly found curious, since both of us looked decidedly Asian. She asked my mom if we were related to "John Downey the POW," and when Mom said yes, the cashier visibly warmed, and said, "You know, I prayed for him every day throughout middle school."

Later on, in my teens, I found out that some of my classmates' parents had had daily mandatory prayer for my dad throughout their years at Catholic parochial school. Over the course of Dad's incarceration, a generation of Connecticut Catholics had transfigured my father into a living martyr. Even though they might have been too young to know much about him at the time, Catholic children throughout the state wove a cosmic web around him, requesting the intercession of the communion of saints on his behalf. Meanwhile, on the material plane, my grandmother led them in a letter-writing campaign to lobby Chairman Mao directly for Dad's release. And in doing so, they were conscripted into not only the service of his physical and spiritual liberation but also the cosmic war against "godless Communism"—little schoolhouse crusaders for both God and country, with Dad as their icon. It's no real wonder that people revered him. They were trained to.

However, for anyone who wasn't a Nutmeg State Catholic Baby Boomer, Dad was probably just an older guy sitting in his car, reading the paper, and drinking Dunkin' Donuts coffee on a Sunday afternoon. In 2005, on the 250th anniversary year of Nathan Hale's birth, my father was presented with Yale's inaugural Nathan Hale Award. Hale, a member of the Yale Class of 1773 and my father, Class of 1951, shared the dubious distinction of having been "two failed spies." Dad mumbled this glibly while we parked the car and made our way toward the Hewitt Quadrangle in the heart of the school's downtown campus. This surreal, desolate courtyard of white and gray stone is adorned with memorials to Yale's wartime dead. For several months at the tail- end of the 1960s, it housed the Claes Oldenburg sculpture *Lipstick (Ascending) on Caterpillar Tracks*—as the name suggests, an enormous steel lipstick pointed skyward, mounted on the chassis of a "tank"—which briefly functioned as a rallying point for antiwar rallies before being moved to a less prominent location to deter vandalism. But on this Veterans Day, several dozen gathered in the shadow of Yale's limestone World War I cenotaph, as Yale president Rick Levin heaped praises on my dad:

> When honored, he deflects applause with self-deprecation and humor. He never speaks with bitterness or recrimination towards his captors. He never complains about his lost years. He has never sought special privilege or advantage. And he has never assumed that in giving so much to his country, he deserved anything in return. . . . Instead, he has lived as if his experience in captivity gave him a special gift of sympathy that was meant to be put in the service of others.[2]

It was the kind of deeply earnest display of public appreciation that my dad found in equal measure moving and disquieting. When it was his turn to speak, he dropped a pearl of wisdom to cut the tension: You know your days are numbered when they start giving you lifetime achievement awards. To which I noted that it must be rarified air to have someone doing the math on your life expectancy in order to best calculate your awards schedule. At the end of the ceremony, the father of an old youth hockey teammate approached me, his eyes welling up: "He never told me any of this." I guess in the decade that they spent together in the stands of rinks all across New England—hundreds of hours—it just never came up.

Afterward, we went down the block to Mory's, an old Yale restaurant founded in 1849. In one of the upper rooms, I sat at an enormous round table with Dad and a dozen or so of his classmates who'd returned to New Haven for the ceremony. Over lunch and drinks, one of them leaned over to me and whispered under his breath, "You realize you're the only one here who isn't a spook?"

My dad's career in espionage has been exceptionally well documented, which, he used to remind me, was a symptom of error. The common response—though never from my father—about the CIA's "legacy of ashes," as one author put it, was that, by design, the public would always disproportionately learn about the Agency's failures, because successful operations remained perpetually secret.[3] Of the dozens of his classmates who were recruited into the brand-new CIA with him, right out of college, many of them had huge gaps in their history that remained shrouded, even to their closest friends and family. Even to fellow classmates-turned-spies.

∗ ∗ ∗

For the majority of my father's twenty-one years as a prisoner somewhere on the outskirts of Beijing, his family knew very little about his life. His mother—my grandma—attempted to gather information about his conditions and the prognosis for his release from the U.S. government. Though she successfully enlisted Dad's dedicated friends and some assorted politicians, she was consistently misled into thinking that the State Department was at all times exhausting every available resource at its disposal to retrieve my father and his partner, Dick Fecteau. In early 1955, John Foster Dulles sent my grandmother a sympathetic and ultimately milquetoast letter that was echoed by other government officials throughout the subsequent fifteen years: declarations of emotional resonance, tethering my father's suffering to the cosmic cause of freedom, and some expression of powerlessness to entertain her requests:

Dear Mrs. Downey:

I want to express to you the deep personal sympathy and concern of your Government in the cruel dilemma which the Chinese Communists have forced upon you through the continued illegal imprisonment of your son. Public opinion throughout the free world will judge the words and deeds of those who have it within their power to end promptly the tragic grief which they have visited upon you.

Only by releasing those they hold can the Chinese Communists convincingly demonstrate concern for the human suffering they have caused.

The increasingly belligerent attitude and actions of the Chinese Communists in recent days have forced this Government to the reluctant conclusion that it would be imprudent for the time being to issue passports valid for travel to Communist China to any American citizens. This decision is made only after careful deliberation and in the belief that it is in the best interest of our nation. In the interest of peace we do not think it prudent to afford the Chinese Communists further opportunities to provoke our nation and strain its patience further.

Knowing the anxiety to which you have been subjected, we cherish the hope that the unremitting efforts to which the United Nations has dedicated itself will secure the release of the imprisoned United States personnel. If the United Nations efforts should be unavailing, we shall renew our own efforts.

With admiration for the fortitude which you have manifested, and with my warm personal sympathy,

Sincerely yours,
John Foster Dulles[4]

The travel passports would come in time. What Dulles—nor anyone from any branch of the government—would never tell her was that the CCP was lobbying for a mutually beneficial accord that would have included Dad and Dick Fecteau's early release. Instead, she was fed a steady diet of platitudes and excuses. Once he was sentenced in 1954, after a two-year information blackout, and his presumed-dead status was upgraded to life in prison, my family's most reliable source of information was often Dad himself, through his regular mail updates and the five visits his mother made to Beijing, beginning in 1958.

Unsurprisingly perhaps, communication engendered a great deal of confusion on all sides. By design, prisons render the incarcerated remote—both physically and psychologically—*even if* they're not on the opposite sides of a global war. This was compounded by the State Department's congenital incapacity to acknowledge what was plainly obvious—that their mission had violated China's territorial sovereignty as part of a sanctioned, if supposedly covert, arm of American intervention in Asia. Information trickled in every direction, obscured by coded language, partial candor, rumor, and misdirection. The most honest assessment she ever got was possibly from Edgar Snow, the exiled journalist casualty of McCarthyism who'd cultivated close ties to Chinese communism:

ADDRESS OFFICIAL COMMUNICATIONS TO
THE SECRETARY OF STATE
WASHINGTON 25, D. C.

DEPARTMENT OF STATE
WASHINGTON

January 27, 1955

Dear Mrs. Downey:

I want to express to you the deep personal sympathy and concern of your Government in the cruel dilemma which the Chinese Communists have forced upon you through the continued illegal imprisonment of your son. Public opinion throughout the free world will judge the words and deeds of those who have it within their power to end promptly the tragic grief which they have visited upon you. Only by releasing those they hold can the Chinese Communists convincingly demonstrate concern for the human suffering they have caused.

The increasingly belligerent attitude and actions of the Chinese Communists in recent days have forced this Government to the reluctant conclusion that it would be imprudent for the time being to issue passports valid for travel to Communist China to any American citizens. This decision is made only after careful deliberation and in the belief that it is in the best interests of our nation. In the interest of peace we do not think it prudent to afford the Chinese Communists further opportunities to provoke our nation and strain its patience further.

Knowing the anxiety to which you have been subjected, we cherish the hope that the unremitting efforts to which the United Nations has dedicated itself will secure the release of the imprisoned United States personnel. If the United Nations efforts should be unavailing, we shall renew our own efforts.

With admiration for the fortitude which you have manifested, and with my warm personal sympathy,

Sincerely yours,

John Foster Dulles

Mrs. Mary V. Downey,
43 Monroe Street,
New Britain, Connecticut.

In 1955, U.S. secretary of state John Foster Dulles wrote a letter to Mary Downey concerning her son's imprisonment in China.

Dear Mrs. Downey:

At my request the Peking authorities furnished me with a copy of the judgment of the military tribunal hearing the case of your son, John. I am not sure whether you ever saw these excerpts but from our conversation I should guess not. In any event I believe you are entitled to know the grave nature of the charges against John and the reasons why the U.|N. was not able to do anything to secure his release with the P.W.'s.

It seems to me reasonable to hope that his release might be secured, as a gesture of good-will on China's part, either in the event of a restoration of U.S.-China relations or of the seating of China in the U.N. Your friend Mr. Bowles would probably know best how to judge that possibility. Even without any such development in the years ahead I would hope for a commutation of his sentence and release on good behavior, if Sino-American relations do not further deteriorate. I shall certainly write to you if I can think of any other means which might be effective, as I deeply sympathize with your feelings as a mother.[5]

All the information Dad received about what was known about their capture was mediated by several layers of filtration—what happened, what the government knew about what happened, what version of that was made known to my grandmother and the general public, and what slice of that was passed back to my father through his screened prison mail. So once Dad was finally permitted to write his mother, he had no way of knowing what she knew, and limited options for discussing the finer points of their botched mission through his censored letters. He occasionally tried to send a coded message, although this often failed, sometimes comically. In one of these early letters, when the circumstances of the capture remained hazy, Dad tried to signal that his Civilian Air Transport (CAT) C-47 plane had been shot down by filling his letter back to his mother with references to cats—black cats, yellow cats, calico cats. He hoped she would pass it to someone in the Agency who could decipher the "code," so at least they would have some basic awareness of how things went down. Instead, about a month later, he received a concerned response from my grandma, asking him if he was still experiencing hallucinations and reminding him that the Downeys were a dog family.

*   *   *

After my Dad and Dick Fecteau had been in prison for almost two years and ten months, mostly in solitary confinement, news of their sentencing reached the United States via Morse code from the Chinese state media company Xinhua (New China News Agency). The announcement of their sentencing was paired with that of the eleven B-29 crew members, who'd been captured shortly after them, and with whom they would be housed for three weeks in December 1954. My father remembers those weeks as incredibly uplifting after so much time previously spent in isolation. In a 1974 oral history interview with the CIA's Office of Personnel, Dad recalled what it was like to be housed with American cellmates:

> One of perhaps the most striking things that ever happened to me was that about two weeks after my sentencing, after I'd been living in solitary confinement for those two years and more, I was called out. They came into my cell, and gestured to me to pick up my gear, and follow them. . . . And then the door was opened, I was ushered into this cell and when I got inside I became aware suddenly that the cell was filled with people. And as I looked around I could not believe my eyes. They were all Americans, and I remember we were all looking at each other and unknown to me they had just had the same thing happen to them. . . . It really boggled me. It was one of the biggest thrills and shocks I ever experienced.
>
> I suddenly found myself thrust in the midst of a bunch of Americans. I mean this really does something, I don't know. . . . It's just within that first five minutes to know I was back among Americans and what that meant and what Americans were like. It was just really tremendous.[6]

But this profound sense of relief was soon replaced with the old sense of desolation when he was separated from them so shortly thereafter. The B-29 crew members were actually the ones who told Dad and Fecteau that the Korean War had ended. When I was little, my father got a little telegram from one of the crew members that contained an iron-on patch, a mouse dressed in human clothes, wielding a whiskey bottle like a baseball bat. It was a callback to the song "Little Brown Mouse," which they used to sing together in the cells, about an intoxicated pub mouse who lapped up spilled liquor off the barroom floor.

Although they were obviously grim circumstances, Dad's memories of his time sharing cells with the B-29 crew and Fecteau all together had a lingering sweetness to them. That Christmas, 1954, Dad wrote my grandmother his second letter:

Dear Mom

Today is Christmas + I thought I'd write a short note to let you know I'm thinking of you. I'm living with several other Americans + we're having a swell holiday—sang carols last night + had peanuts, candy, etc., + tonight the Chinese are providing us with a fancy dinner. I also was given a present of ham + canned chicken from the Chinese, so we've had a real old fashioned Christmas. I wish I could be with you, of course, but I hope the knowledge that I'm alive + well + in good spirits will brighten your holiday. The guys I'm with are all swell guys and we're allowed much freedom to associate, play sports, etc. + members of the Chinese staff are specially assigned to look after our welfare so we're well taken care of.

Did you have a white Christmas? We had some snow a few days ago, although the weather here is generally a bit milder than at home. I'm wearing Chinese style padded clothes + I imagine I look about the size of a house in them—but they are certainly practical, warm + comfortable.

I'll close now, but will write again in the near future + hope to hear from you soon. All love to Joan + Willie + the relatives. God bless you all.

Much love + Merry Christmas,
Jack[7]

At around this time, prison guards were instructed to arrange a kind of candid photoshoot that showed Dad and his fellow prisoners of war in the dark, quilted winter uniforms Dad describes in this letter. Some of them are also wearing Elmer Fudd–style wool hats, with the earflaps pulled back and tied together on top. They are sitting around a table, eating and chatting, some of them playing table tennis. All eleven surviving members of the crew were released the following summer. Steve Kiba, the B-29 radio operator, would later speculate that the Chinese government might've originally planned to release all the Americans together, but that might have been contingent on the United States acknowledging that Dad and Fecteau were CIA. When the airmen returned home, one was quoted: "They told me and the rest of the crew to forget all about Downey and Fecteau. . . . They told us those weeks never existed . . . to act as if it never happened— those were the words the CIA man said."[8]

One of the things that I recall from as early as I knew anything of the outline of Dad's story was that he believed, first, that the Chinese were completely justified in detaining him and his partner, and, second, that he never had any expectation that anyone was coming to save them, no diplomatic horse-trading, no black-ops jailbreak. The most powerful emotion I sensed in Dad's memories of those years was resignation, particularly once they'd been sentenced. He was not bitter at either government because he harbored no expectations that either would go to extraordinary lengths to free them. The only thing that really irked him later in life was the rumor that they'd hopped on the plane as a kind of lark, when they'd actually been ordered to cover for operators whose clearances hadn't passed on account of a paperwork snafu. He knew what he was doing was a breach of international law, and he knew that once captured, his government would disavow any knowledge of the operation. Once he was given a life sentence, he knew that prison was now his world.

Dad said that daily life actually became more manageable for him once the sentence came down. He was no longer waiting for anything, which, in some way, relieved him of the anxiety of expectation. Having been, along with Dick Fecteau, kept in suspended animation for two years while they awaited news of their fate, they now had definitive clarity, even if it was the clarity of a life sentence. Fecteau, with his twenty-year sentence, had an end in sight—if just barely. They determined my father to have been the "boss," seemingly based on nothing other than presumptions about status conferred on him by his undergraduate education—Yale instead of Boston University, Fecteau's alma mater. Dad used to joke that, for all of its upward mobility class privileges, going to Yale really screwed him.

But in some practical ways, their conditions improved after their sentencing. The food was better, more substantial. And they were able to send and receive mail. For my dad, this latter concession was most critical. Of course, it meant that he could communicate with his family and friends. But it also meant that he could petition his mother for care packages of nonperishable American food—which he did with great fervor. He claimed this was the origin of his lifelong addiction to peanut butter, which he slathered on just about anything he could find, including my mother's homemade scallion pancakes—which was an affable culinary abomination. One of my cousins remembered that whenever she'd visit our grandmother, her dining table had been converted into a food distribution center: a measuring scale, jars of jam, canned meat and fruit, and packages of cookies. To provide a little extra cushion, my grandmother wrapped everything in old newspapers, which gave Dad a bit of extra reading material. He carefully scanned even seemingly trivial scraps, like corporate advertisements, which is how he found out that a street back home in New Britain had been renamed in his honor. Dad's shock and curious excitement quickly turned to anxiety that his meager privileges might be withdrawn if guards believed he was becoming a celebrity back home. So he crumpled up the newspaper and ate it.

*   *   *

During the early 1960s, Dad's correspondence restrictions tightened, and he could only receive mail from immediate family—so he came to rely on the *Yale Alumni Magazine* for updates about his old classmates, and they occasionally communicated to him, and about him, in the "class updates" section. During the Vietnam War, some of them played out political disagreements in those pages. In the October 1967 edition, Lew Herbert Abrams, then a Marine pilot operating out of Da Nang Air Base, offered some snarky remarks about an antiwar classmate then puzzled over whether Dad would be catching up on the dispute from within his POW cell. A few months later Abrams was shot down over North Vietnam, and his remains would not be returned to his family until 1997.

One of the few prison stories Dad loved to tell—it was his go-to on just about any occasion when he was expected to speak about his incarceration, but also one that he repeated to me periodically, was his belated vicarious experience of the "Harvard Beats Yale 29–29" football epic of 1968. Coming into the game—the last of the season—both teams were undefeated, making this one of the most highly anticipated rivalries of the year. Yale, led by future NFL standout Calvin Hill, was heavily favored, and predictably dominated the first half. With only two minutes left, they led 29–13. Thinking it was effectively over, our family friend Grace Parker left early, hoping to beat the traffic rush. Knowing my father would be frantically waiting for news, she quickly penned a postcard note about Yale's dominant victory and perfect season, and mailed it off to China. "Yale beat Harvard 29–13." Several weeks later, my father received it—his first news about the game, and he was, of course, elated. But the story had an unexpectedly tragic ending. Stealing a few brief moments together, Dad gloated to Dick Fecteau about New Haven's triumph over Boston. However, several weeks later, Dad received a copy of the *Yale Alumni Magazine*, recounting that episode of "The Game"—still widely considered the most electrifying Harvard-Yale matchup of all time. As Dad told it, "a wail, as from a banshee, reverberated throughout the cellblock." What the conscientious Grace Parker had missed in her enthusiasm to avoid parking-lot gridlock was one of the most incredible comebacks in college football history: "With the help of two Yale fumbles, three Bulldog penalties, and a successful onside kick, Harvard scored two touchdowns in the final 42 seconds, tying the score 29–29. Since overtime was not yet a part of college football in those days, that was how it ended. The *Harvard Crimson*'s now-famous headline told the story all too well: 'Harvard Beats Yale, 29–29.'"[9]

Perhaps most incredibly, Harvard succeeded on back-to-back two-point conversions, within the same minute—something almost completely unforeseeable, even if you were to grant the otherwise improbable touchdown scenario. Overcome with grief, Dad took solace in his daily routines and ran his emotions dry in the miniature prison courtyard "track." Fecteau did not, however, miss his opportunity to exact revenge and savaged my father about Yale's utter collapse, which was, for Fecteau, a triumph of competitive schadenfreude as much as collegiate pigskin. Dad used to say of Fecteau that there's nobody with whom he would've rather been locked up.

This tale was vintage Dad material: a synthesis of comedy and tragedy that was good for a laugh at his own expense. Dad's characteristic sense of absurdity, which extended throughout his post-incarceration afterlife, was a useful coping mechanism tool, which he deployed frequently and seemingly reflexively. It allowed him to acknowledge his deep isolation, and how magnified the importance of relatively small things could become as he was so deprived of sources of joy. That he would be rendered apoplectic might've been indicative of his radical interior desolation. But then again, the man loved Yale football. I spent an enormous percentage of November Saturdays in the 1980s freezing my ass off at the Yale Bowl with him, while he seemed completely unfazed by physical discomfort. In school I had a teacher once say that everyone who loves Dostoevsky's writing secretly identifies with Alyosha in *The Brothers Karamazov*, but I think Dad actually imagined himself more like *The Idiot*'s Prince Myshkin, a figure so guileless that he appeared comically naive to onlookers, while his true nature was that of the "holy fool." However, although Dad was a pretty remarkable Luddite—washing machines, let alone computers and cell phones, remained objects of mystery and wonder—his farcical sense of self contrasted with the reverence he was shown by those around him.

By this time, Dad and Fecteau had been joined on the cellblock by more Americans, including the pilot Philip Smith, whom Dad warmly described as "just as American as apple pie."[10] When they had been paired with the B-29 crew, Dad and Fecteau were both quite young and new to the POW life. But now they were seasoned veterans. Smith and Robert Flynn were captives from a completely different war, one my dad had only read about on newspaper scraps. Smith was a keen observer and quickly profiled his new neighbors. In his memoir, Smith later recalled their first meeting:

> My heart quickened as he [a prison guard] opened the bolt and led the way into the cell. There sat three men, obviously prisoners. Two appeared to be Americans, one Chinese. I was dumbfounded. . . . I had been totally isolated for so long; this was a stunning turn of events.
>
> The cell, I saw at a glance, was the same size as mine, but much more crowded, with two beds, two tables, and now five people. And as I looked around I glimpsed something that made me blink in surprise—and shock. Stacks and stacks of paperback books and American magazines were piled in one corner. . . . Who were these prisoners? And, my God, how long had they been here to accumulate such a vast array of reading materials? I was appalled at the very thought of how long they must have been incarcerated.
>
> I looked at the two Americans, at a loss for words. Nothing had prepared me for this. My joy at seeing them was almost forgotten in a rush of sympathy for what they must have been through. I hesitated, unsure of what to say or do, but they immediately held out their hands and introduced themselves as John Downey and Richard Fecteau. . . .
>
> It was Downey who was so good at getting around Maha ["Ma Hua" in my father's text—a Chinese cellmate who spoke English and who, they believed, was undercover]. Downey was a master at nonverbal communication. He could say more with his eyes and facial expressions than anyone I ever knew. His face alone could tell a story, and when Maha wasn't looking, it often did. He also taught me how to play the game with Maha. Sometimes I'd slip and start to ask a question or make a statement that was not appropriate in front of the Oriental, and Downey quickly shut me up just by looking at me. . . .
>
> The stories they told were incredible, and so were they. My weight had been dropping steadily since I arrived in Peking; I would have expected them to be skin and bones, but they weren't. They seemed to be in fairly good health physically and remarkably good health mentally. In everything they said and did when I was with them they

communicated optimism that some miraculous event would take place and would bring the early release. "This is what happened, we're here and we're going to make it," they said, and they seemed to believe it. I wondered, if I were in their position, if I would have equal fortitude. I could only hope I would.

Talk about tragedy, I thought. These men had been in their early twenties when they were captured and had lost fifteen vital years of their lives. How could Downey, in particular, be optimistic when he'd been sentenced to life in prison? That was a devastating idea to me, but whenever I asked him about it he replied calmly and quietly that he would never give up hope of being released. . . .

Their personalities were very different—Downey was much more extroverted, talkative, and ready to laugh than the more serious and subdued Fecteau. And yet both accepted their fate and their outlook was far more upbeat than my own. I suspected they would have been friends under any circumstances, for they were sensitive and intelligent and shared a love of adventure, sports, and the dangers of their profession.[11]

I only met Smith once, at the premiere of *Extraordinary Fidelity*, the CIA documentary about Dad and Fecteau, which had featured Smith as a commenter. Smith's distinctions between Fecteau and my father continue to strike me as so perceptive: although certainly they had many things in common, Dad and Fecteau were their own people with their own personalities. They were almost diametric opposites when it came to the coping mechanisms they developed. Over the years, by his own admission, my father became heavily obsessive and routinized. This included cultivating neuroses around the organization of his cell but also his exercise regimen. Fecteau, on the other hand, responded quite differently to solitary confinement by finding comfort beneath the waters of his imagination. But for my dad, amplifying voluntarily practices of self-discipline allowed him to organize his daily schedule—stay on task from moment to moment rather than sinking into a vortex of endless monotony—and afforded him a measure of agency in a situation designed to break him by stripping him of control. It also gave Dad the opportunity to track his metrics. In 1955, so relatively early on, one of his letters to a college classmate was printed in the *Yale Alumni Magazine*, and reprinted in the *New Haven Register*, revealing a little bit of his emerging carceral personality: "In the last eight months I've read about 100 books, including Dickens, Thackeray, Scott, Tolstoy, Balzac, Turgenev, Cervantes and many others—show me a book and I've read it. In the same period, I've done some 23,000 calisthenics, run about 55 miles and washed about 100 items of clothing."[12]

It seems perfectly characteristic of my dad that he would brag to classmates about his laundry accomplishments, which he composed on a 1 × 2 piece of paper, cut up from the single sheet that he was rationed every month. Dad attempted to exercise autonomy wherever he could, albeit within a larger context of abject vulnerability—even if that meant keeping statistics on his laundry, which he related with evident pride. At his cardiovascular peak, he ran upward of five hundred laps a day in the two-lane courtyard track in order to hit a goal distance of ten miles. He kept track of days of the month by counting pull-up repetitions, adding one per day to his base count, until he reached the end of the month. At one point he lost nine days, although he was never sure exactly when the error occurred or what days, precisely, he missed. But most of Dad's stories about his prison routine were tragicomically self-deprecating: like the one about how he taught himself Russian, but then realized, a decade in, that he'd learned the alphabet wrong.

* * *

A particular mutation of Catholic guilt that my dad and I shared was rooted in our knowledge that, in a very literal way, we both owed our lives to Richard Nixon. In 1971, there was a quickening in U.S.-China relations, punctuated by Henry Kissinger's secret meeting with Zhou Enlai, the U.S. table tennis team's fabled "ping-pong diplomacy" exhibition tour, and Nixon's announcement that he would end the quarter-century diplomatic boycott of the PRC. Dad's advocates amplified their lobbying efforts. This included my grandmother and other relatives, as well as Ella T. Grasso, then a House representative and future Connecticut governor. Dad's classmates, now in their forties, continued to press. Jerome Cohen, now a Harvard professor with expertise in Chinese law, amplified his long-standing theory that Fecteau and Dad might be released if only the United States would admit the obvious truth about their identities:

> Now that table tennis has introduced "people to people" diplomacy, the prospects for Downey's release may well brighten if the U.S. will admit that it violated China's territorial integrity during a bygone wartime era, apologize for having done so and recognize China's sovereign right to punish offenses against its security.
>
> If the U.S. opposes making individuals the pawns of power politics, it should abandon its preoccupation with "face" . . . and set the record straight. Otherwise Jack Downey may not make our twenty-fifth reunion."[13]

Dad's college roommate, Putney Westerfield, a former CIA officer in Southeast Asia who had since become a publisher for *Fortune* magazine, wrote letters to Henry Kissinger, Secretary of State William P. Rogers, Undersecretary of State for Political Affairs Alexis Johnson, UN Ambassador George H. W. Bush, and Senior Staff Member of the National Security Council John Holdridge, requesting that they pressure Nixon to seek Dad's compassionate release.

But by the time diplomatic priorities finally started tacking in his favor, Dad's expectations for his future had tempered. As he would describe it to me, his range of emotional frequency had narrowed, vibrating neither too high nor too low. So, by the time the unexpected good news arrived that Nixon's very simple, almost absurdly muted pseudo-acknowledgement that "Downey involves a CIA agent" and the news of my grandmother's stroke had motivated his premature release on humanitarian grounds, Dad did not, as you might expect, erupt into spasms of celebratory backflips and fist-pumps:

> My very first reaction to being told I was to be released was almost indifference, and my reaction when I got released was about the same. To this day I haven't had a real. . . . For years I assumed when I got the word I was going to get out or when I stepped over that border, I would just go bananas, but it was just a shrug of the shoulders. I never felt any great thrill or shock and that is kind of strange

I think. My reeling is my reaction when they told me I was going was sort of sincerely, "Well Christ, it's about time, you bastards." That's about the way I felt. Apparently I had gone past the time when I was going to get excited about things like that. . . . So I just sort of, like dropping off a coat, I didn't look back and just felt very . . . this of course is my own judgment here, I think I was very calm and not at all elated or excited, certainly not depressed, but just pleased mildly.[14]

When the time came for him to leave, Dad was watching ping-pong on a communal television. As the guard approached him, Dad reflexively raised his hand to shush him, as the match was midpoint and he was eager to see it to its conclusion. The entire release was quietly anticlimactic. He never got to hit the Hong Kong nightclubs—a long-standing fantastical post-incarceration daydream—as he had to quickly return to be by his mother's hospital bed. News of my grandmother's recent massive stroke was unknown to Dad, but it was an effective pretext for Zhou to immediately commute the remainder of his sentence. First, he was sped away to Manila to be reunited with his brother. My uncle Bill had received the news of Dad's release directly from Richard Nixon, soon followed up by a call from Henry Kissinger, instructing Bill to keep my grandmother on a respirator until Dad lifted off Chinese soil—even in the event of her death—to maintain the illusion of impending filial reunification for the sentimental aging premier. Within two days, Dad was by her side at the New Britain General Hospital. Although she had been in a coma following her second stroke just weeks before, she came out of it for an hour when Dad arrived, before slipping back in for another month or so.

* * *

Jack Downey emerged from his 20 years in prison looking and acting like a man who'd never been in prison, almost a symbol of the détente that now exists between the United States and China. Downey had two recreations in prison, reading and exercising. Together, they saved his sanity.

He came out of prison speaking Chinese and able to read and write Russian, which he learned from Russian cellmates and from the Russian novels his Chinese captors let him have. His friends say he is in excellent physical shape at the age of 42. He can run 10 miles, do 100 pushups and as many as 50 chinups. His weight is 190 pounds, a little less than it was when he wrestled and played varsity football for Yale.[15]

Mom first heard about Dad in the pages of the March 1973 edition of *Time* magazine, reporting on his release after just over twenty years in Chinese prison. That spring, Dad was plastered all over local and national media, which—unsurprisingly perhaps—framed the narrative of his ordeal and return in dramatic terms. But by virtue of his own temperament and after two decades in prison, Dad was not a natural media darling. He avoided extended interviews during his first years back stateside, and even five years later remained unseasoned in the art of discussing himself:

> Indeed, John Thomas Downey does not like talking about those prison years when bits of information filtering through what was once called the Bamboo Curtain made him a figure as mysterious as Tibet's Dalai Lama. . . . He was cordial, open and unpretentious. He was also visibly uncomfortable discussing his former life. If someone can pace sitting down, then Downey paced incessantly in an easy chair in the living room of his newly bought home. . . . He threw his legs first over one arm of the chair, then the other. He leaned forward. He slouched back. He reclined so steeply he seemed about to slide onto the floor. He is physically formidable—there is no difficulty envisioning him bursting from a lineman's crouch—and the chair seemed too small to hold him.
>
> Downey likes to say his prison years were essentially boring. Perhaps he is right.[16]

Decades later, I remember my father recalling the Dalai Lama analogy with nervous laughter, borne out of a sense of lingering sheepish embarrassment. "Just like the Dalai Lama," he chuckled. Media reports about Dad seemed fascinated with his body, describing him as powerful and robust—not at all wasted or waiflike, as readers might have imagined a ravaged POW would be. It was a contrast in type: Dad's patriotic suffering was foundational for his depiction as a heroic figure, while all external signs seemed to indicate that he emerged from his decades behind the "Bamboo Curtain" remarkably intact. It was easy to see why he might've been good at contact sports. Dad was physically insensitive. While my uncle Bill was apparently constitutionally injured throughout his life—he "always had an arse or an elbow" my grandmother would say when they were kids—my father would often simply not notice that he'd been injured in some way. One summer when I was in high school, he flipped over his bike handlebars and split open his face. Instead of rolling around on the ground, he just popped up, reassured gawking onlookers he was fine, and went about his way. Even after enough time had passed for the adrenaline to wear off, Dad seemed to forget he was still bleeding profusely. Another time he put his hand straight through a glass door and sliced up his forearm—the punch line was that he hadn't noticed the door was glass. It was so bad we had to take him to the emergency room, and as he was brought down the hall in a wheelchair, there was so much blood that one of the attendants started projectile vomiting at the sight. The whole time Dad was smiling and waving to passersby like he was the pope on parade. Even as a senior, he had the type of carelessness with his own body that I associate with children who imagine themselves unbreakable but also don't seem to register pain. It made me and Mom anxious every time he picked up a chainsaw.

By the time my mother read about my father in *Time* in 1973, she was living in New Haven, where she worked as a chemist at Yale. She had arrived in Eugene, Oregon, in 1962, and gradually moved out east. She adopted the nickname Betty, inspired by her love for the actress Betty Grable, but this led to some confusion because it was so popular among Chinese immigrants, so she eventually swapped it for Audrey, as in Hepburn. She had just become a naturalized citizen the month before, and her access to mainland China was restricted to CCP state-censored magazines at the Yale Library. Upon his return to Connecticut, Dad would become both leading subject and, eventually, primary informant in her quest for contemporary news of her homeland. Although my future parents were geographically

proximate—converging in New Haven by way of northern China—
there was really no plausible opportunity for them to meet, if not for
my mother's intrepid, almost Pelagian resolve, which makes almost
everyone appear chronically lazy by comparison. After learning of my
father's return and that his mother was convalescing at New Britain
General Hospital, Mom went out on a limb and wrote an introductory letter to Dad, postmarked to my grandmother—the only guaranteed address she could locate. Because of the hundreds of newspaper
and magazine articles chronicling Dad's captivity and return, he
was inundated with all sorts of requests. But her letter was different.
Some weeks later, her phone rang, and it was my dad on the other end
of the line. They went out on their first date the next evening.

When Dad picked Mom up from her apartment in downtown New
Haven, on July 28, 1973, he still dressed like it was the 1950s. Since
it was effectively a blind date, they both looked each other over. My
mother recalled his "ocean-blue eyes" hidden "behind a pair of thick
glasses, under curly, bushy eyebrows." Dad was apparently taken
aback at how tall she was.[17] Mom lived close to Yale's campus, and
Dad cracked a slightly macabre and low-hanging-fruit joke about him
living in China all the while Mom was living just blocks from the site
of his happiest memories, which kept him afloat during his incarceration. Luckily, Mom shared his ironic sense of humor. Throughout my
life, Dad would occasionally try to play cute with Mom by speaking to
her in Mandarin. Apparently that was a habit he picked up immediately. As they drove to dinner, he started singing Chinese communist
songs, hamming it up for dramatic effect. Oddly, this was actually
my mother's first time hearing communist songs, let alone being
sung by a hulking white guy in Connecticut wearing white buckskin
loafers. They swapped stories about their respective—in some ways
inverse—experiences in each other's home countries and compared
notes on congee, the Chinese breakfast staple.

They realized her hometown of Shenyang had also been his first
site of captivity, where he was detained for several months and under-
went his most severe interrogation. During that time, his only relief
was the idiomatic curiosity of his inquisitor menacingly hurling lost-
in-translation accusations at him: "You mixed egg! You turtle egg!
You son of a rabbit!" Small talk about Chinese prison life was a grim

yet unavoidable feature of their first date but also signaled how their overlapping, if inverted, backgrounds undergirded their compatibility as a couple, insofar as my father's reentry process was estranging. As he acclimated to the legacy of the 1960s—a Catholic Church that was no longer Latin, household televisions, highways—he grew hungry for someone to talk with about China who didn't treat it like an Oriental fantasy. And my mother had an equal and opposite hunger to hear about the world she had fled, unfiltered by the lens of either Chinese or American propaganda. Through my father, Mom could compare his experience of the Great Leap Forward and Cultural Revolution with the utopian version depicted in Chinese state narratives. Although China was then in the process of opening, relatively speaking, to outside media, my mother had never been close with someone who'd actually experienced Chinese communism firsthand, even if my dad's circumstances were obviously irregular.

Over supper at the Griswold Inn, a rural eighteenth-century New England tavern, my future parents bonded over conversation about Chinese pickled cabbage. Dad remembered the two pork and cabbage dumplings that prisoners were offered as a special treat on Chinese New Year. When my father realized that he'd stumbled into a potentially bottomless source of dumplings, their relationship really took off. Soon he'd conscripted my mother into a competitive eating challenge: he'd eat as many dumplings as she could put in front of him. Mom found all this dumpling talk a little weird for the season, since they were traditionally a winter food. Dad was so unaccustomed to choosing what he ate, and yet there he was fantasizing about Chinese food, in the middle of a dinner of prime rib and potatoes.

Although they'd quickly moved on to the presumption of a second date filled with dumplings, Mom and Dad still barely knew each other at all. Dumplings, as anyone who's made them from scratch knows, are hard work. The following Saturday, Mom spent the better part of an afternoon chopping, mixing, and kneading dough, folding it all into half-moon-shaped little meat pastries. She steamed enough dumplings to feed a medium-sized family, which turned out to be perfect, because Dad ate *thirty-four* of them. Mom took a head count afterward to confirm. He enthusiastically drowned each of them in soy sauce and reminisced about how his early interrogators used his love for soy sauce as leverage to break him. In the preamble to his ill-fated mission, the aspiring guerillas they'd trained had ribbed Dad mercilessly for his soy sauce cravings. Apparently, one of the Manchurian double agents who gave advance notice of the mission had written profiles of Dad and Fecteau and included some of his culinary preferences. During the early days of his detention, when the pair were still holding out and maintaining anonymity, Dad's interrogator entered the room and said blankly, "You are Jack, you love soy sauce." As Dad recalled, that was the point when he knew he'd been played and had his mission sabotaged from within. Even in the near months after his release, Dad was drawn toward the familiar things that reminded him of the small world from which he'd only just escaped.

You don't have to be a psychoanalyst to notice the peculiar trajectory that led my father, a POW who spent two decades in a Chinese prison, to date and eventually marry a Chinese woman and later become a judge. Later in life, Dad liked to think of himself as the kind of judge who let people out for Christmas, but I imagine that's true for a lot of judges—although I figure my father had above-average cognitive dissonance about his work. He believed in systems and structures without being transformed into a "law and order" enthusiast. I often wondered what it was like, psychologically, for him to sentence people. But there were limits to his identification with the people he saw in court, even if he had more points of recognition than most judges. Dad didn't emerge from prison as an abolitionist. We didn't have those kinds of conversations. I just knew that he seemed to enjoy releasing people more than jailing them. Maybe that was his way of rationalizing his work or reframing his relationship to incarceration.

The irony wasn't lost on him either. Shortly after they started dating, Dad took Mom to meet *his* mother at the hospital, where she was still recuperating, and where he'd become such a regular that the staff greeted him on sight. About two months before, the town of New Britain had hosted a welcome-home celebration for Dad at the Darius Miller Music Shell, a quarter-globe-shaped slice of stage that was built in the style of Los Angeles's Hollywood Bowl. His local celebrity had only grown in the immediate months after his return.

My grandmother was in pretty bad shape by this point, unable to hear or see well. But even as Dad raised his voice to make the introduction, he knew she'd be tickled by their burgeoning romance: "Hi Mom, your wayward son is here to see you! . . . Mom, you won't believe this. I've come all the way back from China and I met a Chinese woman in our backyard, New Haven. She works at a Yale University laboratory. Her name is Audrey Lee—I brought her here to meet you, Mom." Mom mostly stood off to the side to be polite and let Dad have a bit of quality time with my grandmother. She recalled what that first meeting with her future mother-in-law was like:

> Jack updated his mother on his latest activities, telling her about the dumplings I made for him, the movies we saw together, and about the day we spent at the beach. Jack recalled their family summer days at the beach in Madison (Connecticut). Mary listened quietly with a contented smile on her face as he continued his monologue. I noticed how tightly Mary was holding onto Jack's fingers. She was now so thin that her cheeks were sunken; there was hardly a body under her dress, which made her abundant white hair even more striking. After a while, Mary's eyelids grew heavy and her grip on Jack's finger's loosened.[18]

*   *   *

I wish my childhood memories came with footnotes. In 1983, our family traveled to China, as a kind of goodwill exchange tour. My recollections from this early period of my life are few and far between, and what remains is wispy and opaque. Our visit was many things— a return for both my parents, a publicity operation for both governments, a feel-good story of heroism and reconciliation for NBC Broadcasting (that chronicled the trip), and my first visit to my literal motherland. My memories are a fusion of actual caches and reconstructed episodes that have been recounted to me so often that they feel authentic. There are some things I know are my own. The way the imposing karst mountains in Guilin reminded me of candy corn. The weird miniature impromptu international relations summit I had with a Mongolian boy during our visit to the Great Wall as we shook hands and exchanged toys, egged on by a small crowd of enthusiastic Chinese onlookers. I also recall the time I scandalized everyone by punching my mother's uncle—a hapless elder my father nicknamed "Uncle Grim"—when he patted me on the head.

There is an official trip photo of my dad meeting with Wang Bing-nan, the former Chinese assistant foreign minister and ambassador to Poland, who served as chief—albeit unofficial—diplomat to the United States up until the Cultural Revolution, when he was deposed, arrested, and imprisoned for almost a decade until he completed "reeducation" at a cadre school. In the photo, Wang and my father are sitting together on a long couch, flanked by another Chinese representative and our family friend Jim Warner, split by our translator and handler Zhou Bozhi. I'm far off to the side, sitting on my mother's lap, apparently deeply entranced with my own stubby little fingers. Wang's hands, by contrast, are sinewy and knotted— they looked like they had been crushed. He and Dad were a study in contrasts. Wang was jovial, beaming in his gray "Mao suit," while my father leaned in, expressionless in a dark suit and tie, listening intently to him.

In all, we spent three weeks in China. There were several formal meetings, although the one with Wang had the most gravitas. It had been a decade since my father's release from prison and thirty-five years since my mother had left the mainland for Taiwan. We landed in Beijing, as the visit was front-loaded with more "official" activities before we set off for the nostalgic and scenic parts of the trip. We were put up at the Grand Hotel Beijing, just a few blocks east of Tiananmen Square, and just around the corner from the Wangfujing shopping strip. This was, in fact, the same hotel that housed my grandmother and uncle Bill on their visits during Dad's incarceration.

"So, you are the famous John Downey. Your name has been on my lips for many years. I am so glad to finally meet you. You sure have a lot of friends. Welcome back to China." Wang 's friendly effervescence had set a congenial tone. But below the pleasantries were grave moments. His toothy grin and Dad's concentrated blankness obscured the fact that that photograph captured the moment Wang disclosed to my father information he thought my father did not know. The Chinese government had secretly attempted to parlay with the United States and proposed a round of negotiations that would have seen the two prisoners released after only five years—a proposal that was rejected by the United States. Wang revealed that he had prepared to negotiate for Fecteau and Dad's release as early as 1956, which was just a smidge more than three years after their capture— about a quarter of their total imprisonment, or in my father's case, a small fraction of his life sentence. But this was old news to my father, who had first learned of it in a one-thousand-page-long 1958 *Herald Tribune* almanac that Fecteau had received in the mail during his imprisonment. This had made sense of a seemingly impromptu carceral vacation tour they had taken in the spring of 1956, which retrospectively seemed designed to favorably impress the prisoners in expectation of an imminent return back to the United States. Dad chronicled this trip in a letter to his mother:

> Sorry to be late with this letter but I just returned yesterday from a 4 week trip around the country. We visited Tientsin [Tianjin], Nanking [Nanjing], Shanghai, Hongchow [Hangzhou], + Wuhan (Hankou) + if you look them up on the map it will give you some idea of the extent of the trip. Our actual visits covered a wide range of places + things—everything from factories + schools to basketball games and (in Shanghai) a fashion show! . . . I hope this finds you all well, I haven't had time to catch up on back mail yet but wanted to let you know things are rosy at this end. . . . Gave up smoking for Lent _ am glad that's over. Next time I've decided to sacrifice something like spinach or croquet. . . . Drank many a dram of tea on the journey but must admit I prefer beer. . . . Cigarettes are running low ("Luckies" + "Kools" preferred).[19]

However, although Wang's information was not, in fact, new, this reminder—delivered by the principal architect of my father's hypothetical early release—was a harsh reminder of how much of my father's life had been lost to the machinations of U.S.-Chinese foreign policy.

Unbeknownst to my family, Wang had planned a large banquet, which paraded us around a ballroom full of Chinese officials. The intimacy of the earlier meeting quickly transitioned into a formal CCP government spectacle. Dad was asked softball questions about his treatment in prison—the quality of food and the company he kept—which seemed to ignore the fact that he'd spent half his time in solitary confinement. Near the end of the banquet, Wang said to Dad, "We don't blame you for what happened; you were only a young man at the time." And with that, he stood up and toasted with his glass of *baijiu*: "We welcome you, our new friend, back to China. Let me quote an old saying: 'You were a lowly prisoner in the past, a highly honored guest today.' Let us drink to our new friendship." It was one of the rare times Dad ever drank liquor—he was a habitual consumer of relatively bland lagers but almost never spirits. As everyone in the room raised a glass and simultaneously saluted *"Gambei!"* Dad pounded back the *baijiu*, while everyone else politely sipped, and they were visibly taken aback at his enthusiasm. Although it was unusual for Dad to booze, his delivery mechanism was characteristically comical, flamboyant, and unassumingly impolitic. Luckily, everyone seemed to find this charming.

The next day, Barbara Roessner reported the meeting in the *Hartford Courant.*

> John T. Downey dined on Peking duck with an old enemy turned new friend Friday night, and learned some intriguing details of the Sino-American negotiations that swirled around his 20-year incarceration in a Chinese prison camp. . . .
>
> There was one story in particular that caught Downey's interest. Wang said that Downey would have been freed in 1956—after five years in prison—if the Americans had accepted a Chinese proposal to allow American and Chinese journalists to visit each other's countries.
>
> But the United States refused, adhering to the staunchly anti-communist policy of then Secretary of State John Foster Dulles, Wang said.
>
> "That was Dulles' policy. He thought it was blackmail," Downey said of the deal supposedly offered by the Chinese.
>
> Unbeknownst to Downey, U. Alexis Johnson, who was the chief American negotiator at the time, said from Washington, D.C., Friday

that the Chinese never linked their proposal for an exchange of newspaper reporters to Downey's release.

"Wang Bingnan might well have told him that, but they never said that to us at the time," Johnson, now a 77-year-old retiree said with a laugh.[20]

The policy surrounding Dad and Fecteau was implemented, in part, by Johnson, so the story went—so we would not have any particular reason to expect his candor in response to allegations that John Foster Dulles's intransigence to Chinese political power had effectively marooned them. But then again, neither could we assume the complete transparency of Wang's version of history, simply because he was friendly and earnest. The thing was, almost everybody was friendly and earnest with Dad at this point in his life. Both the Chinese and American governments treated him like a dignitary in the years after his release, although both had—inadvertently or not—prolonged his captivity, all while proclaiming their helplessness to free him.

We had an obligatory photoshoot in Tiananmen Square, in front of the famous massive portrait of Mao. We visited boilerplate tourist sites, like the Temple of Heaven, the Forbidden City, and of course the Great Wall, where I had the aforementioned international pseudo-diplomatic summit with the Mongolian child. There is an embarrassing photo of me at the Beijing Zoo, straddling a stuffed tiger like it was a pony—although it was haggard and looked like a zombie. We also visited a state farming commune that my parents soon realized had been staged, at least partially, for our arrival. My mother actually recognized it from the cover of an edition of a Chinese magazine she had read in the Yale Library. Two decades later, I saw this kind of temporary staged façade at the Jokhang Temple in Lhasa, Tibet's capital, as "traditionally" dressed Tibetan performers were ushered into the square to dramatize their Tibetanness for a junket of international reporters and were just as quickly disassembled once the media moved on.

But then again, the entire visit was an orchestrated publicity stunt for everyone involved. I might have been the only one who missed the memo. NBC filmed us much of the time, at least in the more cinematic moments, and every day the videographer sent film back home to be run on morning television. In the early 1980s, China was still something of a novelty, so the curiosity was as much about the footage from Beijing as it was the trip itself. At three years old, I was peaking on the cuteness front, and the camera operator enjoyed shooting me in my fashionable blue OshKosh overall shorts and striped polo shirt, with my standard-issue Asian bowl cut and knee socks.

I didn't appreciate how surreal the trip must have been for my parents until I returned to Beijing as an adult. As a seven-year-old, my mother had stayed in Beijing with her nuclear family for five months after fleeing their home city of Shenyang in 1948 on the front end of the Communist Revolution. They eventually went to Taiwan, some of the many mainlanders who took refuge in Chiang Kai-shek's emerging expat Kuomintang dictatorship. At one point, Mom ducked out from our hotel to visit the old Dong'an Market in the Wangfujing shopping district, which she had visited as a child. Her family had spent all their money there before following my grandfather to Taiwan:

> As our mother reasoned that the [Mainland] currency would be worthless once we got to Taiwan, she decided to spend it all, except for the travel fare, on the Moon Festival. She took all four children to stop at this market. We bought all that we could carry: boxes of mooncakes, juicy peaches, pears, graves, and sausages. We celebrated our last Moon Festival on Mainland China with abundance . . . but we missed our father. The next day, like so many political refugees in mainland China in those days, we started our long journey to Taiwan.[21]

Walking through Dong'an, my mother sank into a nostalgic mist, recollecting her childhood, long-since-passed parents, and the meandering path of her life that led her to the United States and ultimately back to that same Beijing marketplace. She'd spent most of her life fantasizing about Beijing's famous mooncakes, and she was thrilled to stumble across a specialty bakery. The bubble burst when she bit into a mooncake with the same texture and flavor as a hockey puck and quickly ran to the nearest trashcan. Mom's growing disenchantment with modern China—which now seemed hollow and drab compared to her memory—was contrasted against my father's enthusiasm for how much nicer everything seemed compared to *his*. They experienced Beijing at different—both somewhat liminal—inflection points in modern Chinese history. The year 1983 was itself the cusp of another transition. But none of us knew that at the time—certainly, I didn't. We just knew that the mooncakes were hard and tasteless. But while my mother interpreted 1983 as part of a declension narrative, Dad was more optimistic about China's economic ascendency.

After Beijing, we moved on to my mother's hometown, Shenyang, which was about a hundred and fifty miles farther northeast from the North Korean border. When my mother's family of six evacuated in 1948, they left behind her paternal grandparents, two uncles, two aunts, their respective nuclear families, and the medical clinic where her father worked as a physician. My grandfather, Lee Shaotang, also worked as an administrator at a local medical school once under Japanese occupation, later renamed First Medical University of China under Mao.[22] Although many of our relatives had scattered across the region since the Communist Revolution, the Chinese government had located a dozen or so of them, which we found astonishing in the pre-internet world. We had a big family meal, which was a powerful reunion for Mom, and gave Dad an opportunity to meet his extended in-law family and demonstrate his superhuman dumpling consumption.

* * *

John T. Downey, a former C.I.A. agent who became the longest-serving American prisoner of war by surviving more than 20 years in Chinese prisons after he was shot down over Manchuria in 1952, died on Monday at a hospice in Branford, Conn. He was 84.[23]

I watched my father die early in the morning of November 17, 2014. According to the death certificate, it was 12:25 a.m. It was probably a few minutes earlier, as I'd sat with him for a spell before notifying the nurse on duty. He'd been diagnosed with pancreatic cancer about a month earlier, and although he was originally projected to have upward of a year left, anyone who's encountered pancreatic cancer knows it's a fickle illness—rapid, sneaky, and brutal—often so advanced that it's terminal by the time it's detected. Within ten days of his diagnosis, Dad had been admitted to the hospital with an assortment of typical Stage-4 ailments. After a few days it became clear that the only real option was to transition to palliative care.

Although it was, very literally, a morbid affair, Dad's arrival at Connecticut Hospice felt weirdly festive. Dad was looped on painkillers, which really did wonders for his spirits as he was wheeled into the residence. The cold sun was shining that sharp slanted light that comes in the winter months and makes the whole brief daytime look like the golden hour before sunset. The salty wind blowing off Long Island Sound cut through its radiating warmth. An old friend's father and local New Haven musician, Richard Gallagher, happened to be volunteering on-site, and he sang "When the Saints Go Marching In" as Dad was wheeled into his room. Friends had shown up to welcome him. And I think it bears repeating, he was on a lot of painkillers.

The hospice had been at capacity, so we could only get Dad a bed because of the passing of a prior guest. This meant that there was a sort of pecking order in the six-person room he moved into. The higher up the food chain you got, the closer you got to the wall-to-wall window overlooking Long Island Sound. The view was expansive, ocean and sky separated by a sliver of cape that reflects electric magenta at sunset. Little by little, Dad would move his way up the ladder as the roommates who had arrived before him quietly died. In his last days, as his life force retreated inward and he could only drink water through a sponge lollipop, we wheeled his hospital bed around and raised its back, so he could look out into the deep of the Atlantic Ocean. We both had congenital lizard skin—the kind of skin so dry that it would become chapped and brittle in the colder months. But his had become soft and smooth, regaining a level of buoyancy that I'd never seen in him as an adult. He was already in his fifties by the time I was born. In his sickness, his large frame had become gaunt and his skin tightened so that he looked almost young.

One of the peculiar things about dying in a small New England town was that so many of his visitors had loved ones who'd previously died in the same hospice. In some of them, you could see the cycle of tension and release (sometimes followed by more tension), as they passed the room down the hall where their mother had died and entered the room where their father had died to say goodbye to *my* father. Or it was their sister. Or their cousin. Hospices are, of course, places of tremendous gravity. My mother and I swapped shifts, so that there was one of us by Dad's bedside from start to finish, and the other would occasionally go down to the cafeteria to chat with visitors over coffee. At one point, a family friend noticed one of the nurses stopping by to pick up a snack and recognized her as the principal caretaker of his own parent some years prior. After she left, he spoke about her reverently, as if she were some kind of oracle, who could foresee the moment of death as it grew ever closer.

On his last night, I sat alone with Dad, intently watching him draw breath, as his life slowly receded inward, safeguarding the most essential functions for as long as possible. To my untrained eye, he looked like he was sleeping like usual—frail and diminished, but more or less unchanged. Around 11:00 p.m., one of the nurses came in to check on him—the same nurse that another visitor had talked about as though she were a kind of death-clairvoyant. She leaned in for a close look at his face, left the room, and quickly returned with a shaving razor and a pair of warm towels. For the next few minutes, she wiped down his face and shaved his stubble, all the while quietly whispering into his ear words that were unintelligible to me. When she was finished, she gave him a long look, touched me on the shoulder and gently announced, "It won't be long now," as she breezed out the door.

He was dead within the hour. His breath grew softer and softer, and I held his hand in mine and hummed the tune to Wreckless Eric's 1997 single "Whole Wide World." The beats between inhalation and exhalation gradually lengthened, until one time he just didn't inhale. His skin turned to porcelain. Dad's early hospitalization had been a cycle of crashes and resuscitations and frantically beeping life-support machines, but his final moments were serene and almost luminescent. His death was sad but not tragic. One of the last things Dad said to me a few days earlier, maybe as a final attempt to offer some paternal comfort, was "I never thought I'd live this long."

* * *

We had a boilerplate Catholic wake back in Wallingford, Dad's first hometown. He wore a full face of tastefully applied makeup and his favorite suit. A steady line of mourners filed past to pay their last respects. Some of them had been regular visitors during Dad's final months, as he'd battled other ailments long before we had a clear cancer diagnosis. Others were former coworkers, old friends, and several kind locals who'd simply read his obituary in the local paper. A few jammed mementos into his coffin for Dad to take with him—a rosary or two, a pack of Kit Kats, a bottle of Moosehead Lager. Nick Dujmovic, an in-house scholar of CIA history from the Center for the Study of Intelligence—"the real CSI," someone once told us—showed up. He'd been our point person at the Agency during my dad's last few years, and he was as encyclopedic as he was kind. At one point the local diocesan priest paused the train of mourners to offer a few formal words of condolence and lead us in prayer. During the Lord's Prayer, about half of the people there outed themselves as infrequent churchgoers when they recited the outdated English translation that had been replaced six years earlier.

Dad's funeral was a classic *exitus et reditus* cycle completion. The mass was held at Most Holy Trinity Church in Wallingford, his family's original home parish during his childhood, just down the street from my great-grandfather's old saloon. Dad had been an altar boy there until he was summarily dismissed by the priest because he was so clumsy with the incenser. The crowd was standing room only, but I still felt dwarfed by the vast space under the high vaulted ceilings. Someone on the funeral director's team broke the liturgical rules and played "Danny Boy," which made all the Irish hearts swell. Maybe there's no such thing as being too corny during a funeral. There was even a bagpiper at the cemetery when we arrived for the internment. Dad was buried next to my grandfather, who—for reasons that remain unexplained to me—rested in an unmarked grave until Dad finally located it during my high school years. At the end of the service, a twenty- or thirty-something man in a trench coat pulled me aside to let me know that he'd attended on behalf of the CIA, to offer the condolences of his superiors and the larger intelligence community. As with the ceremonial honors Dad received later in life from the Agency, it was a mix of the sentimental and the eerie.

* * *

"Don't worry, we're gonna treat your dad like a rockstar," reassured the affable young staffer on the other end of the line. I was in my late twenties, and the CIA was cold-calling me about arrangements for my visit to the Agency headquarters. Although in retrospect I had just about as much cause to anticipate this eventuality as any person with no interest in joining the intelligence service, I never imagined myself ever visiting CIA headquarters in McLean, Virginia. I also honestly wasn't extremely confident I'd pass their security background check. I only visited twice. The first time was in 2010, for the premiere of *Extraordinary Fidelity*, a documentary about Fecteau and Dad commissioned by the Center for the Study of Intelligence. Before I could visit, there were several stages of logistical preparation. I had to submit personal information before I could be granted access to the headquarters' grounds, which everyone called "Langley" or "Campus," a quaint quasi-collegiate affectation obscuring its position as a hub of global surveillance. Then came this painless, if strange, phone orientation with this chipper staffer—what to do about parking, appropriate attire, and instructions to leave my phone in the car.

The George Bush Center for Intelligence is, in fact, a campus—a constellation of buildings woven together to accommodate the expanding capacity of the Agency. The "Original Headquarters Building," whose façade will be familiar to any casual viewer of CIA-related films or primetime cable shows, was just an idea at the time Dad's plane was shot down. It was built around the midpoint of his incarceration. It houses, among many other things, the CIA Memorial Wall, which includes anonymous black stars memorializing the Agency's killed-in-action. It includes stars for Robert C. Snoddy and Norman A. Schwartz, the pilots who died in the crash. There is also a

Starbucks, a museum, a gift shop peddling CIA kitsch, a library, and a hallway filled with paintings, including one of my father's ill-fated plane flying over Manchuria, lit up by antiaircraft fire. And it is home to the Director's office, where we sat down with Leon Panetta, who greeted me with the stereotypical "challenge coin" handshake, which I'd theretofore presumed was cloak-and-dagger conspiracy fiction. But then again, maybe he was playing things up for me.

Before our audience with Panetta, we had a chummy lunch during which I chatted with Michael Sulick, then director of Clandestine Operations, while Dad sat across the table, preoccupied with his conversation with someone from the Special Activities branch, the current iteration of my father's old Guerilla Warfare unit. This was during the waterboarding scandal era, which added a layer of surrealism. I noticed two things from that lunch. The first was that everyone was so charming, perhaps the greatest conversationalists I've ever met. Eventually I realized this should've been predictable because I was, after all, surrounded by professional spies. The second was that almost all of them had gone to Catholic (and specifically Jesuit) colleges: Fordham, Santa Clara, Le Moyne.

As the staffer had promised, the tone of the whole day was buoyant, with one brief exception. As we exited the Original Headquarters Building on our way to "The Bubble"—the CIA's theater that looked like a mini Epcot Center—a car crashed into a security barricade in the front parking lot, just a few yards away. Everyone, especially Panetta's bodyguard, reflexively tensed. But then we recognized the driver as John Kenneth Knaus, a legendary officer who'd worked with the Chushi Gangdruk Tibetan resistance to Chinese invasion in the early 1960s.

Before the screening, Panetta offered brief introductory remarks. He likened Fecteau and Dad to Jack Bauer from the television series *24*, which didn't strike me as a flattering comparison, but it was presumably made to appeal to the fantastical imaginations of the younger officers in attendance. Dad had no idea who Jack Bauer was, which was fitting, since an aide later confessed to me that Panetta didn't either. The film was a History Channel–style documentary, interesplicing black-and-white footage with dramatic reenactments and interviews. Because it was produced for internal use only, there

were some tonal curiosities, like when George Tenet seems to be sub-
tly reassuring the viewer (presumably a novice officer) that if they
unfortunately suffer a similar fate to Dad and Fecteau, they should at
least come out of it with back pay and a pension. I suppose those are
relevant points for an audience of spies who could plausibly be anxious about being captured abroad and disavowed by their own government. Dad's interviews in the film were about the longest I'd ever
heard him speak about his incarceration at one time. It also included
some brief video footage of the "skyhook" retrieval system that I'd
only seen in the movie *The Dark Knight*. Dad seemed pleased with the
representation. His only gripe was that he thought he should've been
played by Matt Damon. Although *Extraordinary Fidelity* was originally
meant to be private, the film was released to the Associated Press
in response to a Freedom of Information Act request and was soon
uploaded to the CIA's YouTube channel.[24] Afterward, my parents went
out to dinner with some of the film's bottom-liners and guests who'd
come into town for the event. By pure chance, Newt Gingrich was also
dining at the restaurant, and when he came over to greet the party,
Dad—in classic Irish Catholic fashion—stood up and only blurted
out a terse, "I'm a Democrat."

*   *   *

My father's unenviable distinction as the United States' longest-
serving prisoner of war was earned by being captured doing a job he
wasn't particularly trained for on a doomed mission that was itself
an extension of a foreign policy that his superiors knew would make
him unsalvageable if things went wrong. And when they did, he
was left, with his partner, to live out his life in solitary confinement
because it was more politically expedient to maintain the fiction that
they weren't who everyone knew they were. I'm sure people held a
range of impressions of him, and certainly that must have been true
once he became a judge and later had his courthouse rededicated
in his name. In many ways, he cultivated respectability—an aristo-
cratic education, a tragic interlude as a long-suffering patriotic icon,
a series of estimable white-collar public service jobs. It all synced so
nicely with those lost-then-found archetypes.

But this resurrection narrative contrasted with Dad's own image of himself. He saw himself as a kind of bumbling Inspector Clouseau, stumbling into incredibly good fortune and incredibly bad fortune alike. And this made him almost completely incapable of buying into the heroic mystique that was woven around him.

At the end of his 1974 interview, the historian James White asked Dad if he had any larger existential reflections on his decades in prison. In my dad's short responses I see some of his foundational personality traits all together—laconic, self-deprecating, unenchanted, but never *dis*enchanted.

JAMES WHITE: OK, well I think that about covers what I had in mind. Obviously you don't have any bitterness toward anyone, or do you?

JOHN DOWNEY: No, I don't, come to think of it. I mean I would say that's an honest statement. Not even the Chinese for that matter.

JW: Not towards the guy that sent you out?

JD: No, I wouldn't say so. I felt for him. It turned out to be such a goddamned disaster from his point of view.

JW: And the final would be so the so-called lessons, besides not getting caught. Do you have any words of wisdom on that?

JD: Gosh, I don't know. I mean I understand things have changed greatly in the whole orientation, but I've been brainwashed or changed to the extent that I think it's just as well not to put in time trying to overthrow other people's governments if you're not in a state of war with them, you know. And I mean the whole. . . . I really think restricting intelligence agency work to intelligence is probably, in the long run, probably a better move. But that's not very profound. No, I don't know any other great insight. . . .

JW: You still have to pick and choose your words. I guess you value your privacy. For example, in connection with awards, you wouldn't want them public, or would you? Don't let me put words in your mouth. Would you want your award public?

JD: I would want whatever the Agency thought was best. I haven't the slightest. If it happened, if it were announced publicly, that

Jack Downey with his wife, Audrey, and their son, Jack Lee.

wouldn't faze me except no doubt it would bring more phone calls and reporters snooping around. For that reason alone, I'd just as soon skip it, come to think of it, but I have no obsession to keep this secret and on the other hand, if they thought it were better to . . .

[End of Interview.][25]

ACKNOWLEDGMENTS

JACK LEE DOWNEY

It would be just plain rude to start my acknowledgments in any other way than by talking about my mother. This whole project is really hers, even though her name doesn't appear on the cover. She's the one who safeguarded Dad's original manuscript and discovered his prison letters, and she has been the driving force that brought this book to fruition, weathering some of the early storms that threatened to derail the project before it even got off its feet. In his afterlife, Mom has remained the primary custodian of Dad's memory—this has included not only meticulous historical research and granular close reads of his papers but also a massive amount of her own writing on his background. She's the real expert on my father, and this book quite simply wouldn't exist without her.

We had a lot of support throughout the process of trying to find a good platform for my father's original manuscript. Jack Keyes, Nick Neeley, and Bernadette Conway were steadfast companions during Dad's later years, and they encouraged us to see this project through when we might have otherwise given up. Carol Wiske, Penny Snow, Wendy Chen, Judy Clark, and Omi Hodwitz each dedicated *many* hours to working with my mother on our very first attempts at organizing a volume that would have ultimately looked quite different from—but was an integral part of the origin story that led to—this version. Judy Schiff, an acclaimed archivist and now my mother's neighbor, gave invaluable guidance for document preservation and seeded the idea for a posthumous book project before she even knew about my father's manuscript.

One of Dad's great skills was the ability to gather incredible friends. As his prison term stacked years upon years, high school and college classmates—particularly the Yale Class of 1951—kept him tethered to life back home by writing updates and sending him reading materials once he was able to receive mail. Former teammates, fraternity brothers, everyday pals, and even one of his undergrad wrestling coaches, Eddie O'Donnell, lobbied to keep Dad and Dick Fecteau's case from being buried or forgotten. In particular, his old roommate Putney Westerfield and Jerome Cohen—once a college classmate and later his law school professor—went to extraordinary lengths to pressure the Nixon administration to facilitate Dad's release. Additionally, Professor Cohen played an instrumental role in helping our family navigate the contours of publishing this unusual triptych of a book.

It is largely to Professor Cohen's credit that we eventually connected with Tom Christensen and Stephen Wesley at Columbia University Press. As one might imagine, we've been hypersensitive in trying to pair with collaborators who would sync well with our vision for the project, and we have been very grateful to Tom and Stephen for their respectful sensitivity, diligence, and professionalism. Peter and Amy Bernstein were capable matchmakers with CUP, and Geoffrey Menin shepherded us through some rocky moments on the front end of the project, before our partnership with Columbia.

The last but not least in this litany of gratitude is Dick Fecteau, my dad's partner and constant companion during their shared two decades in prison, even when they were separated by cell walls. Mr. Fecteau did us a tremendous service by reviewing Dad's manuscript, even though it forced him to relive their shared past trauma. As I mention in my afterword, Dad always used to say that if he'd been forced to do it all over again, there's nobody he'd rather be captured and held behind bars indefinitely with than Mr. Fecteau—Dad's gallows humor version of the highest possible compliment.

I'd like to dedicate this work to my grandparents—all of whom had passed long before I was born—but particularly to my paternal grandmother Mary V. Downey, who may have been the most unsung of heroes in this story, as far as public notoriety is concerned, but whom I've always known as the stuff of Downey family legend.

THOMAS J. CHRISTENSEN

I must thank William Yuen Yee for his excellent research assistance. I also thank Professor Chen Jian for expert advice and the sharing of some important background research materials. The book is much better for the careful review of the entire manuscript by Professor Nicholas Dujmovic, the scholar and former CIA historian who provided the first authoritative public account of Downey and Fecteau's ill-fated mission. I am grateful to Jack Lee Downey and his mother, Audrey Downey, for asking me to work on this project and for graciously inviting me to New Haven to view the Downey family archive. Stephen Wesley provided editorial advice throughout the drafting of the manuscript and the book is much better for his input. Dr. Henry A. Kissinger graciously agreed to an interview about the Nixon administration's strategy in appealing for Mr. Downey's release.

While writing the analytic chapters, I often remembered another Yale graduate and dedicated public servant, Ambassador James Lilley, whom I felt fortunate to consider not only a mentor but also a friend. I think that he would have liked this book, and I hope that my contribution to it honors his memory. And as with all books in this series, this one honors two extraordinary scholars of United States relations with East Asia whom I also consider mentors and friends, Warren I. Cohen and the late Nancy Bernkopf Tucker.

While this book was in production, a mentor, colleague, and friend, Professor Robert Jervis, passed away. A giant in the study of international politics, he was passionate about analytic diplomatic history and was a long-time consultant to the intelligence community. I spoke with him about this project in his final months and he expressed excitement about it. I regret that he never had a chance to read the book. I dedicate my part of this book to him. May his memory be a blessing. It will always be so for me.

NOTES

EPIGRAPH

John T. Downey, letter to Rufus Philips, October 10, 1952. John T. Downey papers, (MS 2053) Manuscripts and Archives, Yale University Library.

1. A PERFECT AMBUSH

1. Dick Fecteau, letter to Audrey Downey, confirmed that the Red Army used two antiaircraft 50's, to bring down the C-47 plane. "I walked right by them," he wrote, January 2018.
2. The name Peking (in the Wade-Giles transliteration sytem) was used in the West until the 1980s. When the People's Republic of China was established in 1949, the capital became known as Beijing (in the pinyin transliteration method).

2. AN AMERICAN HERO ON A FOOL'S MISSION

1. Nicholas Dujmovic, "Extraordinary Fidelity: Two CIA Prisoners in China, 1952–1973," *Studies in Intelligence* 50, no. 4 (2006), https://www.cia.gov/library /center-for-the-study-of-intelligence/csi-publications/csi-studies/studies /vol50no4/two-cia-prisoners-in-china-1952201373.html.
2. Dujmovic, "Extraordinary Fidelity," 1.

3. Joe F. Leeker, "CAT and Air America in Japan" (Dallas: University of Texas at Dallas, 2013–2015), 53, http://www.utdallas.edu/library/specialcollections /hac/cataam/leeker/history/japan.pdf; the only account that identifies the other two candidates is Roger B. Jeans, *The CIA and Third Force Movements in China During the Early Cold War* (New York: Lexington, 2018), 150–151. Since one was a retired army colonel, the chance for POW status upon capture seems even more plausible.

4. Dujmovic, "Extraordinary Fidelity," 4.

5. Dujmovic, "Extraordinary Fidelity," 4.

6. John Kenneth Knaus, *Orphans of the Cold War: America and the Tibetan Struggle for Survival* (New York: Public Affairs, 1999).

7. For discussion of the enabling legislation creating the Central Intelligence Agency, the Department of Defense, and the National Security Council, see "The National Security Act of 1947," Office of the Historian, U.S. Department of State, https://history.state.gov/milestones/1945-1952/national-security-act.

8. Jeans, *The CIA and Third Force Movements*, chap. 1.

9. Nancy Bernkopf Tucker, *Patterns in the Dust: Chinese-American Relations and the Recognition Controversy, 1949–50* (New York: Columbia University Press, 1983).

10. *Time*, January 3, 1938. For press coverage of Chiang after the war, see Tucker, *Patterns in the Dust*, 145–49.

11. Chen Jian, *Mao's China and the Cold War* (Chapel Hill: University of North Carolina Press, 2001), chap. 3.

12. For excellent coverage of the Marshall Mission, see Richard Bernstein, *China 1945: Mao's Revolution and America's Fateful Choice* (New York: Knopf, 2014) and Daniel Kurtz-Phelan, *The China Mission: George Marshall's Unfinished War, 1945–47* (New York: Norton, 2018).

13. Jeans, *The CIA and Third Force Movements*, 12.

14. Tucker, *Patterns in the Dust*; Thomas J. Christensen, *Useful Adversaries: Grand Strategy, Domestic Mobilization, and Sino-American Conflict* (Princeton, NJ: Princeton University Press, 1996), chaps. 4–5; and David M. Finkelstein, *Washington's Taiwan Dilemma, 1949–50: From Abandonment to Salvation* (Fairfax, VA: George Mason University Press, 1993).

15. Christensen, *Useful Adversaries*, 119.

16. Jeans, *The CIA and Third Force Movements*, xxii–xxiv, chaps. 1–2.

17. Jeans, *The CIA and Third Force Movements*, 169.

18. Jay Taylor, *The Generalissimo: Chiang Kai-shek and the Struggle for Modern China*, (Cambridge, MA: Belknap Press of Harvard University Press, 2009), 467.

19. Jeans, *The CIA and Third Force Movements*, 18.

20. Jeans, *The CIA and the Third Force Movements*.

21. Taylor, *The Generalissimo*, 464, 469.

22. Taylor, *The Generalissimo*, 454.

23. National Intelligence Estimate-10, Communist China, January 17, 1951, in *Tracking the Dragon: National Intellgence Estimates on China During the Era of Mao, 1948–76*, (Langley, VA: National Intelligence Council, 2004), 83–86. For the two million figure, see Jeans, *The CIA and Third Force Movements*, 37.

24. Jeans, *The CIA and Third Force Movements*, chap. 2.

25. For a discussion of the distinctions between Kennan's strongpoint strategy and NSC 68, see John Lewis Gaddis, *Strategies of Containment: A Critical Reappraisal of Postwar American National Security Policy* (New York: Oxford University Press, 1982), chaps. 3–4.

26. Christensen, *Useful Adversaries*, 122–28.

27. Dean Acheson, *Present at the Creation: My Years at the State Department* (New York, Norton, 1969), 375.

28. Michael M. Sheng, *Battling Western Imperialism: Mao, Stalin, and the United States* (Princeton, NJ: Princeton University Press, 1997), 177–78.

29. For the impressive biographies of American OPC officers in Hong Kong in 1949–1950, see Jeans, *The CIA and Third Force Movements*, chap. 1.

30. Jeans, *The CIA and Third Force Movements*, 18–20, 30–32.

31. Jeans, *The CIA and Third Force Movements*, chap. 5.

32. Christensen, *Useful Adversaries*.

33. Nicholas Dujmovic, "Drastic Actions Short of War: The Origins and Application of CIA's Covert Paramilitary Force in the Early Cold War," *Journal of Military History* 76 (July 2012): 797, 799.

34. Jeans, *The CIA and Third Force Movements*, 32.

35. John T. Downey as quoted in Dujmovic, "Drastic Actions Short of War," 804.

36. Dujmovic, "Drastic Actions Short of War," 803.

37. James Lilley with Jeffrey Lilley, *China Hands: Nine Decades of Adventure, Espionage, and Diplomacy in Asia* (New York: Public Affairs, 2004).

38. Dujmovic, "Drastic Actions Short of War," 797.

39. Dujmovic, "Drastic Actions Short of War," 798.

40. Dujmovic, "Drastic Actions Short of War," 791.

41. "John Kenneth Knaus, CIA Officer Who Aided in Tibetan Struggle, Dies at 92," *Washington Post*, May 26, 2016.

42. Knaus, *Orphans of the Cold War.*

43. David Cheng Chang, *The Hijacked War: The History of Chinese POWs in the Korean War* (Stanford, CA: Stanford University Press, 2020), chaps. 4 and 6, especially pages 130–31.

44. Chang, *The Hijacked War*, chap. 6, and pages 201–8.

45. Leeker, "CAT and Air America in Japan," 1.

46. Taylor, *The Generalissimo*, 454.

47. Chang, *The Hijacked War*, 202. One of the teaching edicts for the prisoners was "we shall return to Formosa under any circumstance." Only two of the twenty-one thousand POWs were originally from Taiwan (Formosa).

48. For the 1951 CIA estimates, see Jeans, *The CIA and Third Force Movements*, 47.

49. Dujmovic, "Drastic Actions Short of War," 791.
50. Chang, *The Hijacked War*, chap. 15.
51. Lilley, *China Hands*, 80.
52. Lilley, *China Hands*, 81.
53. Lilley, *China Hands*, 82.
54. Lilley, *China Hands*, 82–83.
55. Leeker, "CAT and Air America in Japan," 54.
56. Lilley, *China Hands*, 82; Jeans, *The CIA and Third Force Movements*, 41; and Taylor, *The Generalissimo*, 455.

3. WHO I AM, WHERE I CAME FROM

1. Thomas Meskill later became a member of Congress; he was the governor of Connecticut in 1973 when Jack returned and later became a federal judge.
2. James Lilley with Jeffrey Lilley, *China Hands: Nine Decades of Adventure, Espionage, and Diplomacy in Asia* (New York: Public Affairs, 2004), 70.
3. Lilley, *China Hands*, 70. Among the one thousand students of the Yale Class of 1951, one hundred joined the CIA.

4. THE KOREAN WATERSHED: THE COLD WAR BEGINS FOR DOWNEY AND AMERICA

1. Rosemary Foot, *The Wrong War: American Policy and the Dimensions of the Korean Conflict* (Ithaca, NY: Cornell University Press, 1985); Ernest May, *Lessons of the Past: The Use and Misuse of History in American Foreign Policy* (New York: Oxford University Press, 1973); Glenn Paige, *The Korea Decision, June 24–30, 1950* (New York: Free Press, 1968); William W. Stueck, *The Road to Confrontation: American Policy Toward China and Korea* (Chapel Hill: University of North Carolina Press, 1981).
2. James Lilley, *China Hands: Nine Decades of Adventure, Espionage, and Diplomacy in Asia* (New York: Public Affairs, 2004), chap. 5.
3. Robert Jervis, "The Impact of the Korean War on the Cold War," *Journal of Conflict Resolution* (Dec. 1980): 563–592; Paul Hammond, "NSC 68: Prologue to Rearmament" in *Strategy, Politics, and Defense Budgets*, ed. Warner S. Schilling, Paul Y. Hammond, and Glenn H. Snyder, (New York: Columbia University Press, 1962), 351–363; and Thomas J. Christensen, *Useful Adversaries: Grand Strategy, Domestic Mobilization, and Sino-American Conflict, 1947–1958* (Princeton, NJ: Princeton University Press, 1996), chapter 4–5.

4. For the impact of the Korean War on the growth of the CIA and the OPC in particular, see chapter 2 above.
5. Jack Downey's personal chronology kindly shared with the author by his family.
6. Deborah Welch Larson, *The Origins of Containment: A Psychological Explanation* (Princeton, NJ: Princeton University Press, 1985), 219, 227, 240.
7. Arthur Vandenberg quoted in Robert Divine, *Foreign Policy and U.S. Presidential Elections, 1952–1960* (New York: New Viewpoints, 1974), 70. For the inside story of the creation of the Truman Doctrine speech, see Joseph Marion Jones, *The Fifteen Weeks: An Inside Account of the Genesis of the Marshall Plan* (Boston: Mariner, 1965). Jones was the author of the speech. For a review of the documentary evidence regarding the thinking of Truman and his cabinet, see Christensen, *Useful Adversaries*, chap. 3.
8. For comparisons of pre-WWII peacetime military expenditures with the budgets from 1948–1950, see Myron Slade Kendrick, *A Century and a Half of Federal Expenditures* (Cambridge, MA: National Bureau of Economic Research, 1955), 12; Warner Schilling, "The Politics of National Defense," in Schilling, Hammond, and Snyder, *Strategy, Politics, and Defense Budgets*, 30.
9. On Kennan's strongpoint strategy and its application to Asia, see John Lewis Gaddis, *Strategies of Containment: A Critical Reappraisal of Postwar American National Security Policy* (New York: Oxford University Press, 1982), chaps. 2–3; and Paul Heer, *Mr. X and the Pacific: George F. Kennan and American Policy in East Asia* (Ithaca, NY: Cornell University Press, 2018).
10. Robert Blum, *Drawing the Line: The Origins of American Containment Policy in East Asia* (New York, Norton, 1982), 179–180, 193.
11. The earliest use of the term may have been by Lewis McCarroll Purifoy, *Harry Truman's China Policy: McCarthyism and the Diplomacy of Hysteria, 1947–51* (New York: New Viewpoints, 1976). For a fuller analysis of the logroll between fiscal conservatives and the China lobby that produced the Asialationist challenge to Truman's European initiatives, see Christensen, *Useful Adversaries*, 69–76.
12. Kennan as quoted in Gaddis, *Strategies of Containment*, 52.
13. Christensen, *Useful Adversaries*, chaps. 3–4.
14. Stueck, *The Road to Confrontation*, 163–64. For the United States' general fear of entrapment in war by smaller Asian allies, see Victor Cha, "Powerplay: Origins of the U.S. Alliance System in Asia," *International Security* 34, no. 3 (Winter 2009/2010): 158–96.
15. For the declassified original document, see National Security Council Document Number 68, *Foreign Relations of the United States*, 1950, Vol. 1: 234–92. For analysis see Hammond, "NSC 68"; Samuel Wells, "Sounding the Tocsin: NSC 68 and the Soviet Threat," *International Security* 4, no. 2 (Fall 1979), 116–58; and Gaddis, *Strategies of Containment*, chap. 4.

16. Schilling, *The Politics of National Defense*, 153; for evidence of public opinion support for such a strategy, see Christensen, *Useful Adversaries*, 47–48.

17. Wells, "Sounding the Tocsin"; Gaddis, *Strategies of Containment*, chap. 4.

18. Paige, *The Korea Decision*; May, *Lessons of the Past*; and William W. Stueck, *The Korean War: An International History* (Princeton, NJ: Princeton University Press, 1997), 43.

19. Chen Jian, *China's Road to the Korean War: The Making of Sino-American Conflict* (New York: Columbia University Press, 1994); Allen S. Whiting, *China Crosses the Yalu: The Decision to Enter the Korean War* (Stanford, CA: Stanford University Press, 1960); and Christensen, *Useful Adversaries*, chap. 5.

20. "Public Attitudes Concerning Formosa," September 26, 1950, Foster Papers, Box 33, File: China, 1949–1952, National Archives.

21. Thomas J. Christensen, *Worse than a Monolith: Alliance Politics and Problems of Coercive Diplomacy in Asia* (Princeton, NJ: Princeton University Press, 2011), 70.

22. For a review of multiple original communications between Stalin and Mao in October 1950 in Chinese-language documents, see Christensen, *Worse than a Monolith*, 89–103.

23. Guy D, Vanderpool, "COMINT and the PRC Intervention in the Korean War," DOCID 304650, in National Security Archive, George Washington University, doc. no. 21, 15; and National Intelligence Council, "Chinese Communist Intervention in Korea," NIE-2, November 6, 1950, in *Tracking the Dragon: National Intelligence Estimates on China During the Era of Mao, 1949–76* (Washington, DC: U.S. Government Printing Office, 2004), 76.

24. For a review of the Chinese-language primary and secondary documents supporting these points, see Christensen, *Worse than a Monolith*, chap. 3.

25. Elizabeth Stanley, *Paths to Peace: Domestic Coalition Shifts, War Termination and the Korean War* (Stanford, CA: Stanford University Press, 2009); Foot, *The Wrong War*; David Cheng Chang, *The Hijacked War: The Story of Chinese POWs in the Korean War* (Stanford, CA: Stanford University Press, 2020); and Chen Jian, *Mao's China and the Cold War* (Chapel Hill: University of North Carolina Press, 2001), chap. 4.

26. Lilley, *China Hands*, 68–70.

27. For a recent analysis of the extent of these efforts, see Austin Carson, *Secret Wars: Covert Conflict in International Relations* (Princeton, NJ: Princeton University Press, 2018), chap. 5.

28. Jon Halliday, "Air Operations in Korea: The Soviet Side of the Story," in William J. Williams, *A Revolutionary War: Korea and the Transformation of the Postwar World* (Chicago: Imprint Publications, 1993); and Jon Halliday, "A Secret War," *Far Eastern Economic Review* (April 22, 1993): 32–36.

29. Halliday, "Air Operations in Korea" and "A Secret War"; also see Paul H. Nitze, *From Hiroshima to Glasnost: At the Center of Decision* (New York: Grover Weidenfeld, 1989), 106–8.
30. "Taipei to the Secretary of State," February 9, 1950, Decimal File 293.1141/2-950, Box 1205, National Archives.
31. Thomas J. Christensen, "Threats, Assurances, and the Last Chance for Peace: The Lessons of Mao's Korean War Telegrams," *International Security* (Summer 1992): 122–154.
32. Morton Halperin, *Limited War in the Nuclear Age* (New York: Wiley, 1963); and Thomas Schelling, *Arms and Influence* (New Haven, CT: Yale University Press, 1966).
33. Christensen, *Worse than a Monolith*, chap. 4.
34. For coverage of Zhou's shock and Kim Il-sung's elation at the changed Soviet position on POWs after Stalin's death, see Chang, *The Hijacked War*, chap. 14.

5. THE MAKING OF A MISSION

1. This name is a pseudonym.

6. THE FLIGHT OVER CHINA

1. John K. Singlaub was a highly decorated former member of OSS and a founding member of the CIA. He later became a major general but was removed from command in Korea for publicly criticizing President Jimmy Carter's decision to reduce American troop strength in that country in 1977.

8. OF SOLDIERS AND SPIES

1. See, for example, Christina Zhao, "Xi Jinping Demands 'Absolute Loyalty' from China's People's Liberation Army," *Newsweek*, August 20, 2018, https://www.newsweek.com/xi-jinping-demands-absolute-loyalty-chinas-peoples-liberation-army-1080484.
2. On the ways in which the CCP disciplinary organs override state anti-corruption processes in extralegal ways, see Jamie Horsley, "What's So Controversial About China's New Anti-Corruption Body?" Brookings Institution, May 30, 2018, https://www.brookings.edu/opinions/whats-so-controversial-about-chinas-new-anti-corruption-body/; also see Ling Li,

"Politics of Anti-Corruption in China: Paradigm Change of the Party's Disciplinary Regime, 2012–2017," *Journal of Modern China* 28, no. 115 (July 2018), https://www.tandfonline.com/doi/full/10.1080/10670564.2018.1497911.

3. Josh Chin, "China Dramatically Boosts Spending on Internal Security," *Wall Street Journal*, March 6, 2018, https://www.marketwatch.com/story/china-dramatically-boosts-spending-on-internal-security-2018-03-06.

4. See Richard McGregor, "How the State Runs Business in China," *The Guardian*, July 25, 2019, https://www.theguardian.com/world/2019/jul/25/china-business-xi-jinping-communist-party-state-private-enterprise-huawei.

5. Secretary of State Michael Pompeo, "Communist China and the Free World's Future," https://www.state.gov/communist-china-and-the-free-worlds-future/; also see "Remarks by Deputy National Security Advisor Matt Pottinger to the Miller Center at the University of Virginia." The White House, May 4, 2020, www.whitehouse.gov/briefings-statements/remarks-deputy-national-security-advisor-matt-pottinger-miller-center-university-virginia/.

6. Robert Burns, "Soldiers' Cold War Ordeal Tied to CIA Link, Mysterious Leak," *Los Angeles Times*, September 13, 1998, https://www.latimes.com/archives/la-xpm-1998-sep-13-mn-22205-story.html. For further public confirmation of the plane's origins at Clark Air Base in the Philippines and the CCP's discovering that the crew had links to a CIA program, see "ASN Wikibase Occurrence #86182," *Aviation Safety Network*, http://aviation-safety.net/wikibase/86182.

7. Burns, "Soldiers' Cold War Ordeal."

8. Caleb Larson, "Operation Moolah: The Secret Plan to Get a Russian Fighter Jet Out of North Korea," *The National Interest*, April 22, 2020, https://nationalinterest.org/blog/buzz/operation-moolah-secret-plan-get-russian-fighter-jet-out-north-korea-147036.

9. Kenneth T. Young, *Negotiating with the Chinese Communists: The United States Experience, 1953–57* (New York: McGraw Hill, 1968), 40–41.

10. Hammarskjöld shared these talking points with the Russian ambassador to the United Nations before he departed for Beijing, knowing that he would dutifully pass them on to Zhou Enlai. For the document from the Chinese foreign ministry archives, see "Minutes of Conversation Between Premier Zhou Enlai and Soviet Ambassador Pavel Yudin Regarding Dag Hammarskjold's Trip to Beijing," January 4, 1955, in Woodrow Wilson Center Digital Archive, https://digitalarchive.wilsoncenter.org/document/113183.pdf?v=c4cdbc8a38b2b7df0921352ec74d89b5.

11. "Telegram from the Representative at the United Nations (Lodge) to the Department of State," January 13, 1955, in *Foreign Relations of the United States (FRUS)*, 1955–57, China, Vol. II, https://history.state.gov/historicaldocuments/frus1955-57v02/d11.

12. Young, *Negotiating with the Chinese Communists*, 36–44.

13. "Telegram from the Representative at the United Nations (Lodge) to the Department of State," January 13, 1955.

14. The U.S. government document first reporting the conviction of Downey, Fecteau, and the B-29 crew was a translation of a wire report from the New China News Agency by the Foreign Broadcast Information Service in Tokyo. See "Text of Spy Judgement," November 23, 1954, 17:22 GMT, FBIS Tokyo in Downey's personal files.

15. "Telegram from the Representative at the United Nations (Lodge) to the Department of State," January 13, 1955.

16. This according to the family's chronology, which was kindly shared with the author.

17. "US Spy's Mission in Flying to Communist China," *Akahita Shimbun*, Tokyo, January 7, 1955, translated by USAF Intelligence Service Squadron, Document IR 69–55 (unclassified), January 11, 1955. This document was in Downey's personal files reviewed by the author.

18. Nicholas Dujmovic, "Extraordinary Fidelity: From a Chinese Prison to CIA's Highest Honor," *Studies in Intelligence* 50, no. 4 (December 2006), reprint, 9. On this issue also see an excellent piece of scholarship by Daniel Aaron Rubin, "Pawns of the Cold War: John Foster Dulles, the PRC, and the Imprisonments of John Downey and Richard Fecteau" (Master's thesis, Department of History, University of Maryland, 2004), 50.

19. Shen Zhihua, "Sino-North Korean Conflict and Its Resolution During the Korean War," *Cold War International History Project*, nos. 14/15 (Fall 2003/Winter 2004): 19; and Thomas J. Christensen, *Worse than a Monolith: Alliance Politics and Problems of Coercive Diplomacy in Asia* (Princeton, NJ: Princeton University Press, 2011), 120.

20. For a comprehensive history of the Chinese POW issue and its impact on the Korean War, see David Cheng Chang, *The Hijacked War: The Story of Chinese POWs in the Korean War* (Stanford, CA: Stanford University Press, 2020). For some of the policy debates on prisoner repatriation, see chap. 9. Also see Elizabeth Stanley, *Paths to Peace: Domestic Coalition Shifts, War Termination, and the Korean War* (Stanford, CA: Stanford University Press, 2009), esp. chap. 6, for U.S. debates on repatriation; and Chen Jian, *Mao's China and the Cold War* (Chapel Hill: University of North Carolina Press, 2001), chap. 4.

21. Chang, *The Hijacked War*, especially chaps. 2, 3, and 5, for some diverse and detailed biographies of CPV "volunteers" who would later become POWs.

22. William W. Stueck, *The Korean War: An International History* (Princeton, NJ: Princeton University Press, 1995), chap. 8; and Chang, *The Hijacked War*, 129–37 on why Taiwanese interpreters were necessary for interrogation. For evidence of brainwashing, see Chang, *The Hijacked War*, chap. 8, and for coercion against the POWs in the vetting process for "voluntary repatriation" see Chang, *The Hijacked War*, chap. 10.

23. Chang, *The Hijacked War*, 128–29.

24. Chang, *The Hijacked War*, 372.
25. Chang, *The Hijacked War*, chap. 15.
26. Chang, *The Hijacked War*, Conclusion.
27. Chang, *The Hijacked War*, chap. 16. I take a less jaded view of Truman and Eisenhower's intentions toward the prisoners, although I fully appreciate the contradictions that Chang has uncovered between concern for the welfare of the individual prisoner expressed in the voluntary repatriation policy and the goal of turning some of those prisoners into agents of subversive political change upon their return. Our difference on this score may result from my even more jaded view than Chang of the oppressive political life of Chinese citizens under the Chinese communists in the 1950s and 1960s. I find it impossible to imagine that having been a former POW in a U.S.-run camp in South Korea would not be a major and dangerous scar on a Chinese citizen's political dossier regardless of the details of what had occurred in the camps.
28. Chang, *The Hijacked War*, Conclusion.
29. Stueck, *The Korean War*, chap. 8.
30. Shen Zhihua, "Jieshu Chaoxian Zhanzheng" ("Ending the Korean War") in *Lengzhan yu Zhongguo*, ed. Zhang Baiji and Niu Jun (The Cold War and China) (Beijing: World Knowledge Publishers, 2002), 182–83; Shen Zhihua, "Sino-North Korean Conflict," 19; Shen Zhihua and Yafeng Xia, *A Misunderstood Friendship: Mao Zedong, Kim Il-sung, and Sino-North Korean Relations, 1949–76* (New York: Columbia University Press, 2018), chap. 2; Christensen, *Worse than a Monolith*, 120; Gregg A. Brazinsky, *Winning the Cold War: Sino-American Rivalry During the Cold War* (Chapel Hill: University of North Carolina Press, 2017), 52–53; and Chang, *The Hijacked War*, 256–66.
31. Christensen, *Worse than a Monolith*, chap. 4, offers detailed documentation from China and Russia to support these points. Also see Shen and Xia, *A Misunderstood Friendship*, chap. 2; and Elizabeth Stanley, *Paths to Peace: Domestic Coalition Shifts, War Termination, and the Korean War* (Stanford, CA: Stanford University Press, 2009), chap. 4.
32. Rosemary Foot, *A Substitute for Victory: The Politics of Peacemaking at the Korean Armistice Talks* (Ithaca, NY: Cornell University Press, 1990), 182–83; and Christensen, *Worse than a Monolith*, 121.
33. Shen Zhihua, "Jieshu Chaoxian Zhanzheng," 200–205.

12. B-29 CREW WERE RELEASED FROM CHINA

1. Dick Fecteau said "I walked by two antiaircraft 50's" in a private letter to Audrey Downey, February 2018.
2. After his release, Baumer had the rest of his foot amputated. His military career ended, and he became a high-school guidance counselor.

3. Dag Hammarskjöld had asked to visit the prison where the American prisoners resided. The Chinese government refused but provided the photographs instead.

4. Bina Cady Kiyonaga, *My Spy: Memoir of a CIA Wife* (New York: Avon, 2000), 137: "Jack Downey still had the presence of mind to seize an opportunity to get an important message out."

14. "YOUR GOVERNMENT DOES NOT WANT YOU BACK": THE FAILURE OF U.S.-PRC NEGOTIATIONS AT GENEVA

1. The release of the B-29 crew is discussed in chapters 8 and 12. For a detailed account of their ordeal, see Robert Burns, "Soldiers' Cold War Ordeal Tied to CIA Link, Mysterious Leak," *Los Angeles Times*, September 13, 1998, https://www.latimes.com/archives/la-xpm-1998-sep-13-mn-22205-story.html.

2. It seems unlikely that Chinese officials would have presented in advance a draft version of the U.S.-PRC agreement that was reached in Geneva on September 10, 1955. For this reason, it seems likely that Downey's recollection was simply off by two or three weeks and that Chou approached him in September, not August.

3. For the full original text, see "Agreed Announcement of the Ambassadors of the United States of America and the People's Republic of China," September 10, 1955, in *Foreign Relations of the United States (FRUS), 1955–57, China*, Vol. III, 85–86.

4. See the memoirs of Wang and Johnson: Wang Bingnan, *Zhongmei Huitan Jiu Nian Huigu* (Review of the Nine Year Sino-American Ambassadorial Talks) (Beijing: World Knowledge, 1985), 18–60; and U. Alexis Johnson, with Jet Olivarius McAlister, *The Right Hand of Power* (Englewood Cliffs, NJ: Prentice Hall, 1984), chap. 8; also see Kenneth T. Young, *Negotiating with the Chinese Communists, 1953–67* (New York: McGraw-Hill, 1968), chaps. 2–4.

5. See Zhang Baijia, "The Changing International Scene and Chinese Policy Toward the United States," in *Re-examining the Cold War: U.S.-China Diplomacy, 1954–73*, ed. Robert S. Ross and Jiang Changbin (Cambridge, MA: Harvard University Asia Center, 2001); Gong Li, "Tensions in the Taiwan Strait: Chinese Strategies and Tactics," in *Re-examining the Cold War*; Nancy Bernkopf Tucker, *Taiwan, Hong Kong, and the United States* (New York: Twayne Publishers, 1994), 38–40; Nancy Bernkopf Tucker, "John Foster Dulles and the Taiwan Roots of the 'Two Chinas' Policy," in *John Foster Dulles and the Diplomacy of the Cold War*, ed. Richard Immerman (Princeton, NJ: Princeton University Press, 1990), 240–42; and Thomas J. Christensen, *Worse than a Monolith: Alliance Politics and Problems of Coercive Diplomacy in Asia* (Princeton, NJ: Princeton University Press, 2011), 135–46.

6. Shen Zhihua, "Yuanzhu yu Xianzhi: Sulian yu Zhongguo de Hewuqi de Yanzhi," (Assistance and Limitations: Sino-Soviet Nuclear Weapons Research and Development), *Lishi Yanjiu* (Historical Studies) (March 2004); Taylor M. Fravel, *Active Defense: China's Military Strategy Since 1949* (Princeton, NJ: Princeton University Press, 2019), chap. 8; and John Lewis and Xue Litai, *China Builds the Bomb* (Stanford, CA: Stanford University Press, 1988), chap. 3.

7. Wang, *Zhongmei Huitan Jiu Nian Huigu*, 48.

8. The author acquired two important declassified top secret documents relevant to the Geneva talks from the PRC foreign ministry archives. In the first decade of this century, these archives were still open to foreign scholars. *Guanyu zhongmei shuangfang dashiji daibiao zai Rineiwa huiyi de fangan* (The Plan Regarding China-U.S. Bilateral Ambassadorial-Level-Representative Talks at Geneva,), Cable No. 273 from the PRC foreign ministry to Warsaw, Geneva, and Moscow, July 18, 1955, Top Secret (*juemi*) Archive No. 111-00014-01; and *Guanyu zhongmei dashiji daibiao zai Rineiwa huitan de zhishi* (Instructions Regarding China-U.S. Ambassadorial-Level Representative Talks at Geneva), Cable No. 481 to Geneva, July 30, 1955, Top Secret (*juemi*) Archive No. 111-0014-03.

9. Chen Jian, *Mao's China and the Cold War* (Chapel Hill: University of North Carolina Press, 2010), 191–92; Young, *Negotiating with the Chinese Communists*, 44–47.

10. Wang, *Zhongmei Huitan Jiu Nian Huigu*, 44–45.

11. In his initial instructions for the August meetings, Johnson is sternly warned not to indicate diplomatic recognition of the PRC in his discussions with Wang. "Letter from the Secretary of State to Ambassador U. Alexis Johnson," July 29, 1955, in *FRUS*, 1955, China, Vol. II, 685–87.

12. "Telegram from the Representative at the United Nations (Lodge) to the Department of State," January 13, 1955, in *FRUS*, 1955-57, China, Vol. II, https://history.state.gov/historicaldocuments/frus1955-57v02/d11.

13. For Hammaskjöld's strategy in the talks with Zhou, intentionally shared in advance with the Soviet ambassador to the UN, see "Minutes of Conversation Between Premier Zhou Enlai and Soviet Ambassador Pavel Yudin Regarding Dag Hammarskjold's Trip to Beijing," January 4, 1955, in Woodrow Wilson Center Digital Archive.

14. Young, *Negotiating with the Chinese Communists*, chap. 3.

15. Wang, *Zhongmei Huitan Jiu Nian Huigu*, 44–45.

16. Yang Gongsu, *Zhonghua Renmin Gongheguo Waijiao Lilun yu Shixian* (The Theory and Practice of PRC Diplomacy), 1996 (internally circulated), 70–73.

17. Wang, *Zhongmei Huitan Jiu Nian Huigum*, 62–63.

18. For Wang's initial categorization of Downey and Fecteau alongside the recently released B-29 crew in the "military" category, see "Telegram from Ambassador U. Alexis Johnson to the Department of State," August 2, 1955,

in *FRUS*, 1955–57, Vol. III, 7–10. For Johnson's reply to Wang that the two spies were civilians, not military officers, and Wang's retort, see "Telegram from Ambassador U. Alexis Johnson to the Department of State," August 4, 1955, in *FRUS*, 1955–57, Vol. III, 14.

19. "Instructions Regarding China-U.S. Ambassadorial-Level Representative Talks at Geneva," July 30, 1955, 4.

20. Burns, "Soldiers' Cold War Ordeal Tied to CIA Link, Mysterious Leak."

21. Wang, *Zhongmei Huitan Jiu Nian Huigu*, 43, 48.

22. "Instructions Regarding China-U.S. Ambassadorial-Level Representative Talks at Geneva," July 30, 1955.

23. Wang, *Zhongmei Huitan Jiu Nian Huigu*, 26.

24. *Zeng Zai Zhongguo Fuxing 21 Nian de Meiguo Qian Te Gong Qu Shi, Zhencha Zhongguo Shi Bei Jiluo* (A Former American Special Agent Who Served 21 Years in China Has Died. [His plane] Was Shot Down While Surveilling China), an unpublished compilation of the relevant history of Downey's case. Li Bingkui, *Meiguo Jiandie yuYi Jiu Wu Si Nian Zhi Yi Jiu Wu Wu Nian Zhong Mei Guanxi Weiji* (U.S. Spies and the 1954–1955 Crisis in China-U.S. Relations), *Zhong Gong Dang Shi Yanjiu* (Chinese Communist Party History Studies) 6 (2008): 65–71.

25. "Telegram from Ambasador U. Alexis Johnson to the Department of State," August 12, 1955 33–34. And as Rubin points out, since the PRC government also considered the B-29 crew to be spies and released them in late July, Wang had some degree of credibility that the status of "spy" did not fully preclude a review of Downey and Fecteau's cases. Daniel Aaron Rubin, "Pawns of the Cold War: John Foster Dulles, the PRC, and the Imprisonments of John Downey and Richard Fecteau" (Master's thesis, Department of History, University of Maryland, 2004), 47.

26. Wang, *Zhongmei Huitan Jiu Nian Huigu*.

27. "The Plan Regarding China-U.S. Bilateral Ambassadorial-Level-Representative Talks at Geneva," July 18, 1955; and "Instructions Regarding China-U.S. Ambassadorial-Level Representative Talks at Geneva," July 30, 1955.

28. Christensen, *Useful Adversaries: Grand Strategy, Domestic Mobilization, and Sino-American Conflict, 1947–1958* (Princeton, NJ: Princeton University Press, 1996), 192.

29. Johnson, *The Right Hand of Power*, chap. 8; and Young, *Negotiating with the Chinese Communists*, chap. 4.

30. Wang, *Zhongmei Huitan Jiu Nian Huigu*, 57–58; and Young, *Negotiating with the Chinese Communists*.

31. "Telegram from the Secretary of State to Ambassador U. Alexis Johnson, at Geneva," August 5, 1955, in *FRUS*, 1955–57, China, Vol. III, 17–18; Young, *Negotiating with the Chinese Communists*, chaps. 3–4; and Johnson, *The Right Hand of Power*, chap. 8.

32. Wang, *Zhongmei Huitan Jiu Nian Huigu*, 50.

33. "Telegram from the Secretary of State to Ambassador U. Alexis Johnson, at Geneva," August 10, 1955, in *FRUS*, 1955–57, China, Vol. III, 26–27.

34. For the original text, see "Agreed Announcement of the Ambassadors of the United States of America and the People's Republic of China," September 10, 1955, in *FRUS*, 1955–57, China, Vol. III, 85–86.

35. Rubin, "Pawns of the Cold War," 53.

36. For an excellent brief bio of Dr. Qian, see Claire Noland, "Qian Xuesen Dies at 98, Rocket Scientist Helped Establish Jet Propulsion Laboratory," *Los Angeles Times*, November 1, 2009, updated September 16, 2014, https:// www.latimes.com/nation/la-me-qian-xuesen1-2009nov01-story.html; also see Michael Wines, "Qian Xuesen, Father of China's Space Program, Dies at 98," *New York Times*, November 3, 2009, https://www.nytimes.com/2009 /11/04/world/asia/04qian.html.

37. Wang, *Zhongmei Huitan Jiu Nian Huigu*, 27, 49; also see "Telegram from Ambassador U. Alexis Johnson to the Department of State," August 8, 1955, in *FRUS*, 1955–57, China, Vol. III, 19–21.

38. Wang, *Zhongmei Huitan Jiu Nian Huigu*, 49.

39. Author's personal experience in China in the fall of 2009.

40. Yang, *Zhonghua Renmin Gongheguo Waijiao Lilun yu Shixian*, 69–73. The quotation is on p. 71. Yang was a PRC ambassador who taught at Peking University in the 1980s and 1990s and trained the next generation of Chinese leaders. The book, which is internally circulated (*neibu faxing*) and lists no publisher, is a collection of his lectures. Yang claims in a footnote that the section here is based on Wang's memoirs and documents from the foreign ministry archives.

41. "The Plan Regarding China-U.S. Bilateral Ambassadorial-Level-Representative Talks at Geneva," July 18, 1955; and "Instructions Regarding China-U.S. Ambassadorial-Level Representative Talks at Geneva," July 30, 1955.

42. Young, *Negotiating with the Chinese Communists*, chap. 4; and Johnson, *The Right Hand of Power*, chap. 8.

43. Young, *Negotiating with the Chinese Communists*, 120; and Wang, *Zhongmei Huitan Jiu Nian Huigu*, 62–63.

44. Wang, *Zhongmei Huitan Jiu Nian Huigu*, 62–64. For an internal expression of concern for the public support gained by journalists who decided to go to China despite the ban, see "Letter from the Director of the Office of Chinese Affairs (McConaughy) to Ambassador U. Alexis Johnson in Geneva," February 11, 1957, in *FRUS*, 1955–57, China, Vol. III, 473–76.

45. On the fear that the U.S. reputation for resolve would be questioned and morale diminished among allies if Washington compromised on journalists, see "Memorandum of Conversation, Department of State, February 12, 1957," in *FRUS*, 1955–57, China, Vol. III, 476–78. On the fear of future detention of Americans if compromises were made with the CCP on journalists, see the long quotation from Dulles's February 5, 1955, press conference in

footnote 3 of "Letter from the Director of the Office of Chinese Affairs," February 11, 1957, 474.

46. John Foster Dulles, letter to Mary V. Downey, January 27, 1955, U.S. Department of State. The author viewed the original letter in Downey's personal files kindly shared by his family. The letter must have been particularly painful for Mrs. Downey to receive because the Office of the Secretary of Defense had written her one week earlier informing her that the PRC government would permit her to visit and that, if she wanted to do so, she should express her interest and relevant information would be provided to her. See General G. B. Erskine (USMC, Ret.), Special Assistant to the Secretary to Mrs. Downey, January 19, 1955, Office of the Secretary of Defense, in Downey's personal files. On Dulles's initial rigidity regarding visits, also see Rubin, *Pawns of the Cold War*, 39–40.

47. Young, *Negotiating with the Chinese Communists*, chap. 5.

48. From the personal chronology of John T. Downey.

49. From the personal chronology of John T. Downey.

50. "Telegram from the Representative at the United Nations (Lodge) to the Department of State," January 13, 1955.

51. For the story of the release of the four fighter pilots in May 1955, see Rebekah Davis, "Harold Fischer Jr., 83, Pilot Was Korean War Ace, POW," *Washington Post*, May 12, 2009, http://archive.boston.com/bostonglobe/obituaries/articles/2009/05/12/harold_fischer_jr_83_pilot_was_korean_war_ace_pow/.

52. Wang, *Zhongmei Huitan Jiu Nian Huigu*, 55–56. Wang also said that Zhou viewed the repatriation of Dr. Qian Xuesen as a major success for the PRC.

53. "Letter from the Director of the Office of Chinese Affairs (McConaughy) to the Ambassador in Czechoslovakia (Johnson)," January 30, 1957, in *FRUS*, 1955–57, China, Vol. III, 466–470, at p.468.

54. "Telegram from Ambassador U. Alexis Johnson to the Department of State," February 14, 1957, in *FRUS*, 1955–57, China, Vol. III, 479–81.

55. "Letter from the Director of the Office of Chinese Affairs (McConaughy) to Ambassador U. Alexis Johnson in Geneva," February 11, 1957, 473–76, 474fn3. The footnote includes the text of relevant portions of Dulles's press conference on the matter on February 5, 1957.

56. "Telegram from Ambassador U. Alexis Johnson to the Department of State," February 14, 1957, 479–81.

57. Barbara Roessner, "Tale of Early Release Offered Spices Downey China Tour," *Hartford Courant*, September 3, 1983.

58. In an excellent master's thesis, Daniel Aaron Rubin makes the important point that the PRC also viewed the B-29 crew as spies but released them before the Geneva talks began, suggesting that Downey and Fecteau's status as spies did not preclude them from release if the United States had accepted Zhou's offer to exchange journalists. See Daniel Aaron Rubin, "Pawns of the Cold War."

59. Johnson, *The Right Hand of Power*, 263.

15. PRISON LIFE

1. After ten years of smoking, Jack quit in 1965, after reading the Surgeon General's warning: "Cigarette smoking may be hazardous to your health."

18. A PINHOLE VIEW ON A MASSIVE TRAGEDY: 1958–1970

1. Wang Bingnan *Zhongmei Huitan Jiu Nian Huigu* (Review of the Nine-Year Sino-American Ambassadorial Talks) (Beijing: World Knowledge Press, 1985), 60.
2. "Letter from the Director of the Office of Chinese Affairs (McConaughy) to the Ambassador in Czechoslovakia (Johnson)," January 30, 1957 in *Foreign Relations of the United States (FRUS)*, China, 1955–57, Vol. III, 466–68.
3. Kenneth T. Young, *Negotiating with the Chinese Communists: The United States Experience, 1953–57* (New York: McGraw Hill, 1968), chaps. 5–6.
4. Young, *Negotiating with the Chinese Communists*, part III.
5. For a fuller account of the links between the Great Leap Forward and the Second Taiwan Straits Crisis, see Thomas J. Christensen, *Useful Adversaries: Grand Strategy, Domestic Mobilization, and Sino-American Conflict, 1947–58* (Princeton, NJ: Princeton University Press, 1996), chap. 6.
6. Thomas J. Christensen, *Worse than a Monolith: Alliance Politics and Problems of Coercive Diplomacy in Asia* (Princeton, NJ: Princeton University Press), chap. 5.
7. Jasper Becker, *Hungry Ghosts: Mao's Secret Famine* (New York: Free Press, 1996 and 2013). For a very frank criticism of the Great Leap Forward by a PRC scholar (without the damning statistics on deaths), see Xie Chuntao, *Dayuejin de Kuanglan, 1958–60* [The Mad Tide of the Great Leap Forward, 1958–60] (Henan: Henan People's Press, 1990).
8. Roderick MacFarquhar, *Origins of the Cultural Revolution, Vol. 3: The Coming of the Cataclysm* (New York: Columbia University Press, 1997), parts 1 and 2 for retrenchment from the Great Leap.
9. On the offshore islands and Chiang's legitimacy on Taiwan, see Jay Taylor, *The Generalissimo: Chiang Kai-shek and the Struggle for Modern China*, (Cambridge, MA: Belknap Press of Harvard University Press, 2009).
10. Christensen, *Useful Adversaries*, chap. 6.
11. For Mao's rivalry with Khrushchev and its international implications, see Christensen, *Worse than a Monolith*, chap. 5.
12. Christensen, *Worse than a Monolith*, chaps. 5–6.
13. On the Sino-Soviet rivalry and its role in Moscow's support for revolution in Southeast Asia and the sending of nuclear weapons to Cuba, see Alexsei

Fursenko and Timothy Naftali, *One Hell of a Gamble: Khrushchev, Castro, and Kennedy, 1958–64* (New York: Norton, 1997), 49–52, 102–3. Also see Christensen, *Worse than a Monolith*. chaps. 5–6.

14. For a recap of Smith's story, see https://www.pownetwork.org/bios/s/s106 .htm; and Jeremy Bendor, "Newly Released NSA Documents Reveal that China Captured American Soldiers During the Vietnam War," *Business Insider Australia*, December 16, 2014, https://www.businessinsider.com.au /nsa-documents-about-american-pows-during-vietnam-war-2014-12.

15. For the story of Colonel Robert Flynn, see Fred L. Borch III and Robert F. Dorr, "2032 Days of Solitary in China," *Vietnam Magazine*, February 2009 at https://www.historynet.com/2032-days-solitary-china.htm.

16. Christensen, *Worse than a Monolith*, chaps. 5–6.

17. MacFarquhar, *Origins of the Cultural Revolution*; for the ideological reasons offered for Liu's and Deng's purges, see Peter Van Ness, *Revolution and China's Foreign Policy: Peking's Support for Wars of National Liberation* (Berkeley: University of California Press, 1970), 238–39.

18. Li Rui, *Du Peng Dehuai zishu* [Reading Peng Dehuai's Autobiography], *Renmin ribao*, April 23, 2014.

19. Van Ness, *Revolution and China's Foreign Policy*, section III; Harold C. Hinton, *The Sino-Soviet Confrontation: Implications for the Future* (New York: Crane Russak, 1976), 9–10; "The Sino-Soviet Struggle in the World Communist Movement Since Khrushchev's Fall," *Central Intelligence Agency*, September 1967, https://web.archive.org/web/20160919005449/https://www.cia.gov/library /readingroom/docs/esau-35.pdf, 44; and "The USSR and China," *Central Intelligence Agency*, https://web.archive.org/web/20160919010913/https:// www.cia.gov/library/readingroom/docs/DOC_0001095916.pdf, 3–4.

20. Van Ness, *Revolution and Chinese Foreign Policy*, 202; and "Mao's Red Guard Diplomacy: 1967," *Central Intelligence Agency*, June 21, 1968, https://www.cia .gov/library/readingroom/docs/polo-21.pdf, 16.

21. Geng Zhihui, *Cultural Revolution Memoirs Written and Read in English: Image Formation, Reception and Counternarrative*. University of Minnesota, 2008. *ProQuest*, http://search.proquest.com/docview/304582613/abstract/A379 Fo5AADC84B31PQ/1, 31–35; and "Growing up in Mao's China." *BBC News*, September 27, 2011, www.bbc.com, https://www.bbc.com/news/magazine -15063195.

22. Shen Zhihua, "Shen Zhihua on Learning the Scholar's Craft: Reflections of Historians and International Relations Scholars," H-diplo essay 267, H-Diplo website, September 15, 2020, https://networks.h-net.org/node /28443/discussions/6426825/h-diplo-essay-267-shen-zhihua-learning -scholar%E2%80%99s-craft.

23. Wang Yuhua. "The Political Legacy of Violence During China's Cultural Revolution." *British Journal of Political Science* 51, no. 2 (April 2021): 463–87.

24. For a CIA history report of the original PRC accusation against Redmond, see "Redmond Was Spy 8 Years, Peiping Says," released November 14, 2003, https://www.cia.gov/library/readingroom/document/cia-rdp75-00001 r000400210017-3. For published recognition that he was indeed a CIA agent, see Maury Allen, *China Spy, The Story of Hugh Francis Redmond* (Sarasota, FL: Gazetter, 1998); Ted Gup, *The Book of Honor: The Secret Lives and Deaths of CIA Operatives* (New York: Doubleday, 2001); and Steven Weinberg, "CIA Tight-Lipped on Names Behind Stars," *Denver Post*, May 28, 2001.

25. Gup, *The Book of Honor*, 396.

26. Roderick MacFarquhar and Michael Schoenhals, *Mao's Last Revolution* (Cambridge, MA: Belknap Press of Harvard University Press, 2008), 258.

27. Liu Xiaohong, *Chinese Ambassadors: The Rise of Diplomatic Professionalism Since 1949* (Seattle: University of Washington Press, 2001), 113.

28. Borch and Dorr, "2032 Days of Solitary in China."

19. FAMILY VISITS

1. When Mary Downey entered the Chinese prison, she had signed many forms; one form forbade them to discuss Jack Downey's crime. It seemed there was a policy change order from higher up in the Chinese government at the last minute.

2. Edgar Snow wrote many books on the rise of communism in China, including *Red Star Over China.* Half of his ashes were buried in Peking University. His monument reads "An American Friend of the People of China, 1905–1972."

20. U.S.-PRC RAPPROCHEMENT AND JACK DOWNEY'S RELEASE: 1968–1973

1. George C. Herring, *America's Longest War: The United States and Vietnam, 1950-75*, 3rd edition (New York: McGraw Hill, 1996), chap. 7. For an excellent analysis of the pessimism about the war created by Tet in American public opinion and in elite politics, see Dominic D. P. Johnson and Dominic Tierney, *Failing to Win: Perceptions of Victory and Defeat in International Politics* (Cambridge, MA: Harvard University Press, 2006), chap. 6.

2. Richard M. Nixon, "Asia After Viet Nam," *Foreign Affairs*, October 1, 1967, www.foreignaffairs.com/articles/united-states/1967-10-01/asia-after-viet-nam.

3. Nelson W. Polsby, *Presidential Elections*, 5th ed. (New York: Scribner's, 1980), 174.

4. For a concise recap of the Prague Spring and the invasion, see Marc Santora, "50 Years After Prague Spring, Lessons on Freedom (and a Broken Spirit),

New York Times, August 20, 2018, https://www.nytimes.com/2018/08/20/world /europe/prague-spring-communism.html; and Olga Pavlenko, "The Events in Czechoslovakia and the Soviet Embassy in Prague in 1967–1968," in *The Soviet Invasion of Czechoslovakia in 1968: The Russian Perspective*, ed. Josef Pazderka (Washington, DC: Lexington, 2019), chap. 6.

5. Taylor Fravel, *Strong Borders, Secure Nation: Cooperation and Conflict in China's Territorial Disputes* (Princeton, NJ: Princeton University Press, 2008), 201–17; Wang Zhongchun, "The Soviet Factor in Sino-Soviet Normalization," in *Normalization of U.S.-China Relations: An International History*, ed. William C. Kirby, Robert S. Ross, and Gong Li (Cambridge, MA: Harvard University Asia Center, 2005); and Robert S. Ross, *Negotiating Cooperation: The United States and China, 1969-89* (Stanford, CA: Stanford University Press, 1995), chap. 2.

6. On Mao ordering the attack, see Gong Li, "Chinese Decision Making," in *Re-Examining the Cold War: U.S.-China Diplomacy, 1954-73*, ed. Robert S. Ross and Jiang Changbin (Cambridge, MA: Harvard University Asia Center, 2001), 327–31; Yang Kuisong, "The Sino-Soviet Border Clash of 1969: From Zhenbao Island to Sino-American Rapprochement," *Cold War History* 1, no. 1 (August 2000), 21–52; and Lyle Goldstein, "Return to Zhenbao Island: Who Started Shooting and Why It Matters," *China Quarterly* 168 (December 2001), 985–87.

7. For a fuller review of these arguments, see Thomas J. Christensen, "Windows and War: Trend Analysis and Beijing's Use of Force," in *New Directions in the Study of China's Foreign Policy*, ed. Alastair Iain Johnston and Robert S. Ross (Stanford, CA: Stanford University Press, 2006), 69–71. For an argument emphasizing international pressures, see Fravel, *Strong Borders, Secure Nation*, 201–17. For an argument that mixes international and domestic factors, see Yang, "The Sino-Soviet Border Clash." For an argument that sees domestic political goals as primary in Mao's thinking, see Goldstein, "Return to Zhenbao Island."

8. Fravel, *Strong Borders, Secure Nation*, 208.

9. Yang, "Sino-Soviet Border Clash," 35–37.

10. Henry Kissinger, *The White House Years* (New York: Simon and Schuster, 2011), 425–36. In his later book, *On China* (New York: Penguin, 2011), 218, Kissinger corrects the mistaken first impression but maintains, correctly in my opinion, that while Mao initiated the attack in March 1969, he did so for broadly defensive purposes in the face of what he saw as a growing and intolerable threat from Soviet forces on China's border.

11. Fravel, *Strong Borders, Secure Nation*, 202.

12. Kissinger, *On China*, 218.

13. Thomas J. Christensen, *Worse than a Monolith: Alliance Politics and Problems of Coercive Diplomacy in Asia* (Princeton, NJ: Princeton University Press, 2011), chap. 6.

14. Christensen, *Worse than a Monolith*, 202–8.
15. Kissinger, *On China*, 220–21.
16. Yafeng Xia, "China's Elite Politics and Sino-American Rapprochement, January 1969–February 1972," *Journal of Cold War Studies* 8, no. 4 (2006): 13; Kissinger, *White House Years*, 1,443.
17. Ross, *Negotiating Cooperation*, 28.
18. Kissinger, *White House Years*, 1,685.
19. Kissinger, *On China*, 230–31.
20. Author's telephone interview with Henry Kissinger, February 12, 2021.
21. Xia, "China's Elite Politics and Sino-American Rapprochement," 15.
22. Xia, "China's Elite Politics and Sino-American Rapprochement," 15.
23. Chen Jian, *Mao's China and the Cold War* (Chapel Hill: University of North Carolina Press, 2001), 259–60; Hong Zhaohui and Yi Sun, "The Butterfly Effect and the Making of 'Ping-Pong Diplomacy,' "*Journal of Contemporary China* 9, no. 25 (2000): 431; and Harry Harding, *A Fragile Relationship: The United States and China Since 1972* (Washington, DC: Brookings Institution, 1992), 39.
24. Kissinger, *White House Years*, 1,585.
25. National Committee on U.S.-China Relations, https://www.ncuscr.org/program/table-tennis-delegation-1972/.
26. Kissinger, *On China*, 233.
27. Kissinger, *White House Years*, 1,586.
28. Harding, *A Fragile Relationship*, chaps. 1–2 ; and Ross, *Negotiating Cooperation*, chaps. 1–2.
29. Alan D. Romberg, *Rein in at the Brink of the Precipice: American Policy Toward Taiwan and US-PRC Relations* (Washington, DC: Henry L. Stimson Center, 2003), chap. 2; and Richard C. Bush, *Untying the Knot: Making Peace in the Taiwan Strait* (Washington, DC: Brookings Institution, 2006).
30. Winston Lord to Kissinger, "Your November 23 Night Meeting," enclosing memorandum of conversation, November 23, 1971, National Archives, Record Group 59, Department of State Records, Records of the Policy Planning Staff, Director's Files (Winston Lord), 1969–1977, Box 330, China Exchanges (October 20–December 31, 1971), The National Security Archive, Washington, DC, https://nsarchive2.gwu.edu/NSAEBB/NSAEBB106/index2.htm#12, cited in William Burr, "Nixon's Trip to China," National Security Archive, December 11, 2003; Zhou Enlai and Alexander Haig, "Memorandum of Conversation." January 3, 1972, Box 1037, 6, The National Security Archive, Washington, DC, https://nsarchive2.gwu.edu/NSAEBB/NSAEBB70/doc24.pdf; and Henry Kissinger, "Memorandum of Conversation." February 23, 1972, 2, The National Security Archive, Washington, DC, https://nsarchive2.gwu.edu/NSAEBB/NSAEBB106/NZ-4.pdf.
31. Li Danhui, "Vietnam and Chinese Policy Toward the United States," in *Normalization of U.S.-China Relations* (Cambridge, MA: Harvard University Asia Center, 2005), 193; James Mann, *About Face: A History of America's*

Curious Relationship with China from Nixon to Clinton (New York: Knopf, 1998), 34; and Christensen, *Worse than a Monolith*, 202–8.

32. This frustration and disappointment is clearly evident in the family's archived chronology of Jack Downey's life and in the annotated version of his memoirs, which contains detailed retrospective commentary by family members on what was happening on the home front during the time that he was in prison in Beijing. An annotated version of the memoir and a chronology of Downey's life was graciously provided to the author by the Downey family.

33. Author's telephone interview with Kissinger, February 12, 2021.

34. Declassified documents from the U.S. archives are discussed in detail below.

35. See, for example, Gong Li, *Kuayue Honggou: 1969-79 Zhong Mei Guanxi de Yanbian* [Across the Chasm: The Evolution of U.S. China Relations from 1969-1979] (Henan: Henan People's Press, 1992), 202–3; and Mei Xingwu, "Weijian Changbaishan Kongjiang Meiguo Jiandie" [Surrounded and Liquidated: The U.S. Spies Who Fell from the Sky at Changbai Mountain], *Yan Huang Chun Qiu* 2 (2020): 34–35.

36. Author's telephone interview with Kissinger, February 12, 2021.

37. Author's telephone interview with Kissinger, February 12, 2021.

38. Author's telephone interview with Kissinger, February 12, 2021.

39. Author's telephone interview with Kissinger, February 12, 2021.

40. "137. Memorandum for the President's File," *Foreign Relations of the United States (FRUS)*, 1969–1976, Vol. XVII, China, 1969–1972, U.S. Department of State, July 1, 1971, https://history.state.gov/historicaldocuments/frus1969 -76v17/d137.

41. "9. Memorandum from the President's Assistant for National Security Affairs (Kissinger) to President Nixon," *FRUS*, 1969–1976, Vol. E-13, Documents on China, 1969-1972, U.S. Department of State, July 14, 1971, https:// 2001-2009.state.gov/r/pa/ho/frus/nixon/e13/72417.htm. Italics added by author for emphasis.

42. "164. Memorandum from the President's Assistant for National Security Affairs (Kissinger) to President Nixon," *FRUS*, 1969–1976, Vol. XVII, China, 1969–1972, U.S. Department of State, November 1971, https://history .state.gov/historicaldocuments/frus1969-76v17/d164.

43. "72. Message from Nancy Oullette to the President's Deputy Assistant for National Security Affairs (Haig), Paris, December 10, 1971," *FRUS*, 1969–1976, Vol. E-13, Documents on China, 1969–1972, U.S. Department of State, https://history.state.gov/historicaldocuments/frus1969-76ve13/d72.

44. During his February 1972 trip to China, Nixon expressed his understanding that the two airmen would only be released with other Vietnam War POWs. Memorandum of Conversation, Beijing, February 25, 1972, 5:45–6:45 p.m, FRUS, Documents on China, 1969–72, U.S. Department of State, February 25, 1972, https://history.state.gov/historicaldocuments/frus1969-76v17/d200

45. "Harbort" refers to an American student arrested in China and released in 1971.

46. Memorandum of Conversation, Beijing, February 25, 1972, 5:45–6:45 p.m, FRUS, Documents on China, 1969–72, U.S. Department of State, February 25, 1972 https://history.state.gov/historicaldocuments/frus1969-76v17/d200

47. The Downey family's annotated version of Jack Downey's memoir, kindly shared with the author.

48. "106. Memorandum of Conversation, Shangha, i, February 27, 1972, 11:30 a.m.–1:55 p.m.," FRUS, 1969–1976, Vol. E-13, Documents on China, 1969–1972, U.S. Department of State, February 27, 1972, https://history.state.gov /historicaldocuments/frus1969-76ve13/d106.

49. "229. Memorandum from Richard H. Solomon of the National Security Council Staff to the President's Assistant for National Security Affairs (Kissinger)," FRUS, 1969–1976, Vol. E-13, Documents on China, 1969–1972, June 9, 1972, https://history.state.gov/historicaldocuments/frus1969-76v17/d229.

50. "No. 146. Memorandum of Conversation, Beijing, June 22–23, 1972, 11:03 p.m.–12:55 a.m.," FRUS, 1969–1976, Vol. E-13, Documents on China, 1969–1972, June 9, 1972, https://history.state.gov/historicaldocuments/frus1969 -76v17/d229.

51. President Nixon's News Conference, January 31, 1973. The full transcript was made available in the New York Times, February 1, 1973, https://www .nytimes.com/1973/02/01/archives/transcript-of-the-presidents-news -conference-on-foreign-and.html.

52. Downey family's annotated chronology of Downey's life.

53. Author's telephone interview with Kissinger, February 12, 2021.

54. Jerome Alan Cohen, "Will Jack Make the 25th Reunion?" New York Times, July 7, 1971. I viewed this piece in the family's archive. It is available online at https:// www.nytimes.com/1971/07/07/archives/will-jack-make-his-25th-reunion.html.

55. "10. Memorandum of Conversation," FRUS, 1969–1976, Vol. XVIII, China, 1973–1976, U.S. Department of State, February 17, 1973, https://history.state .gov/historicaldocuments/frus1969-76v18/d10. Italics added to quotation by author for emphasis.

56. See, for example, Mei Xingwu, "Weijian Changbaishan Kongjiang Meiguo Jiandie," 34–35.

57. Mrs. Mary Downey as told to J. Robert Moskin, "My Son a Prisoner in Red China," Look, December 6, 1950, 78.

AFTERWORD

1. John T. Downey to Rufus C. Phillips (July 10, 1952). "Fats" was a sarcastic term of endearment that Dad first picked up in middle school. Post-Depression era gallows humor, perhaps.

2. Richard C. Levin, *Yale Bulletin & Calendar* 34, no. 12 (November 18, 2005); http://archives.news.yale.edu/v34.n12/story11.html.

3. Tim Weiner, *Legacy of Ashes* (New York: Anchor, 2008).

4. John Foster Dulles to Mary V. Downey (January 27, 1955).

5. Edgar Parks Snow to Mary V. Downey (January 28, 1961).

6. John T. Downey interview with James J. White (April 26, 1974), 16.

7. John T. Downey to Mary V. Downey (December 25, 1954).

8. "CIA Supposedly Stated 'Downey Doesn't Exist,'" *New Britain Herald* (March 15, 1973), 3.

9. George Howe Colt, "The Tie That Binds," *Yale Alumni Magazine* (November/December 2018), https://yalealumnimagazine.com/articles/4802-yale-harvard-1968-tie.

10. Interview with James J. White, 16.

11. Philip E. Smith, *Journey into Darkness* (New York: Pocket, 1992), 155, 159–60, 161.

12. John T. Downey, "Milady Given Short Shrift By Downey," *New Haven Register* (December 14, 1955).

13. Jerome A. Cohen, "Will Jack Make His 25th Reunion?" *New York Times* (July 7, 1971), 37.

14. Interview with James J. White, 18.

15. Thomas O'Toole, "Downey: A CIA Agent in from the Cold," *Washington Post* (March 18, 1973), A7.

16. Joel Lang, "He's out of Prison, But Can Jack Downey Escape His Past?" *Hartford Courant Sunday Magazine* (October 8, 1978), 3.

17. Audrey Lee Downey, unpublished manuscript, 244.

18. Audrey Lee Downey, unpublished manuscript, 264–65.

19. John T. Downey to Mary V. Downey (April 15, 1956).

20. Barbara T. Roessner, "Tale of Early Release Offered Spices Downey's China Tour," *Hartford Courant* (September 3, 1983), A1, A10.

21. Audrey Lee Downey, unpublished manuscript, 324.

22. Audrey Lee Downey, unpublished manuscript, 328–29.

23. Douglas Martin, "John T. Downey Dies at 84; Held Captive in China for 20 Years," *New York Times* (November 19, 2014), https://www.nytimes.com/2014/11/20/us/john-t-downey-dies-at-84-held-captive-for-20-years-.html.

24. Lee Ferran, "CIA Releases Film on Blown China Spy Mission," *ABC News* (June 2, 2011), https://abcnews.go.com/Blotter/cia-releases-film-chinese-capture-torture-agents/story?id=13743541.

25. Interview with James J. White (April 26, 1974), 21, 22.

INDEX